The Ethics of Professional Practice

Richard D. Parsons

West Chester University

D1303564

Allyn and Bacon

Boston • London • Toronto • Sydney • Tokyo • Singapore

Editor-in-Chief, Social Sciences: *Karen Hanson*
Senior Editorial-Production Administrator: *Joe Sweeney*
Editorial-Production Service: *Walsh & Associates, Inc.*
Composition Buyer: *Linda Cox*
Manufacturing Buyer: *Julie McNeill*
Cover Administrator: *Brian Gogolin*

Copyright 2001 by Allyn & Bacon
A Pearson Education Company
160 Gould Street
Needham Heights, MA 02494

www.abacon.com

Library of Congress Cataloging-in-Publication Data

Parsons, Richard D.
    The ethics of professional practice / Richard D. Parsons
        p. cm
    Includes bibliographical references and index.
    ISBN 0-205-30878-3
    1. Professional ethics.   I. Title
BJ1725.P37 2000
174—dc21   00-041629

Printed in the United States of America

15 14 13 12 11 10 9 8 7   09 08 07 06

Conrad Parsons
A man of conviction . . .
An ethical man . . .
and most importantly . . .
a Loving Father.

CONTENTS

PREFACE

For those working in the helping profession, the power of the helping process—be it as a counselor, therapist, or consultant—is more than evident. Equally evident is the fact that this process carries a similarly powerful and awesome set of responsibilities. Sadly, by omission or commission, not all those serving as professional helpers respect the power of the helping process and as a result fail to protect the welfare of their clients. One need only to turn on a television talk show or read a local paper to find examples of unethical therapists who have sexually abused their clients, counselors who have ignored their clients suicidal pleas for help, or even medical and social workers who have personally gained from the misfortune of others.

As helpers we are given the responsibility to care for individuals who, by definition of needing help, are often those who are most vulnerable to manipulation. And, while these premeditated and blatant abuses of client welfare are the exception and not the rule, they demonstrate the power of the helping relationship, even when the "helper" chooses to do harm. Equally deleterious to client welfare—even if unintended by the helper—are those instances when ignorance of ethical standards of practice mitigates client help or causes harm. These helpers may appear (to themselves or others) to be acting on behalf of the client, but their ignorance of the nature of the helping relationship and the process of purposeful change debases even the most fundamental caveat of helping: to do no harm. Thus, in instances where a counselor acts without a clear theoretical framework, influencing others from a reference of unexamined values and employing untested or inappropriate treatment strategies, or when a helper violates client rights in order to satisfy institutional policies and practices, the client suffers and the profession fails to advance.

Standards of Practice

Professional help givers need standards of practice and guidelines for making the many complex ethical decisions encountered in the practice and performance of their duties. This text will expose you to the standards of ethical practice established and maintained by professional boards and organizations as well as the array of ethical considerations that emanate from the unique nature of the helper and relationship.

To BE Ethical

This is not the first text to discuss the unique challenges and needs for ethical professional practice. As with many of the other texts, this book cites ethical standards as explicated by professional organizations such as the American Counseling Association (ACA), the American Association of Marriage and Family Therapists (AAMFT), the American Psychological Association (APA), and the National Association of Social Workers (NASW) (see

Appendix A). Throughout the book, the principles advanced by these organizations are defined and illustrated with fictional case illustrations. Knowing one's professional codes of ethics is essential. However, knowledge alone is insufficient.

We must move beyond simply knowing the ethical principles of practice—to becoming ethical practitioners. If professional helpers expect to **BE** ethical in all manners of their professional life, then they must know and experience ethics at their most personal level. The helper must travel a personal journey of discovery, assessment, and explication of those factors that will influence his or her professional work. Only then will this helper be able to truly appreciate and master the essential standards of ethical practice as espoused by the helping professions. It is only then that this person will **BE** ethical in his or her professional thought and action.

Focus

This text has been designed to move the reader from being a passive recipient of the information presented to becoming an active participant in the process of value and ethics clarification. The text will provide the following emphasis.

1. A THEME that posits that ethical practice is more than something to do, it is the essential way to BE. The emphasis throughout the text will be on challenging the reader to assimilate the material into his or her own value structure, thus becoming an ethical practitioner.
2. While points of similarity across professional disciplines will be reviewed, the text will bring the human experience to the review of ethical standards. The intent is to make "professional ethics" more than a simple compilation of the ethical principles provided by the major professional organizations (e.g., APA, ACA, NASW, AAMFT).
3. The cases presented, as well as the guided exercises, are all designed to facilitate the reader's application of the principles discussed. Given this emphasis on application, each chapter employs multiple case illustrations, simulated case situations, and guided practice.
4. In addition to such a cognitive focus, the text targets the reader's affective domain as well. Throughout the text exercises will be provided that engage the reader's own valuing processes. The purpose of these exercises is twofold. First, it is hoped that the exercises will help to clarify the points under discussion. Second, and more importantly, it is hoped that the exercises will help the reader personalize the material presented and assimilate values, which are in line with professional ethics, into his or her practice.

Chapter Overview

In the first major part of the text, *Helping: The Role and Influence of the Helper*, the nature of the helping relationship and the role of helper characteristics are discussed. The material presented within Chapters 1 and 2 demonstrates that helping is more than the sterile application of techniques or procedures. It is a process in which each participant mobilizes his or her values, beliefs, needs, and even dreams in order to make the very best of an increasingly intimate relationship. Thus, it is argued, that it is imperative that the helper be aware of his or her own values.

Part Two, *Ethics and Standards of Practice*, reviews specific standards of practice and their underlying operating values. Further, the material in Part Two reviews the relationship between professional ethics and the law. The chapters presented in Part Three of the text (*The Nature of the Helping Relationship*) address specific ethical concerns that emerge as a result of the unique nature of a helping relationship. Issues such as Ethical Conflicts: The System and the Interests of Others (Chapter 5), Informed Consent (Chapter 6), Confidentiality (Chapter 7), and Boundaries and the Ethical Use of Power (Chapter 8) are presented in detail, highlighting the subtle challenges to the ethical practitioner. The final section of the text, Part Four, *The Process of Helping*, discusses the specific ethical challenges confronting the ethical practitioner as he or she attempts to provide competent and effective treatment (Chapter 9) and remain accountable for the efficacy of that treatment (Chapter 10).

A Final Thought

This book, like most other texts can be an impersonal factual disseminator of information. Hopefully, the case illustrations and the exercises will help to make it less impersonal. The real key, however, is you, the reader. As you read this book, make the material personal. Invest yourself in the exercises: The more of you placed into your reading, the more the material will be able to stimulate your growth as an ethical helper.

This preface ends with a reminder that ethics is not simply a thing to be memorized. The principles of ethical practice go beyond a demand for comprehension and a demonstration of that comprehension by performance on pencil and paper test. Ethics in and of itself is valueless. It is in **being ethical** that life is given to these principles and the *raison d'être* for our helping is enacted.

ACKNOWLEDGMENTS

Throughout the upcoming pages of this text, a single theme will be apparent. Ethics isn't what we know or what we do, it is how we are. I have been very fortunate to have had many ethical people in my life, all of whom have helped give shape to this textbook.

My parents modeled for me the fundamental values of autonomy, beneficence, justice, and altruism that serve as the core to our professional ethics. I have had many fine professors—especially Joel Meyers and Roy Martin—who helped me to understand and embrace the professional code of ethics, and professional colleagues—especially Bob Wicks and Wally Kahn—who have served as reminders and resources at times of ethical conflict. I also would like to acknowledge my graduate students. Their clear interest and concern in being the best they could be "for their clients" serves as a constant reminder of the reason I (we) am (are) in the helping profession. I am indebted to the input and time provided by my reviewers: Cheryl Sibilsky, Lansing Community College; Stephen Kehoe, El Paso Community College; Robert Scheurell, University of Wisconsin, Milwaukee; and Kimberly Battle-Walters, Azusa Pacific University. Finally, I would like to say a special thank you to Kelly A. Malaney for her assistance with typing and Joseph Mark Diamond not only for the many hours he provided in cross referencing the various codes of professional conduct but also for putting up with my ribbing and developing sense of humor.

Helping: The Role and Influence of the Helper

1 An Introduction to the Formal Process of Helping

Maria: Hi. Are you Ms. Wicks? I'm Maria. Mr. Brady told me that I had to come talk with you.

Thus, with what appears to be a simple social introduction, begins a process of helping. A process which, while appearing so natural, so easy, is in truth, complex and filled with challenges for both the helper and the client. Helping another person cope with a problem or facilitating that person's movement toward a specific outcome is a very responsible process. It is a process involving at least two people. While various names and labels can be applied to the person providing the help (e.g., psychologist, counselor, advocate, social worker, etc.), we will refer to this person simply as the helper and the person receiving the help as the client.

Ms. Wicks, a social worker consulting at a local school district, is about to engage as a helper with Maria (the client) in a process that will require her to employ special knowledge and skills along with a unique sensitivity. She will be called upon to make numerous decisions as she guides Maria through this process. Helping for Ms. Wicks, or any helper, is a process for which there are no clear-cut formulas or recipes to follow.

The process of helping another, the direction it takes, and the outcomes will all be influenced by the person of the helper. It is not just the helper's technical knowledge or skill that influence and give shape to the helping process, it is also his or her values, beliefs, and operating ethics. The unique role and influence of the helper within the developing ethical helping relationship is the focus of the current chapter.

Chapter Objectives

The chapter will present the role that the helper's beliefs, values, and ethics play in shaping the decision making that occurs within the helping dynamic.

After reading this chapter you should be able to do the following:

1. Define helping as a dynamic process, reflecting both an artistry and a science.
2. Describe the unique ethical responsibilities and roles of the professional helper within a helping relationship.
3. Identify the salient characteristics of the effective helper and the degree to which you currently possess these characteristics.
4. Identify the reciprocal roles and responsibilities of both the client and the helper in an ethical helping relationship.

The Helping Process: A Blending of Art and Science

The effective helper understands and appreciates the fact that helping is not simply the sterile application of techniques or procedures. While a helper's understanding of what to do may be grounded in theory and research, the "when" and "how" to do it require a sensitivity that extends well beyond theoretical knowledge and technical efficiency. Consider the many options and decision points afforded the helper working with Kim in the following case illustration (Case 1.1).

In reviewing Kim's complaint did you feel that the roommate was the problem or was something else on Kim's mind? Was there a problem? While Kim was verbally expressive, what did you notice about her behavior, her style of communicating? Should the RA have stopped Kim and asked a question at any point? Should the RA have confronted Kim? So many questions—with no simple, clear answers.

As previously suggested, helping is a process for which there is no one tried and true sequence of steps to be applied. Helping is not an automatic, cold, and distant process of problem solving. It is truly an awesome human encounter, one engaging clients' and helpers' feelings as well as their minds. The complexity and dynamic nature of the helping process is infused with subjectivity, intuition, and often confusion, rendering its facilitation as much of an art as a science. It is important to realize that as with any art—the product— reflects not only the subject, or in this case the client, but also the artist. Each participant mobilizes his or her values, beliefs, needs, and even dreams to make the very best of an increasingly intimate relationship.

As a contributor to this product and process, what might the RA, depicted in Case Illustration 1.1 have contributed to the dynamic with Kim? What did the RA feel? What

---

CASE ILLUSTRATION **1.1**
Kim's

Kim is a college freshman. During her first week of school she came to speak to her residence assistant (who is an upperclassman). On entering the RA's room she stated that she had a "minor complaint" and before the RA could respond, Kim continued to speak, stating:

> I know school has just started, and I am just a naive, little, helpless freshman, but I (looks down on to the floor), well, I . . . (voice becomes quiet) have a kind of . . . well of a . . . I guess you could call it a small, but not real small problem, with my roommate. Look, I don't want to seem like a complainer. I'm not, am I? But (fidgeting a little), gads, this is kinds of embarrassing to talk about, I mean you're a guy (giggles), of course you know that, but. . . . oh HELL I'm just gonna say it. I think my roommate . . . is . . . well, she—let's say is nothing like me. No, what I mean to say is . . . I really like guys (smiles flirtatiously) even though I haven't had a chance to meet anyone here, except the freshman boys, but anyway . . . I don't think she does, if you know what I mean. Well anyway, you get the idea. Don't you? I just need another room!

EXERCISE 1.1
You as Helper—You as Artist

Directions: Return to Kim's case. As you read the descriptions and review Kim's presentation, try to develop a complete image of the interaction. Imagine you are the RA. What does Kim look like? Where are you standing? What might you have been doing prior to her coming to see you? How might that affect your interest and availability to speak with Kim?

After developing a real sense of the scenario with you as the RA, respond to the following questions:

> What meaning did you make of all of the varied verbal, nonverbal (looking down, flirting, etc.) communication?
> How do you interpret the para-verbals (i.e., intonation in her voice, volume, etc.) messages?
> What elements of her style or her message did you pay attention to? All of it?
> How did you "feel" about Kim?
> What did you want to do?

Compare your observations and conclusions with a colleague or classmate: Did he or she focus on other data? Have other feelings? If so, what effect might the "person" of the helper play in defining the problem or selecting a path for problem resolution. How might the unique characteristics of the helper influence the nature of the interaction?

---

needs and concerns did the RA bring to this interaction? What feelings, thoughts, and behaviors were stimulated or elicited by Kim? The uniqueness of the helper tints the process and outcome of the helping relationship. Two different RAs working with Kim may have attended to different pieces of her story or her style and may have moved toward different outcomes or the same outcome through different paths. Exercise 1.1 provides an opportunity to identify the way the personal uniqueness of each helper can influence the very nature and outcome of the helping encounter.

The Helping Process: The Meeting of Client and Helper

Albeit a very unique and special relationship, the helping relationship is *first and foremost* exactly that, a relationship. It is important to note that too often in our eagerness to be of assistance, we rush in with our answers, our directions, our solutions, trying desperately to do something to "solve the problem." We must remember that helping is *realized* in the context of a helping relationship (Parsons, 1995). The quality of the relationship is therefore the keystone to the helping process and thus needs to be of primary concern to all seeking to develop their helping skills.

Helping: A Special Kind of Interpersonal Process and Response

Social encounters and social relationships are not unfamiliar. The normal chit-chat nature of these encounters is more or less familiar and comfortable for all of us. What makes the helping process or the meeting of a client and helper so different?

Client's Needs as Primary

Helping is a process by which one person, the helper, interacts with another in a way to facilitate this other's (the client's) movement toward some specific outcome. Unlike most social exchanges, *primacy is given to one member*, the client. It is the client's needs, concerns, and goals that are the focus of the encounter. It is the client's welfare that is the focus of the relationship and the driving force behind the ethical helper's decision making.

As a result of this "focus on one," the purpose and outcome of the interaction reflect the needs and goals of that "one" and these are specified and terminal. Unlike other social encounters that may be open-ended with both parties remaining engaged as long as their individual needs are being met, the helping relationship is designed to achieve some specific goal and terminate with the achievement of that goal. Once the goal is attained the need for the helping relationship no longer exists. This outcome-specific and terminal nature of helping cannot be forgotten. Nor can the helper forget that it is the needs, concerns, and goals of the client which are primary to the shaping and development of the helping relationship. Consider the helping exchange presented in Case Illustration 1.2. The interaction takes place between a crisis hotline worker and a woman whose child is choking. The exchange demonstrates the unique elements of a helping relationship when contrasted to other social elements.

CASE ILLUSTRATION **1.2**
Telephone Crisis Worker

CRISIS INTERVENTION WORKER: Yes, ma'am. I can hear that you are very upset. I know it seems scary. Yes, ma'am, I am here, I am listening. Could you describe what is happening?

CLIENT (voice on the phone screaming):   My baby is turning blue ... oh, my God ... my baby ... my baby

HELPER: (interrupting) ... Ma'am! Ma'am!

CLIENT: Yes? (trying to catch her breath)

HELPER: It is important for you to try to focus on what I am telling you—can you hear me?

CLIENT: Yes ... but my ...

HELPER: (interrupting) I know its hard for you but keep listening to my voice—you must try. Roll your baby over on her stomach, place your left hand under her belly, and lift her stomach off the floor. Now with your right hand give her a gentle yet

> firm slap in the middle of the back, between her shoulder blades. Go ahead—you do that and tell me what's happening—I can hear you.
>
> (The helper continues talking as she listens to the mother.) Good . . .I can hear the baby now, the baby is crying—that's good—open the baby's mouth, put your finger in and clear out anything that may be inside her mouth.
>
> Great . . . her cries are clear and strong.
>
> **CLIENT:** (sobbing) She . . . she is looking better, she coughed up a plastic grape. Thank you, thank you . . . you saved her life.

Like other social encounters, this one is marked by verbal exchanges and sharing of information. While it is certainly an interaction, it differs from the more typical social exchange, not just in the content of the interaction, but in the fundamental nature of that content. In this and all helping exchanges the nature and substance is the matter of the client. As with other social encounters there is a goal implied—but this again reflects the need and current state of the client, not the helper, and emphasizes the utilization of the client's resources and movement toward a specific outcome (Parsons, 1995). While the helper in this situation may have been about to take a coffee break or may have felt anxious and wished she could have simply handed the phone to another, it was not her needs that were central to this encounter.

When the needs, wants, and concerns of the helper take center stage at the expense of the client, we have the potential for unethical behavior and a less than helping exchange. Exercise 1.2 should help to clarify this important distinction between a helping encounter and other social interactions.

EXERCISE **1.2**
Helping as a Unique Social Encounter

Directions: As with most of these exercises, it would be valuable to complete the exercise and then share your responses with a colleague or classmate to see how individual differences can impact the responses and the potential for the helping process.

Part I: Below you will find three different types of social encounters in which you may be currently engaged or may be seeking to develop. Select one of these encounters and write your response to the questions that follow.

Relationships:
1. A relationship with a member of the opposite sex
2. A relationship with a person of authority who evaluates your performance (e.g., professor, supervisor, boss, etc.)
3. An encounter with a possible employer.

Questions:
1. What is your primary goal for this encounter? That is, what would you like to achieve or gain through this relationship.

2. Assuming that your goal is achieved, what need(s) within you would be met?
3. How might your need and your desire to achieve this specific goal impact your style of interacting? What would you share or not share? How would you share it? How would you behave? As you interacted with this other person what thoughts and concerns might you experience?

Using your written responses regarding your goal, needs and interactional style, how might these factors affect the nature of a helping relationship should you, the helper, bring them to this exchange?

The Role of the Client in the Process of Change

At a surface level, the roles and functions of the participants in this formal helping process are clear. The client brings concerns to a trained helper and expects the helper to help formulate appropriate goals and to employ cost/effective strategies that will realize those goals. What could be simpler? But helping is a relationship in which the unique roles and responsibilities of the participants are not always simple or clear.

Some helpers, in their eagerness to be of assistance, deprive the client of the opportunity to take an active role within the helping process. These helpers often relegate the clients to the role of a "victimized party" in need of the helper's assistance and thus place the brunt of the responsibility of the process of change on the helper's shoulders.

The perspective taken here is that helping is a collaborative process with both the helper and the client having responsibilities and roles to be played within the process. The ethical standards for helpers articulated by the various professional organizations (e.g., AAMFT, ACA, APA, NASW) (see Appendix A) define the reciprocal roles of helper and client—specifying the rights of the client and the responsibilities of the client. As noted by Hare-Mustin and colleagues (Hare-Mustin, Marecek, Kaplan, & Liss-Levinson,1995), the helper responsibilities and clients' rights converge on issues such as freedom of choice, disclosure of information, and protection of human dignity.

While there is a unique role to be played by the helper, the client also has both a role and responsibility within the relationship. Clients are expected to choose wisely, to make use of the information provided, and to assume control of their participation in the helping process (Arbuckle,1977). However, it is the ethical responsibility of the helper to assist the client to assume this role, with the client's welfare always being the point of focus (see Table 1.1).

Freedom and Responsibility to Choose Wisely

If we revisit the client-helper exchange that opened this chapter, we might question both the "freedom" and the "choice" afforded Maria, the client. It is clear, at least from her initial presentation, that her perspective was that she "had to come to talk with" Ms. Wicks.

While absolute freedom may not be afforded clients under certain conditions (such as those who are involuntarily committed), even these clients have the freedom and responsibility to choose wisely within the more narrowed range of choice provided (see Chapter 6). Through open communication with the helper, the client will develop a realistic expectation

TABLE 1.1 Ethical Principles Promoting the Welfare of the Client(s)

Professional Organization	Ethical Principle
American Counseling Association (1995)	A.1. Client Welfare a. Primary Responsibility. The primary responsibility of counselors is to respect the dignity and to promote the welfare of clients.
American Psychological Association (1995)	Principle E: Concern for Others' Welfare Psychologists seek to contribute to the welfare of those with whom they interact professionally. In their professional actions, psychologist weigh the welfare and rights of their patients or clients, students, supervisors, human research participants, and other affected persons, and the welfare of animal subjects of re-search. When conflicts occur among psychologists' obligations or concerns, they attempt to resolve these conflicts and to perform their roles in a responsible fashion that avoids or minimizes harm. Psychologists are sensitive to real and ascribed differences in power between themselves and others, and they do not exploit or mislead other people during or after professional relationships.
National Association of Social Workers (1996)	1.01 Commitment to Clients Social workers' primary responsibility is to promote the well-being of clients. In general, clients' interests are primary. However, social workers' responsibility to the larger society or specific legal obligations may on limited occasions supercede the loyalty owed clients, and clients should be so advised.
American Association of Marriage and Family Therapists (1998)	1 Responsibility to Clients Marriage and family therapists advance the welfare of families and individuals. They respect the rights of those persons seeking their assistance and make reasonable efforts to ensure that their services are used appropriately.

about treatment and treatment outcome. With this knowledge the client can decide if and to what degree he or she wants to be engaged in this helping relationship. Even Maria has the freedom to choose to come, to stay, or to even talk. The helper, Ms. Wicks, can assist Maria to understand these options along with the possible consequence for each. It is then Maria's role, as client, to decide what she wants from the helping process and what she is willing to do to get what she wants.

Assume Control of Their Participation in the Helping Process

Helping is not something one *does to* another, it is a process that one *does with* another. Helping works best when clients enter it voluntarily and assume some control over the process. Even when a client is required, forced, or coerced to come for help, progress will be facilitated by assisting the client to affirm the relevance of the helping and to develop a willingness to participate in the process. This is true even if the only control clients wish to exert is to terminate the relationship, which is their right (Bennett, Bryant, VandenBos, & Greenwood, 1990).

It is incumbent on the ethical helper to assist the client to see the potential benefit of this helping relationship while affirming his or her right to assume control over his or her participation. Case Illustration 1.3 reveals how a helper who "believes" that the client has the right and responsibility to assume control can facilitate the development of a helping relationship in which control and direction is shared.

Imagine the impact on this helping relationship and the possibility of providing Maria "help" if Ms. Wicks, the helper, took a rigid, authoritative stance: "Sit young lady—if Mr. Brady sent you here, you will stay here!"

The specific details over what falls within the realm of control of the client and what belongs to the helper is not predefined. Early in the development of each helping relationship roles and boundaries need to be established (see Chapter 8). The specifics will vary according to the nature of the problem at hand, the therapeutic approach employed, and the specific orientation and values of the participants.

Make Use of the Information Provided

It is hoped that the client will assume a role that shows both an interest in understanding the nature of the current situation and a desire to develop either a different coping style or a

---

C A S E   I L L U S T R A T I O N 1.3
Maria Assumes Control

The following exchange occurred shortly after Ms. Wicks greeted Maria and invited her to take a seat.

MARIA: I don't want to be here—I didn't do anything.

MS. WICKS: You sound like you don't want to be here, but you are. Would you like to return to class?

MARIA: No way! He's a jerk!

MS. WICKS: Well, we have 20 minutes before the next change of class. If you would like, maybe you could tell me what happened? Maybe in talking about it we could come up with a plan to make it better.

MARIA: I don't like talking.

MS. WICKS: Well, you don't have to—if you would rather, you could spend the rest of the period in the career center or reviewing college brochures. But you do look and sound upset and I would like to help if I could.

MARIA: Let me just take a minute. Can I get a drink of water? I'll be right back and I'll tell you what happened.

different life position. It is, however, a role that they have a right not to embrace. A helper may make recommendations and suggestions that if accepted by the client may facilitate the achievement of his or her goal. The client, however, is under no obligation to follow the specific recommendations or suggestions of the helper. The client can and will decide how he or she will employ the information provided.

The fact that a client can decide to use or not use the advice, the information, or the insight gained by working with a helper may appear obvious. Yet, it is not unusual for a helper who has extended himself or herself to a client, to feel disappointed, perhaps even angry, at a client who appears to be less than compliant. This point may become a bit more clear after completing Exercise 1.3.

When a helper has invested time, energy, and part of the self into supporting a client, it may be hard for him or her to accept the client freedom to use or not use the help provided. This is more dramatically brought home in situations in which the client choice to

---

EXERCISE **1.3**
A Client Chooses to Reject Help

Directions: The following is a brief exchange between Alice (the client) and Tim (social worker). Tim has been working with Alice in a program geared to help single mothers find employment. This is the sixth time they have met.

As you read the vignette, try to place yourself in the shoes of the helper. After reading the case illustration, respond to the following questions. As with previous exercises, it may prove beneficial for you to share your responses with a colleague.

> **ALICE (the client):** Hi, sorry I'm late, but I got a phone call from an old friend just as I was going out the door.
>
> **TIM (the helper):** Well, Alice, we have approximately 20 minutes left in your appointment. How about we use the remainder of the session to discuss how well you did with your telephone calls?
>
> **ALICE:** I know I agreed to attempt to call at least three jobs for possible interviews but this was a busy week, plus I had a friend in town and we wanted to hang out a little. So I just kinda figured we could do it another time.
>
> **TIM:** Okay, but in addition to making the calls, you also agreed to complete the interest inventory I gave you. Maybe we could review your profile. Do you have that?
>
> **ALICE:** Gads, you know what, I remember you giving it to me but I think I must have misplaced it or something. Do you have another one? I could try to complete it for next time.
>
> **TIM:** Alice, I am a bit confused. We have been meeting for 6 weeks and even though you stated that you really want to work on identifying a possible career path and to get back to work you seem to have some difficulty following through on the things we discuss. Each time we have decided on a "homework," like to clip ads from the paper, or to go speak with a nurse's aide about her experiences in that career, or the telephoning and interest inventory—you have had difficulty completing the tasks.

ALICE: Well, I'm sorry, but a lot of the things you suggest seem dumb. And other things are just not convenient for me to do! So what should I do now?

1. If you were the helper in this scenario, how might you be feeling about Alice?
2. How might your feelings about Alice be manifested in your interchange? How may they impact your desire to work with Alice?
3. How would you respond to Alice's comment that "a lot of the things you suggest seem dumb."
4. At this point how easy is it for you to remember that the client has a right to choose the degree to which he or she will follow your recommendations?
5. If the client called and wanted your assistance with another problem, would you be willing to help?

ignore the helper's recommendations and advice results in the client's loss of life (see Case Illustration 1.4).

While it may be hard for any helper to accept a client's refusal to accept and follow a recommendation designed to maintain life, the fact remains that the decision—even this life and death decision—rests with the client. It is the client who will ultimately decide if and how to use the information, and the assistance provided—even when not following such assistance, results in his or her death.

The Role of the Helper in the Process of Change

As noted throughout the previous section, the helping process is clearly a joint venture with significant roles to be played by both the client and helper. But even with the assumptions

---

CASE ILLUSTRATION **1.4**
A Client Chooses Death

Roberto is a 67-year-old widower with two adult children. At the age of 60, Roberto was diagnosed with ALS. Over the course of the last year Roberto has experienced a rapid decline in his health and has become depressed. Dr. Sebring (a pastoral counselor) has been working with Roberto for his depression. Dr. Sebring has been employing a number of cognitive techniques to help Roberto reframe his life condition in such a way as to reestablish meaning even with his disease. Roberto has been very engaged in his counseling and employed the various techniques and strategies suggested by Dr. Sebring. As a result of his involvement in counseling, Roberto has found relief from his depression.

Roberto's disease has been progressing and within the last week he has lost his ability to swallow. Roberto's physician wants to insert a feeding tube but Roberto has refused this procedure. Dr. Sebring has continued to work with Roberto encouraging him to embrace life and to follow his physician's recommendation. Roberto, however, is clear and determined that he does not want to be admitted into a hospital, nor does he want to have the feeding tubes inserted. Roberto refuses to accept the recommendations of either his physicians or Dr. Sebring knowing full well that his refusal will result in his starvation and death.

about client responsibilities, one cannot forget that the client comes to the helping relationship often confused, anxious, and most certainly vulnerable. Helping is a relationship of power: The helper is entrusted to use that power wisely and ethically, with the client's welfare being central. This concern for *client welfare* serves as the organizing principle behind the various roles assumed by the helper within the helping relationship. Most standards (see Table 1.1) include statements such as that found in the ACA Statement of Ethical Standards (1995).

> The member's primary obligation is to respect the integrity and promote the welfare of the client(s) (Section A.1.A).

Although the specific way this obligation and role of the helper is manifested will be influenced by the theoretical approach, the nature of the problem, the unique characteristics of the client, and the context within which the help is provided, there are a number of responsibilities that universally fall to the helper in a helping relationship. Helpers are generally responsible for the following: (1) defining and maintaining a helping relationship; (2) facilitating a helping alliance; and (3) facilitating the client's movement toward some specific outcome. Each of the these responsibilities have as their primary purpose to "respect the integrity and promote the welfare of the client(s)" (ACA Code of Ethics, Section A.1.a).

Defining and Maintaining a Helping Relationship

The helping relationship is oftentimes very intense and almost always intimate. Clients are invited to disclose the very personal details of their lives and their situations. A helping relationship is characterized by a power differential that leaves the client vulnerable to the helper's actions (Keith-Spiegel & Koocher, 1985; Pope & Vasquez, 1991). Therefore, it is the helper who is ethically responsible for the relationship (Adleman & Barrett, 1990). The helper is responsible for creating and maintaining the boundaries that keep the client safe during these vulnerable times (see Chapter 8).

Unlike other relationships, in which the goal is to respond to and care for each other's needs, in helping it is the helper's responsibility to address the client's needs and NOT the other way around. Relationships in which the helper is using the interaction with the client to meet his or her own needs threaten this principle of professional contact. Consider the following case illustration (Illustration 1.5) as it elucidates this point.

Returning, for example, to the American Counseling Association Code of Ethics (ACA, 1995), we see the following mandate: "counselors are aware of the intimacy of the relationship . . . [and] maintain respect for the clients and avoid activities that seek to meet their personal needs at the expense of the client" (Section A.5.a). The helper is responsible for defining and maintaining some control over the types of information being discussed and the nature of the relationship as appropriate to the client. To successfully and ethically fulfill this role, this responsibility, helpers need to be aware of their unmet needs and the effect that these may have on their objectivity and helping relationships.

Self-Awareness of Helper's Needs. Since the directive for the ethical helper is to avoid engaging in activities that seek to meet the helper's personal needs at the expense of the

---

CASE ILLUSTRATION 1.5
A Helper Who Needs to Be Needed

Aneesha is a guidance counselor in a public middle school. She has working for the past month with Leonard, a seventh-grade student. Leonard was referred to the school counselor by his homeroom teacher. The teacher expressed her concerned that Leonard was very shy and somewhat vulnerable to being manipulated by his peers. The teacher thought that Leonard could use some assertive training.

Aneesha has recently divorced. She has found herself feeling lonely and has tried to compensate by spending more time at work. Aneesha comes early to school and stays late. She has begun to contact students with whom she had previously worked, checking on their status, and asking if they would like to come into talk with her.

Aneesha worked with Leonard for the past five weeks and his home- room teacher has noted a change in Leonard. Leonard appears more verbally expressive, both in class and with peers. Further, Leonard has made it very clear to his teacher that he would like to discontinue counseling. Leonard explained to his teacher that he had asked Aneesha if he could stop coming for a while and she said that it wasn't time yet. Leonard asked if the teacher would talk to the counselor.

The teacher shared her observations with the counselor along with Leonard's request. However, the counselor responded in no uncertain tone that she was the professional and "knew when it was right to stop."

---

client, it is essential for helpers to be aware of their own unmet needs (e.g., power, approval, nurture, control, intimacy) so that they do not seek satisfaction via the helping relationship.

The power of the helping relationship, the vulnerability of the client, and the intensity of the helping encounter can exert subtle influences on the parties involved and can prove quite seductive to the unaware helper. Consider the following exercise (Exercise 1.4) as it raises your own awareness of the potential for such boundary violation.

Ability to Maintain a Degree of Emotional Objectivity.   Recognizing the potential negative impact that one's unmet needs and concerns may have on the helping relationship is an essential, yet not sufficient, step. In addition to recognizing these unmet needs, the ethical helper needs to be able to maintain emotional objectivity throughout the helping encounter. Such emotional objectivity is often difficult to maintain, a point which is highlighted in Chapter 8.

The Use of Contracts.   One strategy employed by many helpers in establishing and maintaining the helping relationship is to formally define the nature and boundaries of the relationship in terms of a helping contract (Sills, 1997). Ethical helpers inform clients about the purpose and nature of the helping process (see Chapter 6).

This process of providing information not only facilitates the clients' ability to willingly participate and choose wisely, but also sets the boundaries of the helping relationship. The use of a contract can serve as a means for clarifying the nature, limits, responsibilities, and rights of the helping relationship. In developing a contract the helper encourages the

EXERCISE **1.4**
Recognizing a Helper's Unmet Needs

Directions: Along with a classmate or colleague, review the following case description. Then read the description of the five helpers listed below. Next:

1. Identify each helper's possible unmet needs.
2. Discuss the ways that the various helper characteristics and potential unmet needs may negatively impact the helping relationship.

The case situation and client description: The client is a 45-year-old mother of four. She came to a marriage counselor, complaining that her husband was insensitive to her needs as a woman and as a person. In her sessions she described her husband as traditional and somewhat chauvinistic. She stated that while he was a good provider, he was not willing to allow her to go back to school and develop a career of her own. When discussing their sexual relationship, the woman complained that her husband had a low sex drive while she was very sexual and would like to experiment with creative sexual activities.

Five potential therapists:
1. A female therapist who divorced her husband, returned to school, and just completed her degree.
2. A male therapist who comes from a traditional family and who himself has a stay at-home-wife and three children.
3. A male therapist who is married and is currently having financial difficulties.
4. A therapist who came from a broken home in which the divorce process was very drawn out and painful.
5. A therapist who has been without an intimate partner for over two years.

---

client to specify goals and expectations, as well as to affirm the boundaries of the relationship. While there are no hard and fast rules about the elements of a helping contract, items that seem to be essential to the informing nature of contract have been identified by Bennett and colleagues (1990) and are presented in Table 1.2.

It should be noted that not all helpers endorse the value of a contract. Handelsman and Glavin (1995) cite research that questions the value of a contract for the client. These authors question the client's capacity to give informed consent or to agree to a contract. Even with this as a possible caveat, clients have the right to have the helping process explained to them. The ethical helper will share information within the capacity of the client to understand that information and do so in language appropriate to the clients level of comprehension (see Chapter 6).

Facilitating the Development of a Helping Alliance

A second responsibility of a helper is to facilitate the development of a working relationship with the client. It is important for the helper to attempt to reduce the client's initial anxiety by providing the facilitative conditions for helping. Creating a warm and workable

---

TABLE 1.2   Elements of a Written Contract

While we are not suggesting the use of a contract as a risk management technique, one should consult local laws that govern contracting, especially in terms of consumer rights. If a contract is employed, the following are some of the elements to be considered for inclusion.

- Name of helper and client
- A preliminary schedule of sessions
- A date when sessions will begin
- A statement of goals
- A description of the model, techniques, and strategies to be used
- A description of potential negative effects of treatment
- A description of alternatives techniques that might be employed, along with a willingness to assist the client to find these alternatives
- Fee structure and payment schedule
- Statement regarding fee policy for missed appointments, telephone contacts, etc.
- A statement regarding the limits of confidentiality
- A statement of "no guarantee" of success and invitation regarding freedom to renegotiate the terms of the contract at any time.
- Signatures that identify client understanding and acceptance.

(Adapted from Bennett, Bryant, VandenBos, & Greenwood, 1990)

relationship in an atmosphere of understanding and acceptance is primary to the helping process.

Therefore, in addition to increasing our self-awareness of the limiting and potentially negative impact our biases may have on the helping process, it is also clear that we, as helpers, need to develop a number of values and attitudes that assist the client to begin to share his or her story.

The effective, ethical helper will demonstrate qualities of *acceptance, warmth,* and *genuineness* (Berenson & Carkhuff, 1967; Carkhuff & Berenson, 1977; Parsons, 1985; Truax & Carkhuff, 1965). While these conditions may not be sufficient for positive outcomes in every case, it does appear that they are key to the helping alliance and contribute in a facilitative way to the positive outcomes of helping (Ivey, Bradford-Ivey, & Simek-Morgan, 1993). So just as it may be assumed that ethical helpers are knowledgeable and skilled, they must also be people who can demonstrate these facilitative qualities of acceptance, warmth, and genuineness.

Facilitating the Client's Movement Toward Some Specific Outcome

In addition to providing the structure and conditions of a helping relationship, the helper is expected to bring special knowledge and skill to the interaction, which, when applied within the helping process, will assist the client to more effectively cope with the issue at hand. A fundamental principle to which all professional groups subscribe and one that will be more fully discussed in Chapter 2 is that a helper must be aware of the limitations of his/her professional competencies and not exceed those limitations in the delivery of his or her services (see Chapter 9).

Helpers need to bring specialized knowledge and skills to the process of helping. Ethical helpers do not employ procedures or techniques for which they are not properly trained, nor do they extend their helping to those individuals whose problems are well beyond their scope of training and expertise.

When operating alone in our offices, with no faculty member or supervisor looking over our shoulder, our real desire to help the client before us may seduce us into trying new techniques or approaches or even attempting to help with problems that are beyond our training and our experience. Knowing the limits of our competence; being willing to seek ongoing training, supervision, consultation; or making a referral to another helper are all characteristic of an ethical helper (Parsons, 1995). This issue of competence will be discussed in greater detail in the next chapter (Chapter 2).

Case Illustration

We began the chapter with a brief introduction to Maria, a client seeking the assistance of the school social worker, Ms. Wicks. We will continue to follow the development of the helping encounter between Marie and Ms. Wicks throughout the upcoming chapters.

As you read the case illustration, try to identify the presence of the various concepts and important terms described within the chapter. Further, as you read the case, place your self in the role of the helper and begin to identify the various concerns and areas of ethical consideration you might experience in that role.

Client: Hi. Are you Ms. Wicks? I'm Maria. Mr. Brady told me that I had to come talk with you.

Helper: Hi. Yes, I am Ms. Wicks (getting up to shake Marie's hand). Why don't you come in and have a seat? (Ms. Wicks makes a mental note about Maria's appearance. Maria, while appearing annoyed, is a very attractive girl. She looks you in the eye as she speaks and appears self-confident. Maria's manner of dress is somewhat seductive. Her skirt is very short and tight and her sweater has a very low neckline.)

MARIA: I don't want to be here—I didn't do anything.

MS. WICKS: You sound like you don't want to be here, but you are here. Would you like to return to class?

MARIA: No way! He's a jerk!

MS. WICKS: You certainly sound angry. Maria, I know you said you don't want to be here, but since you are I would love to hear what happened and see if I could be of some help? We have 20 minutes before the next change of class. If you would like, maybe you could tell me what happened? Maybe in talking about it we could come up with a plan to make it better.

MARIA: I don't like talking.

MS. WICKS: Well you don't have to, it really is your choice. If you prefer you could spend the rest of the period in the career center or reviewing college brochures? But you do look and sound upset and I would like to help if I could.

MARIA: Let me just take a minute. Can I get a drink of water? I'll be right back and I'll tell you what happened.

MS. WICKS: (After Maria comes back). Well, how was that? Better? You know I really do understand it is a bit strange to talk to someone you don't know. But, I've been able to meet and talk with a lot of the people here at school and it has been my experience that sometimes this has been very helpful. You may or may know but I am a social worker and I have been trained to help people problem solve. Do you have any questions about what I do here or what a social worker is?

MARIA: No, not really. You spoke with one of my friends who was having problems with his mom and dad. Did you see Jose Ramirez?

MS. WICKS: You know Maria one of the things I think is very important when I work with people is that I respect their privacy. In fact, when you and I talk about some things I will keep them in confidence. I mean, I won't tell anyone about what we talk about without your permission. Now there are some exceptions to that—like if you tell me you are going to hurt yourself or try to hurt someone else then I can't keep that secret. Your life is too important to me so I would want to get as many people as possible to help me keep you safe.

MARIA: Yeah, I know about confidentiality—I've gone to a shrink before.

MS. WICKS: Since we have a few more minutes maybe we could talk about getting together later today so that you could tell me what happened and maybe together we could decide if you and I could work on it? What do you think?

MARIA: Yeah, that's cool. I have a report to give in my next class but then I have study hall after that. Could I come back then?

MS. WICKS: (Looking at her calendar). Yes, I'm free. That's my lunch time. How about if we share a sandwich here in the office and get to know each other a bit better?

MARIA: Okay.

MS.WICKS: (Reaching in her desk). Here is a pass. So I'll see you at 12:15. There's the bell. Get back to your class—and give a great report! See you in a bit!

Reflections

1. Did you see any evidence of the creation of boundaries to this relationship?
2. Did Maria enact the role and responsibilities of a client, which were discussed within the chapter?
3. If you were the helper in this situation, how might have Maria's appearance, style, or story impact your objectivity or ability to be an effective, ethical helper?
4. What do you think Ms. Wicks needs to consider as she prepares to continue to enact her role as an ethical helper, meeting with Maria at 12:15?

Cooperative Learning Exercise

The purpose of this chapter was not only to introduce you to the nature of the helping process, the roles to be played by both the client and the helper, and the unique ethical challenges to be confronted within this role of helper, but also to have the you think about your own self in the role of helping. Being in touch with what you bring to the helping encounter is an essential first step to becoming an ethical and effective helper. Therefore, before proceeding to the next chapter, reflect on the following and discuss your reflections with a supervisor, colleague, or classmate.

1. Review your responses to this chapter's exercises. Were you honest? Did you invest energy in responding? If not, why not? What might this suggest about your investment in becoming an effective, ethical helper?
2. What did you learn about yourself as a helper? What specific elements of helping—as presented within this chapter—excite you or concern you?
3. Which particular characteristics of the effective, ethical helper do you feel you possess most strongly, and which do you feel you need to focus on developing?
4. How might you approach the reading, the exercises, and the reflections in the next chapter to maximize your development as a more self-aware, ethical helper?

Summary

The Helping Process: A Blending of Art and Science
The complexity and dynamic nature of the helping process is infused with subjectivity, intuition, and confusion, rendering its facilitation as much of an art as a science. While a foundation of theory and research serves as the base for effective helping, the dynamic process is highly influenced by the personal application and artistry of the helper as he or she adapts technology and research findings to the unique characteristics of individual clients.

The Helping Process: The Meeting of Client and Helper
Like other social encounters, helping is marked by verbal exchanges and sharing of information. Unlike most social encounters, however, helping is one in which the focus is given to one member, the client.

Helping is a process by which one person, the helper, interacts with another in such a way so as to facilitate this other's (i.e., the client's) utilization of his or her resources as he or she moves toward some specific outcome.

The Role of the Client in the Process of Change
Ethics not only ensures clients' rights but places corresponding responsibilities on them. Clients are expected to choose wisely, to make use of the information provided, and to assume control of their participation in the helping process. It is the client's role to decide what he

or she wants from the helping process and what he or she is willing to do to get what is wanted

The Role of the Helper in the Process of Change

The helper's primary obligation is to respect the integrity and promote the welfare of the client. This is accomplished in part by (1) defining and maintaining a helping relationship (2) facilitating a helping alliance, and (3) facilitating the client's movement toward some specific outcome.

IMPORTANT TERMS

acceptance	emotional objectivity
art	facilitative attitudes
assume control	genuineness
boundary violation	helper
client	helping alliance
conditional valuing	helping relationship
congruent	promote the welfare of the client
contract	science
competence	specific outcome
defining and maintaining a helping relationship	use of the information
dynamic process	warmth

SUGGESTED READINGS

Bersoff, D.N. (1995). *Ethical conflicts in psychology.* Washington, DC: American Psychological Association.

Parsons, R.D. (1995). *The skills of helping.* Boston: Allyn and Bacon

Rave, E.J., & Larsen, C.C. (1995) *Ethical decision making in therapy: Feminist perspectives.* New York: Guilford Press.

Sills, C. (Ed.). (1997). *Contracts in counseling.* Thousand Oaks, CA: Sage Publications.

2 Helper Variables: What the Helper Brings to the Helping Relationship

Ms. Wicks: Maria, let me see if I understand what you are saying. You are sexually active and you don't care that you are engaged in unprotected sex. The possibility of becoming pregnant or contracting a sexually transmitted disease, even AIDS, doesn't concern you. Is that what you are saying?

Ms. Wicks, the counselor in our sample case, appears to be actively listening and accurately reflecting Maria's explicit message. However, one must wonder about the manner in which she reflects that message. As a trained professional, Ms. Wicks is most likely attempting to remain objective as she continues her work with her client, Maria. But objectivity does not mean emotionally detached or without one's own values and beliefs.

Ms. Wicks has feelings, expectations, biases, and values regarding adolescents engaging in unprotected sex, and while she is attempting to maintain a professional objectivity, to assume she can remain value free is naive at best and "from an ethical perspective, dangerous" (Newman, 1993, p.151). Does Ms. Wicks' tone of voice, inflection, or even body language reveal her own biases and beliefs regarding unprotected adolescent sexual behavior?

The complexity of a helping process as a problem-solving venture, along with the potential for intense emotional reactions to be experienced by all involved, makes the helping process highly vulnerable to the influence of the needs, interests, beliefs, and expectations of both helper and client. We enter a helping relationship—as we enter all relationships—full of personal expectations, biases, and values. Further, as with any of our encounters, these expectations, biases, and values cannot help but influence the helping relationship, often in profound ways.

The ethical helper needs to be aware of her or his values, biases, and expectations, along with circumstances wherein these personal values, biases, and expectations may interfere with the effective helping of another. It is these affective and subjective factors that the helper brings to the relationship along with clinical knowledge and skill that serve as the focal point for the current chapter.

Chapter Objectives

Extending the discussion started in Chapter 1, which illustrated the role of the helper in the process of change, the current chapter will discuss the role that a helper's values, cultural biases, and professional model plays in giving shape to the helping process and this process of change. After reading this chapter you should be able to do the following:

1. Explain the need for helpers to increase self-awareness of personal values, beliefs, and expectations.
2. Describe the steps to be taken when helper–client values conflict.
3. Discuss the value of a helper having a theoretical model.
4. Define what is meant by "helper competence."
5. Discuss what is meant my the concept of cultural sensitivity.

Helper Values

While it is expected that the client's needs, values, and desires will give shape to the goals of the helping encounter and the nature of each helping interaction, what may not be expected is the role that the helper's values, needs, beliefs, and interests play in coloring the helping process. Consider the following case illustration as it demonstrates the potential influence that the helper's personal values, needs, beliefs, and interests may exert within the helping process (Case 2.1).

Clearly, Michele's personal interest in childbearing and current experience of sadness and grief around her inability to conceive is making it difficult for her to remain emotionally detached as she listens to Judy's story. While professional boundaries are essential for ethical helping, the concept of helper detachment and total objectivity is truly a myth, one that if gone unchallenged can prove detrimental to the helping relationship.

Helpers: Detached and Objective

The fact that helpers' biases, expectations or values are active in the helping process may run contrary to your own belief that helpers must be totally objective, totally value-free. It is neither possible nor desirable to be "scrupulously neutral with respect to values in the counseling relationship" (Corey, Corey, & Callanan, 1988, p. 67). The potential influence of a helper's values, needs, beliefs and interest within the helping relationship is a point of concern and interest for all professional organizations (Table 2.1).

While professional organizations cannot police personal values—they do highlight the importance of recognizing the existence of these values. Further, the various professional organizations have attempted to codify a set of values to guide professional practice and present these in the forms of codes of professional conduct and ethics. However, one cannot simply compartmentalize the "ethics" of the professional helper versus the virtue, value, and ethics of the person of the helper. As such, it is imperative for all ethical helpers to increase awareness of their own personal values, beliefs, and expectations as well as their roles in giving shape to their professional identify and behavior within the helping dynamic.

CASE ILLUSTRATION **2.1**
Michele: Maintaining Objectivity

Michele is a social worker for the Department of Human Services in a large metropolitan city. From all accounts, she is a consummate professional, respected by her peers and supervisors and truly embraced by all her clients. Because of her own competence, Michele is often given some of the hardest cases to handle.

Michele and her husband of five years have, for the past two years unsuccessfully tried to have a child. Michele has just found out that she is unable to get pregnant because of scar tissues lining her fallopian tube. This news has been very upsetting to Michele, and she is currently in counseling.

Michele has continued to go to work and to date has been able to maintain an active, professional calendar. Michele has just been assigned a new case. Judy, is an 18-year-old, single women who is currently living in a halfway house for people progressing through a drug treatment program. The following is part of the intake interview between Michele and Judy.

MICHELE: Hi, Judy. Please come in and have a seat. Thanks for coming.

JUDY: No problem.

MICHELE: As you know I am a social worker for the Department of Human Services, and I will be your case worker while you are at Hansen House (the halfway house). I will help you coordinate your work and therapy schedules and work with you in trying to develop a career development plan.

JUDY: Yeah—I kind of know what you do—I've done this before.

MICHELE: You have?

JUDY: Well, not the halfway house, drug thing. But I had a social worker when I was 11 and another time, like at 13 or 14, living in Detroit.

MICHELE: So you worked with a social worker before. Could you tell me what that was like?

JUDY: It was okay—I had to go 'cause I was living on the street and I got pregnant a couple of times and tried to abort myself.

MICHELE: You were pregnant?

JUDY: Duh, yeah.

MICHELE: But you were just a kid! Just 11!

JUDY: Yeah—so? I was having sex when I was like 9 or 10. I must have gotten pregnant like four times—with two abortions and two "whatevers."

MICHELE: Whatever? Judy, you are talking about human life here.

JUDY: Whoa, cool it . . . that was then . . . I thought you were supposed to be helping me with this career thing? I don't need another person preaching at me!

TABLE 2.1 Ethical Principles Regarding Objectivity

American Association of Marriage and Family Therapists (1998)	3.2 Marriage and family therapists seek appropriate professional assistance for their personal problems or conflicts that may impair work or performance or clinical judgment.
American Counseling Association (1995)	A.5.b Counselors are aware of their own values, attitudes, beliefs, and behaviors and how these apply in a diverse society, and avoid imposing their values on clients.
American Psychological Association (1995)	1.13 Personal Problems and Conflicts (a) Psychologists recognize that their personal problems and conflicts may interfere with their effectiveness. Accordingly, they refrain from undertaking an activity when they know or should know that their personal problems are likely to lead to harm for a patient, client, colleague, student, research participant, or other person to whom they may owe a professional or scientific obligation. (b) In addition, psychologists have an obligation to be alert to signs of, and obtain assistance for, their personal problems at an early stage, in order to prevent significantly impaired performance. (c) When psychologists become aware of personal problems that may interfere with their performing work-related duties adequately, they take appropriate measures, such as obtaining professional consultation or assistance, and determine whether they should limit, suspend, or terminate work-related duties.
National Association of Social Workers (1996)	1.06 Social workers should be alert to and avoid conflicts of interest that interfere with the exercise of professional discretion or an impartial judgment. Social workers should inform clients when a real or potential conflict of interest arises and take reasonable steps to resolve the issue in a manner that makes the clients' interests primary and protects clients' interests to the greatest extent possible. In some cases, protecting clients' interests may require termination of the professional relationship with the proper referral of the client.

Helper Values and Expectations: Shaping the Helping Relationship

Many professional helpers (e.g., counselors, therapists and social workers) present themselves as totally objective, totally value-free. As noted above, total objectivity is not possible. It is possible that the feelings experienced in the helping encounter or the values and expectations with which the helper enters the relationship can distort the helpers' objectivity and interfere with the effective utilization of an appropriate helping process. These feelings can oftentimes be quite subtle in their development and thus can go unrecognized until they have done their damage (see Case Illustration 2.1).

EXERCISE **2.1**
Identifying Areas of Helper Value Conflict

Directions: Part 1: Review the characteristics and experiences of each of the follow-ing helpers and assume that his or her unique experience may cause biases in a partic-ular direction. Next identify a type of client problem for which the helper will have very strong feelings (for or against) and thus may have difficulty remaining nonjudgmental and objective.

Discuss with your colleagues or classmates the impact such bias may have on the help-ing process.

COUNSELOR A: A female professional who had to pay for her own college and post-baccalaureate education even as her family objected that a place for women is in the home.

COUNSELOR B: A divorced professional who experienced and continues to experi-ence a bitter dispute over child custody.

COUNSELOR C: A person who was raised in a very strict, bible-oriented religious family and who identifies herself as a Christian fundamentalist.

COUNSELOR D: An overachieving, highly successful, somewhat driven helper who has been accused as being a workaholic by his coworkers.

Part 2: For each of the following clients, identify one of the counselors (listed above) who may have difficulty in remaining objective and nonjudgmental

CLIENT A: A person considering an abortion

CLIENT B: A person considering suicide

CLIENT C: A child abuser

CLIENT D: A person having an extramarital affair

CLIENT E: A person wishing to break away and becoming independent of her parents.

Helpers cannot always keep their own values out of the helping process. Helper value systems do influence the helper's view of goals, strategies, and even topics discussed (Young-gren, 1993). While helpers cannot be totally value-free, this does not mean they have free license to make helping an indoctrination process (Grimm, 1994). Exercise 2.1 will help illustrate the potential conflict that can exist between helper values and client needs.

As may be evident in the illustrations provided in Exercise 2.1, helper values and biases can interfere with effective helping. Establishing professional boundaries and main-taining professional detachment and objectivity in service of the client, while never absolute, remains a goal of ethical helping (see Chapter 8). In service of this process it may be necessary for the helper to not only clarify but also articulate his or her personal and professional values and the role they may play in the helping process (Newman, 1993). A client has a right to know where the helper stands on various issues presented within in the helping process (Corey, Corey, & Callanan, 1998). To do less is to deprive the client of self-determination (Brace, 1997). Therefore, the ethical helper will attempt to identify and understand the role personal values may play in her or his enactment of the role as helper prior to engaging in a helping relationship. Through such heightened self-awareness, a helper may be more able to monitor the potential influence that his or her values and expectations may have in the helping relationship.

It may be hard for you as a helper to anticipate the type of client problems with which you will be invited to work. As such it may be hard to predetermine how your values may help or hinder your effectiveness as a helper. Exercise 2.2 is designed to increase self-awareness of values and bias. As with each of the exercises it is suggested that responses are shared and discussed with your colleagues or classmates.

The challenge for the ethical helper is to use personal values to enhance the helping process without abusing the power of the relationship or the vulnerability of the client. While it is clear that the ethical helper will resist the temptation to become a missionary for a particular value, she or he will also be "honest enough to recognize how one's value commitments may not promote health"(Bergin, 1991, p. 399).

When Values Conflict

The mutual nature of the helping process almost ensures that there will be times when the individual values, beliefs, and needs of the helper and client may conflict. While respecting

---

EXERCISE 2.2
Areas of Personal Bias

Directions: Part 1: For each of the following identify your belief, your attitude, or your value about the issue presented. Along with a classmate or colleague, discuss the potential impact your position on each of these issues may have as you engage in the helping process.

> Equality of genders
> Fidelity in marriage
> Children's rights
> The recreational use of drugs
> Date rape and the responsibility of the person raped
> Cheating in school
> The viewpoint that one should be able to pull himself or herself up by the bootstraps
> The sanctity of marriage
> A women's right to choose an abortion
> Alternative lifestyles

Part 2: Through personal reflection and discussion of your responses to Part 1, identify those items in Part 1 for which you have *strong* opinions, attitudes, or values. Identify the type of client problems for which these values may interfere with your ability to remain objective and nonjudgmental.

the client and accepting the client's right to choose his or her own vales, a helper may not agree with or embrace those values. Consider the Case Illustration 2.2.

Under these conditions, the ethical helper will expose those values in conflict and then along with the client, review these areas of value conflict in order to decide how they may impact the decisions made in the helping process. When the conflict is such that it interferes with the helper's ability to effectively assist the client, the ethical helper will prepare the client for referral to another helper who is more in line with the client's needs and values (see Chapter 9).

Helper Orientation: A Theoretical Agenda for Helping

In addition to having our practice decisions influenced by personal values and expectations, our view of the "reality" of the helping encounter will be shaped by the model of helping we have embraced and employ. The information presented by each client often appears somewhat disjointed and disconnected. Each helper needs to weave a thread of consistency

---

CASE ILLUSTRATION 2.2
Conflicting Values

Howard is a clinical psychologist who is married with three children, ages 9, 14, and 18. Howard married at the age of 20 and worked full-time as he finished his senior year in college and continued as a graduate student. When his wife, Lisa, became pregnant the couple mutually decided that Lisa would stop working and would be a stay-at-home mom at least until their children were in high school. Both Lisa and Howard value the importance of children having a full-time parent at home, especially during what Howard calls the formative years.

Howard has just received a call from a new client, Tangelique. In a brief telephone intake, Howard learns that Tangelique is 31 years old, a member of a major law firm, on track to become a partner. Tangelique's husband, Ralph, is a physician completing his surgical residency. Tangelique is three months pregnant and, according to Tangelique, she and Ralph are fighting a lot and having "serious marital conflict." The conflict centers on the issue of child care following delivery. Tangelique wants to return to work as soon as possible and feels that the baby can do very well receiving "good, professional child care." Ralph strongly believes that it is essential for a parent to be at home especially during these early years. Ralph stated he would be willing to stay at home if he had completed his residency, but he has a year and a half to finish. He wants Tangelique to stay home for the next two years and then they can decide what to do. Tangelique is willing to cut back on her 60 hours a week to 30 or 40, but this is totally unacceptable to Ralph.

As Howard listens to the presenting concern he becomes very aware of his strong feelings of agreement with Ralph, even prior to meeting the couple. Tangelique stated that she and her husband agree that professional counseling is important at this point in their relationship, and they would like to schedule an appointment.

or find a theme within the information so that she or he can understand what is "really" going on and how best to approach this situation. Most helpers find that making sense out of the information provided by the client is aided by the use of a theoretical model or framework.

Theories of helping such as behavioral theory, psychoanalytic theory, cognitive theory, systems theory, and the like provide frameworks for understanding the meaning of a person's actions as well as offering prescriptions for how to help the person move to a more fully functioning life.

However, just as these theoretical models help us to "make sense" of the information provided by the client, we must be sensitive to the possibility that such a model can impose "sense" on the data offered (see Case Illustration 2.3).

While it is possible that Jimmy is having difficulty resolving issues around his own sexuality, father–son relationship, and so on and therefore acts silly in class because he is anxious, it is just as likely that Tom is simply making him laugh. Peggy's interest in a psy-

---

CASE ILLUSTRATION **2.3**
Finding or Imposing Meaning

Peggy is a recent graduate with a master's degree in counseling. Peggy has always wanted to be a counselor and has been very taken by the psychodynamic view of helping. Peggy intends to go on for additional training and someday become a psychoanalyst.

Peggy is currently employed as a middle-school counselor. She is currently meeting with Jimmy, age 11. Jimmy was sent to her office by his health-science teacher who is very concerned with Jimmy's tendency to giggle and "act silly" during health class. When asked about his behavior in class, Jimmy described the following.

> I sit next to Tom. He's my best friend. But he is a goof. He is always making funny noises or saying things about what we are talking about in class—and I can't help it I just start to laugh. I always get caught and Tom gets away with it.

Peggy asks Jimmy to tell her what they are studying and what type of things Tom may say.

Jimmy responds:

> I don't know . . . something to do with becoming a man and a woman, puberty or something like that, I don't know . . .

At this point, Peggy starts to challenge Jimmy and ask other information about his relationship with his parents.

> Jimmy, you keep saying you don't know. Is it that you don't know or that you find it difficult to talk about these type of things?
>
> Jimmy, it would be helpful to me if you could tell me a little about your family and your relationship with you parents, especially your Dad.

choanalytic theory as well as her own limited training may be directing her to see meaning where none exists.

The ethical practitioner needs to be competent and grounded within the theory and research supporting the helping process (see Chapter 9). Beyond being able to identify the model from which one approaches the helping process, it is also imperative that as an ethical helper, one remembers that theories and models provide only tentative frameworks, not absolute directives, and need to be tested for validity in each situation.

Reflecting and Validating Interpretations

Theoretical models can assist a helper to gather data, connect the information provided, and draw hypothesis and tentative conclusions about the meaning of that data. The ethical helper will keep focused on the "hypothesis testing" nature of this process (see Chapter 9).

As data are provided, the effective helper needs to hazard tentative guesses about meanings and connections to previous data. Once these hypotheses have been established the helper needs to go about the process of finding more information to validate his or her hypotheses or revise these hypotheses as new information is revealed.

The ethical helper will not only continue to identify and articulate his or her model of helping but will remain vigilant in his or her evaluation and testing of the validity of that model. Table 2.2 provides a number of questions that should guide the helper's reflections.

Helper Competence: Beyond Knowledge and Skill

The ethical helper is a competent helper. While competence implies the possession of the knowledge and skill required to practice (see Chapter 9), it also implies the ability to implement and apply that knowledge and skill. Competence goes beyond simply knowing—it requires doing. As such, helpers need to be self-aware and self-caring so as to provide the best care they can.

TABLE 2.2   Guidelines for Reflections of Operating Model

Our theoretical, operative models help give shape to how we see our clients, their problems, prognosis, goals and pathways to those goals. It is important to check the utility and validity of our models for each of our clients and helping encounters.

Questions to consider in reflecting on our operational models of helping:

1. Can I explain the major assumptions and tenets of my model to a colleague?
2. Is it employed by others within the field?
3. Is there support—clinical, anecdotal, empirical—for this model?
4. Can I demonstrate its utility and validity for understanding this current case?
5. What are the limitations and inherent biases built into this model?
6. Are there specific clients, or client problems, for which this model will not be effective?

Care of the Helper—Essential to Maintaining Competence

The failure of the helper to take appropriate care of herself or himself can result in stress and burnout which, in turn, will threaten competence and ethical practice. The ethical helper maintains his or her well-being by seeking physical and psychological care when it is needed, by being alert to the signs of stress and burnout, and by evaluating the decisions he or she has made in relation to the needs of his or her clients (Bennett, Bryant, Vanden-Bos, & Greenwood, 1990, p. 25). The helping process can take a toll on the helper. For example, Farber (1983) found that conducting therapy had decreased the therapists' emotional investment in their own families as well as their ability to be genuine, spontaneous, and comfortable with friends. Clearly, such an ongoing experience can not only jeopardize the helper's own emotional well-being but will interfere with her or his ability to perform competently with her or his clients (Skorupa & Agresti, 1993).

While there may be subtle differences in both the experience and definition of burnout, most agree that it is an ongoing process of depletion of energy, increased fatigue, and a general debilitation of one's functioning. A number of researchers have noted that overly stressed, burned-out helpers can actually contribute to the dysfunctioning and suffering of their clients rather than reduce it (e.g., Emerson & Markos, 1996; Stadler, 1990). Various codes of ethics (see Table 2.3) address the issue of practitioner impairment and have application to the stressed and burned-out helper.

It is the ethical responsibility of all helpers to take the steps needed to protect themselves, their clients, and even colleagues from the potentially damaging effect of such stress and burnout (Benningfield, 1994). While professional help may be required to reduce the impairment resulting from stress and burnout, there are other steps that all ethical helpers can do in attempting to reduce the potential negative effects of helper stress. In fact, rather then simply focusing on the identification of impairment and the introduction of effective remedial programs, the ethical helper will attempt to employ preventive steps, such as continued education, personal therapy, supervision, and peer interaction (Guy, 1987). Specific steps that may help to reduce the potential impact of stress on the functioning of the helper are the following:

1. *Set realistic expectations.* Ethical helpers recognize that they are not omnipotent. Deutsch (1984), in a survey of therapists, found that practitioners with exceptionally high goals often reported high levels of stress. The healthy, ethical helper sets realistic expectations for him- or herself, the client, and the outcome of any one helping relationship.

2. *Take care of self.* It is important for helpers to eat properly, rest, and exercise. Helping is a energy-draining activity, and the ethical, healthy helper will take steps needed to ensure her or his own health is maintained.

3. *Organize and manage.* Boundaries need to be established that not only organize your professional day but help to distinguish the professional from the personal aspects of your life. The ethical, healthy helper will schedule variations into the day, including sufficient breaks to take care of paperwork, personal needs, or even to to take a moment's breather.

4. *Keep perspective.* Helpers need to remember that helping is part of their life, not all of their life. The effective helper will also establish mechanisms for ongoing professional support (e.g., supervision, personal counseling, peer involvement) that are geared to help

TABLE 2.3   **Selected Statements on Professional Impairment**

American Counseling Association (1995)	C.2.g: Counselors refrain from offering or accepting professional services when their physical, mental, or emotional problems are likely to harm a client or others. They are alert to the signs of impairment, seek assistance for problems, and, if necessary, limit, suspend, or terminate their professional responsibilities.
American Psychological Association (1995)	1.13.c. When psychologists become aware of personal problems that may interfere with their performing work-related duties adequately, they take appropriate measures, such as obtaining professional consultation or assistance, and determine whether they should limit, suspend, or terminate their work-related duties.
National Association of Social Workers (1996)	4.05.b. Social workers whose personal problems, psycho-social distress, legal problems, substance abuse, or mental health difficulties interfere with their professional judgment and performance should immediately seek consultation and take appropriate remedial action by seeking professional help, making adjustments in workload, terminating practice, or taking any other steps necessary to protect clients and others. (NASW, 1996, 4.05.b.)
American Association of Marriage and Family Therapists (1998)	Marriage and family therapists seek appropriate professional assistance for their problems or conflicts that may impair work performance or clinical judgement.

the helper maintain objectivity and professional distance, especially when working with particularly difficult cases.

In addition to these preventive steps, ethical practitioners will be aware of the various conditions leading to stress and burnout as well as the warning signs and symptoms of stress in their own life. In a somewhat classic discussion on the issue of burnout, Freudenberger and Richelson (1980) offer a "burnout scale" in which a helper can assess himself or herself along a continuum from "doing fine" to "in dangerous place." Exercise 2.3 provides an adaptation of the original scale and, along with Exercise 2.4, can be used to assess your own current state of stress and burnout.

Helper Sensitivity to Diversity and Culture

Human behavior—human problems—and the process of helping occur within a social and cultural context. For a human service professional to view individual concerns or a person's problems as separate from that person's social, cultural context is to misunderstand them.

EXERCISE 2.3
Recognizing Burnout—Personal Signals

Directions: For each of the following, check the symptom or signal that you have experienced within the last three months. Discuss the symptoms that you have or are experiencing with a colleague, supervisor, or another professional helper in order to develop strategies for reducing such symptoms.

———Hoped that a client would cancel or not show up

———Feel apathetic and uncaring

———Finding it harder to pay attention in the sessions

———Have been forgetting assignments, appointments, etc.

———Don't seem to laugh as much as usual.

———Don't seem to find things as enjoyable as usual

———Lost patience with a client

———Complain about cases to others

———Feel extremely fatigued at the end of the day

———Feel overly tense when with a client

———Experiencing headaches, muscle tension, or stomach problems

———Feel increasingly sad or irritable

Adapted from H. Freudenberg & G. Richelson (1980) *Burn-out: How to beat the high cost of success.* New York: Doubleday.

EXERCISE 2.4
Assessing Potential for Stress and Burnout

Directions: Consider each of the following questions as they reflect your own personal approach to stress and stressful situations. The questions have been adapted from those originally presented by Bennett, Bryant, VandenBos, and Greenwood (1990). Identify those patterns that may increase your risk of burnout and develop a plan to modify those patterns.

1. Do you tend to ignore problems because of fear?
2. Have you learned stress management techniques? For example, do you employ relaxation techniques, time management strategies, etc.?
3. Are you aware of your own personal needs, and are you able to take care of these personal needs?
4. Are you familiar with the warning signs and symptoms of stress and burnout? Are you sensitive and aware of the appearance in these signs as they may signal your own developing level of stress?

5. Do you listen to others (e.g., members of your family, friends, colleagues) when they attempt to point out their concern for your health and wellfare or when they suggest stress may be affecting you?
6. Do you consider seeking help and support when you become aware that you are experiencing stress?

The helper who is culturally unaware and unaware of the values, assumptions, and beliefs that he or she brings to the encounter is vulnerable to unethical practice (Sue, Ivey, & Pederson, 1996).

All helping is to some degree multicultural. Both helper and client bring unique cultural values and social roles to the interaction. As noted by Speight, Myers, Cox, and Highlen (1991) multicultural helping is not restricted to white helpers working with ethnic clients. It applies to female counselors working with male clients, lesbian helpers with straight clients, Jewish helpers with Buddhist clients, even elderly helpers working with youth. In fact, it has been argued that counselors who do not integrate cross-cultural factors (e.g., sex, race, age, social class, or sexual orientation) into their practice infringe on the client's cultural autonomy and basic human rights, and they lessen the chances of establishing an effective therapeutic relationship. Clearly, these conditions would serve as fodder for unethical practice.

All professional organizations emphasize the ethical imperative for helpers to maintain cultural sensitivity and the importance of practitioners recognizing the special needs of diverse client populations (see Table 2.4). The APA Code of Conduct, for example, requires psychologists to obtain the necessary training, experience, consultation, or supervision "where differences of age, gender, race, ethnicity, national origin, religion, sexual orientation, disability, language, or socioeconomic status significantly affect psychologists' work concerning particular individuals or groups" (APA, 1992, Standard 1.08).

To be an ethical helper, one must be open to the values and beliefs of his or her client and be aware of how these relate to his or her own values and beliefs. More specifically, Sue, Arrendondo and McDavis (1992) proposed standards for multicultural counselor competencies that we believe have relevance to all ethical helpers and, as such, will be discussed in some detail. These include the following:

1. Awareness of their own assumptions, values, biases, and limitations and how these can affect the minority client.
2. Understanding the world view of culturally different clients and how these relate to oppressive sociopolitical forces in the United States and to traditional counseling theories.
3. Development of a wide repertoire of appropriate intervention strategies that include verbal and nonverbal communication and out-of-office activities when necessary.

TABLE 2.4   Selected Statements on Cultural Diversity and Sensitivity

American Counseling Association (1995)	A.2.a. Nondiscrimination. Counselors do not condone or engage in discrimination based on age, color, culture, disability, ethnic group, gender, race, religion, sexual orientation, marital status, or socioeconomic status.
	A.2.b. Respecting Differences. Counselors will actively attempt to understand the diverse cultural backgrounds of the clients with whom they work. This includes, but is not limited to, learning how the counselor's own cultural/ethnic/racial identity impacts her or his values and beliefs about the counseling process.
American Psychological Association (1995)	1.08 Psychologists should obtain the necessary training, experience, consultation or supervision "where differences of age, gender, race, ethnicity, national origin, religion, sexual orientation, disability, language, or socioeconomic status significantly affect psychologists' work concerning particular individuals or groups."
American Association of Marriage and Family Therapists (1998)	1.1. Marriage and family therapists do not discriminate against or refuse professional service to anyone on the basis of race, gender, religion, national origin, or sexual orientation.
National Association of Social Workers (1996)	1.05 Cultural Competence and Social Diversity
	Social workers should understand culture and its function in human behavior and society, recognizing the strengths that exist in all cultures.
	Social workers should have a knowledge base of their clients' culture and be able to demonstrate competence in the provision of services that are sensitive to clients' cultures and to differences among people and cultural groups.

Self-Awareness

The effective helper appreciates that her or his view of life, and more specifically her or his view of a client and a client's problem, is highly influenced by world or cultural viewpoint. To be an effective, ethical helper, therefore, one must become sensitive to: (1) his or her own cultural framework and the way it biases his or her attitudes, values, behaviors, and approach to helping, and (2) the client's cultural makeup and the role this cultural element plays in the creation and resolution of the problem presented. The goal is not to become expert and master of all cultural nuance. The goal is to be aware of one's own cultural background as it serves to filter and color client information. The following case (Case Illustration 2.4) illustrates the potentially negative impact one's ignorance of personal cultural bias may have on the accurate understanding of the client's information.

Ms. Thompson, the counselor in this case illustration, was certainly well-meaning. While she most likely values the family unit, it appears that, unlike Lida, Ms. Thompson sees the family as a springboard from which the individual child individuates by moving on. From this perspective, college serves as an excellent resource to stimulate that individ-

---

CASE ILLUSTRATION **2.4**
School Counselor—Filtering Client Information

Ms. Thompson is a senior high counselor working with college placement. She has been recognized as extremely competent and quite successful at assisting her students to gain entrance to the colleges of their choice. Ms. Thompson also prides herself on being able to help her students gain entrance to the "best colleges."

Ms. Thompson is about to meet with Lida Alvarez, a transfer student who has shown an aptitude for mathematics. Lida's family recently moved to this district, having lived in a neighboring district for the past six years. Lida's family is originally from Argentina. Her family (Lida, an older brother, mother, father, and paternal grandparents) moved to the United States when Lida was 10 years old.

Ms. Thompson: Hi, Lida. I'm Ms. Thompson, your college counselor. I see from your records that you are and have been a very good student. You appear to have a real knack for mathematics. I would be interested in knowing what colleges you have begun to consider.

> **LIDA:** I am not thinking about going to college, at least not right after I graduate from high school.
>
> **MS. THOMPSON:** Lida, if it is a financial issue there are a number of scholarships for which you would be a great candidate. I have a lot of success getting students money.
>
> **LIDA:** No, it's not the money. I'm going to work with my mom and dad in our family restaurant.
>
> **MS. THOMPSON:** That is nice, Lida. However, don't you think that a person with your abilities should consider doing something beyond restaurant work?
>
> **LIDA:** It's not just restaurant work—it is our family's restaurant. It was originally my grandfather's and has been in our family for fifty years. They started it in Argentina, which my uncle's family continues to run, and we have had this one in the United States for six years now. This has been my grandfather's dream to bring his restaurant to the United States.
>
> **MS. THOMPSON:** I didn't mean to suggest it is not a good restaurant. I just thought you may find it more stimulating and challenging to go on to college, maybe before you work in the restaurant.
>
> **LIDA:** Ms. Thompson, I am sure you mean well, but this really isn't about college, the restaurant, money, or any of that . . . it is about family, and for now my family needs me to work in the restaurant—and I want to be part of the tradition my grandfather started. There may be a time, later, when I will want to consider something else, including college, but for now I am looking forward to graduating and helping out with my family. But, thanks for your help.

ual development. Lida, however, values family and her ability to contribute to its maintenance. Ms. Thompson missed Lida's perspective on family and her role in it. Lida's tight
family commitment and the importance of tradition in maintaining the family business is
clearly a value that is directing her decisions, one in which she takes pride and feels a sense
of satisfaction.

The ethical helper needs to acknowledge the impact that ethnicity and culture has on
one's behavior and take these factors into account when working with clients with diverse
cultural backgrounds. Further, the ethical helper will seek out educational and training
experiences to enhance understanding of the influence of his or her own cultural values and
the variety of values embraced by their clients so that he or she can address the needs of
these populations more appropriately and effectively.

Understanding the World View of Culturally Different Clients

The ethical and culturally sensitive helper is aware of the limitedness and narrowness of
any one single cultural perspective, even if, and perhaps especially when, that perspective
represents the cultural mainstream. The ethical helper is aware that the "truth" is culture
colored and is therefore sensitive to a larger worldview.

It is not the intent to suggest that each helper be skilled and knowledgeable in all cultures or that a person abandon his or her own cultural perspective. Nor is it the intent to suggest that to be ethical one should only counsel those of similar culture backgrounds. Not
only would such a suggestion be unrealistic, but evidence for ethnical matching in counseling is less than convincing (Atkinson, 1983). What is suggested, however, is that the ethical helper will accept and *value* as legitimate the culturally diverse perspective presented
by clients. To see the client, the client's concerns, and the impact of the therapeutic process
through the cultural lense of the client is both a challenge and an ethical responsibility.
Exercise 2.5 highlights the challenge posed by such a call to cultural sensitivity.

Development of a Wide Repertoire of Appropriate Intervention Strategies

In addition to being aware of the biasing influence of one's own culture and accepting the
culture perspective of the client, the ethical helper will attempt to employ intervention
strategies that are in concert with the client's culture. The ethical, culturally sensitive helper
will understand the institutional and cultural barriers that may interfere with the client's use
of particular strategies and interventions. Further, the ethical helper will be aware of and
respectful of the indigenous helping practices and intrinsic help-giving networks found in
various cultures and communities. For example, Sue and Morishima (1982) reported a cul-
ture-specific intervention that involved the use of an older uncle to serve as an intermedi-
ary to help resolve a conflict between an immigrant Chinese daughter and her immigrant
mother-in-law. Such mediation was a common practice in Chinese culture and thus
reflected a sensitivity and utilization of indigenous helping practices.

EXERCISE 2.5
Cultural Value Preferences

Directions: For each of the scenarios provided use the table below to identify areas in which the culture of the helper may interfere with the efficacy of the helping process.

Scenario 1:
Arnold is a first generation Asian American who has come to discuss his career choices with Mr. Adams, the school counselor. Mr. Adams is very excited about Arnold's academic abilities and is eager to develop a career path that will maximize Arnold's achievement.

Scenario 2:
Latisha is an African American woman who has come to counseling because of what she describes as feelings of depression and thoughts of worthlessness. Dr. Jong has been trained in a nondirective, client-centered form of therapy. She places emphasis on highlighting the client's awareness of her experiences and the internal processes she or he employs in choosing a life path.

Scenario 3:
Alex is a bright, upper-middle-class, Caucasian male. Alex is finishing his senior year in college and has been experiencing panic attacks. Dr. Linda Handsen is attempting to work with Alex, using meditation and guided imagery.

Area of Relationship	Asian American	Native American	African American	Hispanic American	Middle-Class White American
Nature/ Environment	Harmony with	Harmony with	Harmony with	Harmony with	Mastery over
Time	Past-present	Present	Present	Past-present	Future
People	Collateral	Collateral	Collateral	Collateral	Individual
Mode of Activity	Doing	Being-in-becoming	Doing	Being-in becoming	Doing
Nature of Humans	Good	Good	Good and bad	Good	Good and bad

Source: Adapted from *Family Therapy with Ethnic Minorities* (p. 232) by M.K. Ho, 1987, Newbury Park, CA: Sage. Copyright 1987 by Sage Publications.

TABLE 2.5   Culturally Sensitive Interventions

Client Reference Group	Culturally Sensitive Intervention	Recommended Reading
African American	Involvement of clergy and church network as support resources for families in crisis.	Richardson (1992)
Hispanic (Latinos)	Minuchin's family systems approach, which emphasizes generational boundaries instead of equal rights of each family member.	Falicov (1982)
Native Americans	Cooperation with traditional healing approaches of shamans and medicine men and also the involvement of extended family of aunts, uncles, and grandparents.	Thomason (1993)
Asian Americans	Including family members as agents of therapy. This is based on the cultural belief that the family is supposed to deal with personal problems, thus, such clients may resist talking about themselves.	Sue & Sue (1990)

While it is important to note that individual variation *within* cultures exists and that no single statement or strategy is applicable to all members of that culture, Table 2.5 provides a number of examples of culturally sensitive interventions for a variety of reference groups.

The Need for Ongoing Training

The importance of cultural awareness and sensitivity cannot be overemphasized, and yet many helpers fail to approach helping encounters with the appropriate cultural sensitivity and skill. As noted by Sue and Sue (1990), one of the reasons for therapeutic ineffectiveness in cross-cultural counseling "lies in the training of mental health professionals" (p. 7). The ethical helper whose previous formalized training failed to provide cross-cultural training needs to take steps to not only raise personal awareness of cultural factors but also to increase understanding and expand techniques that are appropriate for cross-cultural counseling. Cultural competence has been deemed so important that at least one state (Pennsylvania) has taken a position that mandatory continuing education in cultural diversity be established for license renewal (Knapp, 1998).

The Ethics of Therapeutic Choice

Licensed and certified mental health providers are required to not only provide clients with care that an ordinary, average person should exercise under such circumstances, but to provide services that compare to that of their professional peers. A mental health professional who fails to meet the relevant standard of care, when compared with that of other professionals in the same community with comparable training and experience, is not only performing unethically but may also be found to be negligent in his or her duty to provide care. The evidence for such negligence will rest on the clinical correctness and efficacy of the treatment that was given, along with the practitioner's judgment in choosing it (Bennett et al., 1990).

Ethically and legally, a practitioner needs to not only be competent and skillful in the application of her or his helping skills but needs to employ those skills and approaches that have generally been accepted within the profession as appropriate and customary. Professionals who employ "innovative strategies" not only run the risk of malpractice based on the principle of negligence, but at minimal run the risk of failing their ethical responsibility to provide the best care possible.

Selecting the Appropriate Treatment

All ethical mental health practitioners attempt to make decisions that result in the best approach to use with their clients. Choices within a helping dynamic may occur at an intuitive level as well as a critical evaluative level (Kitchener, 1986). However, as noted by others (e.g., Corey, Corey, & Callahan, 1993; Kitchener, 1986) reliance on feelings and intuition alone in professional decision making may result in poor decisions.

Practitioners need to move from intuitive decision making to more critical evaluative methods (see Chapter 9). Practice decisions need to be made following a practitioner's explorations of his or her feelings and beliefs, a review of codes of ethics and guidelines, consultation with colleagues regarding customary and accepted practice, and critical understanding of the current state of theory and research guiding practice.

It is not only an ethical imperative but a legal reality that practitioners must employ those strategies demonstrated to be best practice in each given situation. When techniques have some general acceptance and are not used, the practitioner runs the risk of not only performing unethically may also be held legally accountable and found to be negligent in their professional duty to provide care. In areas for which there is not solid research to direct best practice, or for which the standard of the profession is not clearly articulated, the ethical practitioner will employ those techniques for which there is a theoretical rationale and evidence that at least the local community and the ordinary, average practitioner would employ these as customary practice. Awareness of the standards of practice defining accepted intervention strategies as well as familiarizing oneself with customary modes of service is essential for ethical practice. Exercise 2.6 has been designed to assist you in this process.

Professionalization, Professional Ethics, and Personal Response

Professionalization is "the process by which an occupation, usually on the basis of a claim to special competence and a concern for the quality of its work and benefits to society, obtains the exclusive right to perform a particular kind of work, to control training criteria

EXERCISE 2.6
Customary and Accepted Practice

Directions: For each of the presenting problems listed do the following:

1. Contact a human service professional in your community and inquire into his or her general approach or strategy employed in this situation.
2. Review the research in the past five years pointing to the efficacy and outcome for specific interventions when employed with this type of problem.
3. Identify your own approach to this situation along with your rationale.

Problem Area	Human Service Professional	Research	Personal Approach
Depression	Dr. Wicks: Employs cognitive behavior Therapy (CBT), (Beck, Rush, Shaw, & Emery, 1979)	NIMH studies demonstrating effectiveness of CBT (Elkin, Shea, Watkins, Imber, Sotsky, Collins, et al., 1989)	I would use CBT plus referral for medication if warranted. Supported by research and local practice professionals
An 11-year-old child diagnosed with ADHD			
A 35-year-old woman diagnosed with agoraphobia			
A 42-year-old man arrested Driving Under the Influence with longstanding history of alcoholism			
A child (6 years old) who appears (burn marks) to have been and may continue to be abused			
A hostile 28-year-old male, reporting a desire to "severely hurt his boss"			

and access to the profession, and to determine and evaluate the way the work is to be performed" (Chalk, Frankel, & Chafer, 1980, p. 3). Once professionalized, an occupation develops professional associations or societies that promote the profession, safeguard the rights of their members, and facilitate the exchange of information. These professional associations and societies also develop codes and standards of practice that are created to enhance the quality of the professional work performed by their members. It is these standards—these codes of ethics—as applied to the practice of helping that will serve as the basis for the remainder of this text.

Codes of Ethics

In professional fields, such as helping, national professional organizations develop rules for appropriate conduct for their memberships (e.g., American Counseling Association, American Psychological Association, National Association of Social Workers, American Association of Marriage and Family Therapy). These codes become the moral standards for these groups and provide practitioners with a guide to making ethical decisions (Bennett et al., 1990; Corey et al., 1993). These sets of practices and implicitly recognized principles of conduct evolve over the history of every profession (Bennett et al.,1990) and serve as a mechanism to ensure that members of a profession will deal justly with the public (Bersoff & Koeppl, 1993; Keith-Spiegel & Koocher, 1985).

The primary reasons for ethical codes are to protect the public from unethical or incompetent professionals and to protect the profession from unethical practices by any of its members (Keith-Spiegel & Koocher, 1985). By themselves, ethical standards do not always provide clear choices for helpers to avoid conflict, make the best decisions for all involved and maintain freedom from legal entanglement. They are simply guidelines that require selection and application to individual situations using the helpers best personal and professional judgment. These standards present "only a rationale for ethical behavior that can be difficult to apply to specific situations" (Engels, Wilborn, & Schneider, 1990, p. 115).

Moving Beyond Professional Standards to Personal Response

As mental health and human service providers, we need to have a clear understanding of professional standards along with knowledge of local, state, and federal policies that impact professional practice. Beyond this understanding and knowledge, however, the ethical practitioner needs to work to move knowledge to action by making these principles personal values and guided moral responses.

Sadly, for many practitioners, the ethics and practice guidelines that they were taught in school lose definition and impetus as they become absorbed within the experience of daily practice. The pressures of everyday life may lead practitioners to view these codes of ethics as abstract concepts that they think about only when they hear or read about an ethics violation by a colleague. Some practitioners view ethics either as rules designed to hinder practice decisions or to serve as a lever to remove colleagues who may not be as concerned about themselves, their clients, or the profession as we might be (Bennett et al., 1990, p. 7).

TABLE 2.6   Eight Steps of Ethical Problem Solving

1. Describe the parameters of the situation. *married women*
2. Define the potential ethical-legal issues involved. *info liability the father*
3. Consult ethical-legal guidelines available that might apply to the resolution of these issues.
4. Evaluate the rights, responsibilities, and welfare of all affected parties.
5. Generate a list of alternative decisions possible for each issue.
6. Enumerate the consequences of making each decision. Evaluate the short-term, ongoing, and long-term consequences of each possible decision.
7. Present any evidence that the various consequences or benefits resulting from each decision will actually occur.
8. Make the decision. Consistent with the codes of ethics, helpers accept responsibility for the decision made and monitor the consequences of the course of action chosen.

Adapted by Jacob-Timm & Hartshorne (1998) from the model originally articulated by Keith-Spiegel and Koocher (1985, pp. 19-20).

We need to move beyond simply seeing codes of ethics as abstract concepts, leverages, or hinderances and begin to view them as personal ethical imperatives.

To this end it has been suggested that each practitioner develop a decision making strategy that is rooted in ethical principles, concern for the dignity and free will of the individuals involved and a concern for the norms of societies (e.g., Haas & Malouf, 1989; Jacob-Timm & Hartshorne (1998); Kitchener, 1986; Pryzwansky, 1993). Jacob-Timm and Hartshorne (1998) provide an eight-step problem-solving model that they adapted from Keith-Spiegel and Koocher (1985, pp. 19–20). These steps are outlined in Table 2.6.

Case Illustration

Returning to our ongoing case of Ms. Wicks and Maria, we can see that Ms. Wicks has identified a number of values or beliefs that are currently giving shape to Maria's decision making. As you continue to read the case, place yourself in the role of the helper and consider your position and reactions as they parallel or contrast those exhibited by Ms. Wicks. After reading the interaction, consider the points raised in the section entitled *Reflections*. How might your personal reactions guide your interaction and decision making in regard to Maria's situation?

> **MS. WICKS:**   Maria, let me see if I understand what you are saying. You are sexually active and you don't care that you are engaged in unprotected sex. The possibility of becoming pregnant or contracting a sexually transmitted disease, even AIDS, doesn't concern you. Is that what you are saying?
>
> **MARIA:**   Well, the way you are saying it—it sounds like I'm stupid.
>
> **MS. WICKS:**   No, I apologize if that is how it sounded. I guess when I heard you say that you were engaging in unprotected sex and I assumed you were at risk of contracting AIDS, that upset me. Maybe that's what you heard in my tone?

Date
0/9/06

Format
paragraph
spacing
Double

MARIA: Not that it is any of your business—but I am sexually active—but in terms of the becoming pregnant—I would like that. I would like to have his child of love!

MS. WICKS: So you feel relatively certain that both you and your boyfriend are free of any sexually transmitted diseases and that as long as you stay monogamous that shouldn't be a problem?

MARIA: Yeah—we've even talked about it!

MS. WICKS: But I don't quite understand your view of becoming pregnant. You seem to want that?

MARIA: Hey—I'm a woman and my man is a man—real macho—our love should be blessed by God. A baby would be proof of our love!

Reflections:

1. What is your current level of competence in regards to working with adolescent, Latino females? How might that impact your ability to work with Maria? What specifically might you have difficulty with?

2. Ms. Wicks has accepted that her own values and beliefs may have influenced the tone of her response. In an attempt to share her own perspective while valuing the position of the client, she offers the clarification regarding her tone of voice.
   How would you have responded to Maria's challenge that you thought she was stupid? The same as Ms. Wicks? More strongly? Not at all?

3. Maria is introducing a number of value-laden issues (e.g., adolescent premarital sex, out-of-wedlock pregnancy, children as evidence of maturity, gifts from God, etc.). How is your perspective similar? Different? How might your perspective give shape to your response?

4. What goal would you have for this encounter? How has that goal been influenced by your own values, family experience, and culture?

Cooperative Learning Exercise

Helping Decisions Shaped by Helper Values

The purpose of the chapter was to both familiarize you with the role that specific helper variables—such as values, theoretical orientation, competence, and cultural sensitivity—play in the formation of a helping process, and to have you begin to increase your awareness of your helper variables as they may inform your professional decision making.

Part 1: Identify your own values as they impact your opinion on each of the following:

   a. Divorce

   b. Abortion

   c. Extramarital sexual affairs

   d. Spanking

   e. Marijuana

    f. Homosexuality

    g. Children's rights

    h. Importance of schedules and planning

    i. Importance of success and achievement

    j. Spirituality

Part 2: For each of the following identify a goal and a treatment strategy that you may employ. After identifying your own goals and strategies share these with a supervisor, colleague, or classmate and attempt to identify alternative goals and strategies that would be appropriate and helpful. Finally, identify how your own opinions, biases, values, and culture experiences may have influenced your selection of goals and treatment strategies for each of the following.

    a. A woman, age 38, who has been married for eleven years and has, over the course of the past eight months, had an affair with her husband's business partner. The affair has resulted in her becoming pregnant. She is stressed and is asking for direction as to what she should do.

    b. A 12-year-old has been referred to you by his parents who found "drug stuff" in his room. The child disclosed to you that he has been smoking marijuana since the beginning of the school year (last three months) and has found that it makes him feel less stressed and depressed. Further, he disclosed that he is upset because he knows he is gay and doesn't know if his parents will accept that. He has asked you NOT to tell his parents.

    c. You are working with a senior in high school who has been referred by his teacher. The student, while having a documented IQ of 148, is currently barely passing his classes. When confronted, he explains that he is simply placing more value and importance in getting in touch with his spiritual side and his "connectedness to all living things" and that he has decided to learn and attend to things that have personal relevance regardless of grades and class rankings.

Summary

Helper Values

It is neither possible nor desirable to be neutral with respect to values in the counseling relationship, and to assume such could be ethically dangerous. Ethical helpers need to increase awareness of their own personal values, beliefs, and expectations and the role they play to in giving shape to their professional identity and behavior within the helping dynamic.

    Establishing professional boundaries and maintaining professional detachment and objectivity in service of the client, while never absolute, remains a goal of ethical helping. In service of this process it may be necessary for the helper to not only clarify, but also to articulate his or her personal and professional values and the role they may play in the helping process.

When client and helper values conflict, the ethical helper will expose those values in conflict and then, along with the client, review these areas of value conflict in order to decide how they may impact the decisions made in the helping process. When the conflict is such that it interferes with the helper's ability to effectively assist the client, the ethical helper will prepare the client for referral to another helper who is more in line with the client's needs and values.

Helper Orientation

A helper's theoretical orientation and model not only provide a framework for understanding the information provided by the client, but can also impose meaning on the data offered. The ethical helper will not only continue to identify and articulate her or his model of helping but will remain vigilant in her or his evaluation and testing of the validity of that model.

Helper Competence

The ethical helper is a competent helper. Competence goes beyond simply knowing—it requires doing. As such, helpers need to be self-aware and self-caring so as to provide the best care they can. The failure of the helper to take appropriate care of him or herself can result in stress and burnout that, in turn, will threaten competence and ethical practice.

Specific steps that may help to reduce the potential impact of stress on the functioning of the helper include (1) setting realistic expectations, (2) taking care of self, (3) organizing and managing personal and professional life, and (4) maintaining objectivity and professional distance.

Helper Cultural Sensitivity

All professional organizations emphasize the ethical imperative for helpers to maintain cultural sensitivity and for practitioners to recognize the special needs of diverse client populations.

To be an ethical helper, one must be open to the values and beliefs of his or her client and be aware of how these relate to his or her own values and beliefs. The ethical helper will (1) be aware of her or his own values, biases, and cultural orientation; (2) understand the world view of culturally different clients; and (3) develop a wide repertoire of culturally appropriate intervention strategies.

Therapeutic Choice

Licensed and certified mental health providers are required to not only provide clients with care that an ordinary, average person should exercise under such circumstances, but to provide services that compare to that of their professional peers. A mental health professional who fails to meet the relevant standard of care, when compared with that of other professionals in the same community with comparable training and experience, is not only performing unethically but may also be found to be negligent in his or her duty to provide care.

Practice decisions need to be made following a practitioner's explorations of his or her feelings and beliefs, a review of codes of ethics and guidelines, consultation with colleagues regarding customary and accepted practice, and critical understanding of the current state of theory and research guiding practice.

Professionalization

Professionalization is the process by which an occupation, usually on the basis of a claim to special competence and a concern for the quality of its work and benefits to society, obtains the exclusive right to perform a particular kind of work, to control training criteria and access to the profession, and to determine and evaluate the way the work is to be performed.

The helping professions have established practices and implicitly recognized principles of conduct that serve as a mechanism to ensure that members of a profession will deal justly with the public. The primary reasons for ethical codes are to protect the public from unethical or incompetent professionals and to protect the profession from unethical practices by any of its members.

IMPORTANT TERMS

burnout
codes of ethics
competence
cultural sensitivity
customary practice
decision-making strategy
hypothesis testing
indigenous helping practices
multicultural

practitioner impairment
professionalization
professional boundaries
professional objectivity
self-determination
standard of care
theoretical model
value-free

SUGGESTED READINGS

Haas, L.J., & Malouf, J.L. (1989). *Keeping up the good work: A practitioner's guide to mental health ethics.* Sarasota, FL: Professional Resource Exchange.

Hopkins, W.E. (1997). *Ethical dimensions of diversity.* London: Sage Publications.

Rave, E.J., & Larsen, C.C. (1995). *Ethical decision making in therapy: Feminist perspectives.* New York: Guilford Press.

Sue, D.W. (1990). *Counseling the culturally different* (2nd ed.). New York: Wiley.

PART TWO

Ethics and Standards of Practice— The Profession's Response

3 Ethical Standards: Guidelines for Helping Others

Maria: Gee—being a counselor is a great job!

Ms. Wicks: Yes, it is, Maria, I enjoy it very much.

Maria: I mean you get to sit in this office and just listen to people complain—you know chat—AND get paid for it!

It is not that unusual to find individuals who believe that "helping" is simply a process of social chatting and that helpers—be they counselors, psychologists, social workers, and so on—are at best nice people and at worse frauds. Contrary to this view, those in the helping profession know and appreciate that as a formal process and a profession, helping is a powerful, awesome, process that carries with it equally powerful and significant responsibilities.

Sadly, it is all too easy to find examples of helpers who have abused this power and responsibility. One need only to turn on a television talk show to find examples of unethical therapists who have sexually abused their clients, counselors who have ignored their clients' suicidal pleas for help, or even medical and social service workers who have personally gained from the misfortune of others. As helpers, we are given the responsibility to care for individuals, who by definition of needing help are often those who are most vulnerable to manipulation. Given the potential vulnerability of their clients and the power of the helping, helpers need guidelines for professional decision making that not only protect but care for those seeking their help. Professional ethics and codes of conduct provide those guidelines.

Chapter Objectives

The decision making of the professional counselors, psychologists, social workers, and marriage and family therapists is formed through training and acquired knowledge and skills and guided by their professional codes of conduct and ethics. The chapter will introduce you to the ethical guidelines employed by counselors, psychologists, marriage and family therapists and social workers. While the uniqueness of each of these professions is reflected within their own ethical principles and codes of conduct, each share common concern for the welfare of the client. The current chapter discusses the need for these ethical principles and highlights the commonality of ethical principles shared across these professions.

After reading this chapter you should be able to do the following:

1. Describe common values and points of concern evidenced in various professional codes of ethical practice
2. Describe what is meant by autonomy, beneficence, and nonmaleficence
3. Describe what is meant by informed consent, competence, confidentiality, and professional boundaries

Formal Ethical Standards: The Evolution of a Profession

Ethics, including professional ethics, are articulated values and beliefs that are believed to help make sound moral judgments (Bersoff & Koepl, 1993). Professional codes of ethics and conduct do not bloom from a vacuum. They reflect the meaningful experiences and discussions of the members of a profession. In fact, in a very real way the existence of these standards of practice or codes of behavior help to establish a particular practice as a profession. These standards, these codes of conduct, communicate to the public that members of these associations and these professions, are competent and act in ways that minimize harm to those they serve. These professional codes of ethics serve to educate the public and the members of that profession as to the specific responsibilities and expectations of that role, thus providing a mechanism for monitoring professional accountability and providing for improvement of practice. For example, the American Counseling Association's Code of Ethics and Standards of Practice (1995), states:

> The specification of a code of ethics enables the association to clarify to current and future members, and to those served by members, the nature of the ethical responsibilities held in common by its members (Preamble).

Similarly, the American Psychological Association's Ethical Principles of Psychologists and Code of Conduct (1992) states:

> This Code is intended to provide both the general principles and the decision rules to cover most situations encountered by psychologists. It has as its primary goals the welfare and protection of the individuals and groups with whom psychologists work. (Preamble)

Codes of ethics not only serve to communicate competence to those served by the profession but also to provide practitioners with guidelines for judging decisions and actions against a standard accepted by the members of that profession.

Thus, when confronted with choices, a practitioner can decide as to the rightness or wrongness of each option, using the code of conduct and ethical principles for that professions as the guideline (see Case Illustration 3.1)

CASE ILLUSTRATION 3.1
Making an Ethical Decision

Dr. Louise Thompson is a licensed clinical social worker in private practice. She has been working with Alfonso a 52-year-old, construction worker who was self-referred for depression. Dr. Thompson has been working with Alfonso for approximately eight sessions. In the course of her work she has identified a primary contributor to Alfonso's depression. Alfonso is currently on physical disability from his job and now that his physical condition appears to be healing, he has many self-doubts about his ability to return to work. As stated by Alfonso, "he wishes that he could stay on disability forever."

Dr. Thompson has just received a certified letter from the disability insurance company asking her (1) to assess and report on her client's ability to return to work and (2) to send all of her records for their review. Dr. Thompson is concerned that while Alfonso's physical condition is on the mend, his depression impairs his ability to problem solve, which may be a problem and potential danger given his line of work. Further, Dr. Thompson has recorded in her notes some of Alfonso's quotes regarding his disdain for his foreman at work, his desire to stay on disability, and his fantasies about damaging the current construction project. She is worried about how these will be interpreted by the company's insurance firm.

Dr. Thompson is not sure if she should even respond to these requests, especially not being completely sure of her competence to judge capability to return to work. Also, in terms of her clinical notes, she wonders if she should edit her notes or refuse to send some file information. It appears that in some ways what is best for the client may be not to honor the request or to do so after carefully filtering the information. But her concern is whether that is legal. Is it ethical? Dr. Thompson wants to do what is best for her client, while practicing within the standards and codes of conduct for her profession. But the standard is not clear, at least to her, so she is unsure what to do. Luckily, Dr. Thompson belongs to the National Association of Social Workers. She has contacted the association and its legal/ethical consultants and in dialogue with them has decided on a plan of action. Without her awareness of the complexity of these requests or her ability to refer to her professional association, Dr. Thompson may have decided in ways that not only would harm her client, but legally and ethically jeopardize her ability to practice.

Professional associations, however, are not attempting to govern social or personal morality. In fact, it is possible for an action viewed as ethical within a profession (e.g., facilitating a therapeutic abortion) to be considered immoral by another group or organizations within society (e.g., religious organizations) or even by an individual member of that profession. Even though these codes do not attempt to dictate morality, as professional codes of conduct they serve as a base from which associations can govern ethical practice within that profession. Behind each profession's code of ethics is a mechanism of governance that gives substance to the ethical principles. Through the use of articulated educational requirements, members of a profession are guided in the development and enactment of their professional roles. Further, when these members fail to perform or practice within the established standard, procedures for disciplining and sanctioning these members are also enacted (see Case Illustration 3.2).

CASE ILLUSTRATION **3.2**
Sanctioning a Member

While it is rare, any single incident of sexual misconduct is one too many for a profession that operates on the implicit trust of its clients. The following reflects one case (significant details have been modified in order to insure anonymity), in which the sexual misconduct of one practitioner came to the attention of a second.

Dr. L., a clinical psychologist, was working with a new client who presented herself as depressed and anxious. In ascertaining some background material, Dr. L. discovered that the client had been in therapy, for the past four years with a certified marriage and family therapist. Additional data gleaned over the course of the next five sessions revealed that this therapist had seen the client and her husband for marriage counseling but in the course of the counseling, referred the husband to another therapist and began treating this client for her "sexual dysfunctions."

As revealed by the client, the previous therapist started a sexual affair with her that continued for one year while she was still under his professional care. The client said that she had become increasingly depressed in the past few months as a direct result of her previous therapist terminating both the sexual contact and the therapeutic relationship. The explanation he provided was simply that she was too needy and too dependent for him to help her. To make matters worse, she works in the same organization as the therapist, and rumor has it that he is currently having an affair with another client.

The client expressed her anger and disgust as well as guilt over the affair. Dr. L worked on helping her understand that maintaining appropriate boundaries was not her responsibility but that of the therapist. As a result of their sessions together, the client, while not seeking or desiring any legal recourse, shared her concern that this man had access to other vulnerable female clients and that she would not feel good unless she could stop that. Together, she and Dr. L. contacted the American Association of Marriage and Family Therapists, which was the professional association of the previous therapist. After an exhausting fact-finding period, the AAMFT Board concluded that not only was this claim valid, but that a history of such behavior existed. The board revoked his certification, provided him with a treatment and mentoring plan, and forwarded their decision to local state board of licensing. The therapist, in addition to holding a certificate as a marriage and family therapist, also was licensed to practice within his state. As a result of AAMFT's action, his license was revoked.

Thus, these codes of conduct, and these ethical principles exist not simply as statements of aspiration but are in fact mandates and standards of professional practice.

Codes of ethics are continually evolving and developing. The ever-changing state of our arts provides the base from which professional ethics similarly evolve. They reflect the knowledge and general consensus of the profession at a given time. For example, most codes of conduct prior to the 1990s didn't provide for increased sensitivity toward (1) diversity and multicultural issues, (2) responding to clients with HIV/AIDS, or (3) sexual relationships between helper and clients following termination of the formal helping relationship. The ongoing awareness among professionals about the importance of these issues has been given voice within the latest editions of these evolving codes of ethics. Because the codes are evolving, it is important that practitioners maintain participation within their professional associations and remain informed about the latest research and literature regarding the ethics of practice.

Across the Professions: A Review of Ethical Standards of Practice

Typically, practitioners within a profession also hold membership within the associations representing that profession (see Appendix A). Most counselors, for example , belong to the American Counseling Association (ACA), psychologists, to the American Psychological Association (APA), marriage and family therapists, to the American Association of Marriage and Family Therapy (AAMFT), and Social Workers, to the National Association of Social Workers (NASW). These professional organizations provide their members with specific statements of guidelines for ethical practice (see Appendix B) and help give clarification to the uniqueness of the role and function of that profession.

The Ethical Principles and Codes of Conduct included within this text (see Appendix B) reflect the latest versions of these standards. It is important for the practitioner to not only know these standards but to review association news and updates regarding ethics and codes of conduct.

Common Concerns and Shared Values Across the Professions

The specific codes of conduct as articulated by each professional organization (see Appendix B) constitute the mandatory ethics of that profession, reflecting the unique demands and responsibilities of those within that profession. However, beneath these specific guidelines lies certain fundamental principles and values that appear to cut across the uniqueness of each individual professional organization

Kitchener (1984) described four fundamental principles that serve to underpin each of these professional codes of conduct (Table 3.1).

Autonomy: The value of self-determination (autonomy) serves as a foundation for all professional decisions reflecting the need to reduce client dependency and maintain client informed consent throughout the relationship.

Beneficence: While concerned with client self-determination, all professional helpers attempt to promote the health and well-being of the client. This promotion of good for others is considered beneficence and is reflected in each of the codes of ethics.

Nonmaleficence: Nonmaleficence means to do no harm. Professionals must take steps to ensure that their decisions do not intentionally or inadvertently risk hurting clients. This includes the imposition of helper values and personal needs into the helping dynamic.

Justice: The ethical professional will respect and protect human and civil rights and not knowingly participate in or condone unfair discriminatory practices.

TABLE 3.1 Fundamental Principles Underlying Professional Codes of Conduct

Professional Organization	Autonomy/ Self-Determination	Beneficence/ Promote Good	Nonmaleficence/ Avoid Harm	Justice/ Equal Treatment
American Psychological Association (1995)	PRINCIPLE D: RESPECT FOR PEOPLE'S RIGHTS AND DIGNITY Psychologists accord appropriate respect to the fundamental rights, dignity, and worth of all people. They respect the rights of individuals to privacy, confidentiality, self-determination, and autonomy . . . and they do not knowingly participate in or condone unfair discriminatory practices.	PRINCIPLE E: CONCERN FOR OTHERS' WELFARE Psychologists seek to contribute to the welfare of those with whom they interact professionally. In their professional actions, psychologists weigh the welfare and rights of their patients or clients, students, supervisees, and human research participants.	1.14 Psychologists take reasonable steps to avoid harming their patients or clients, research participants, students, and others with whom they work, and to minimize harm where it is foreseeable and unavoidable.	1.10 Nondiscrimination. In their work-related activities, psychologists do not engage in unfair discrimination based on age, gender, race, ethnicity, national origin, religion, sexual orientation, disability, socioeconomic status, or any basis proscribed by law.
American Counseling Association (1995)	A.1.b. Counselors encourage client growth and development in ways that foster the client's interest and welfare; counselors avoid fostering dependent counseling relationships.	A.1.a The primary responsibility of counselors is to respect the integrity and promote the welfare of the client.	C.5. Public Responsibility e. Unjustified Gains. Counselors do not use their professional positions to seek or receive unjustified personal gains, sexual favors, unfair advantage, or unearned goods or services.	A.10.c In establishing fees for professional counseling services, counselors consider the financial status of clients and locality. In the event that the established fee structure is inappropriate for a client, assistance is provided in attempting to find comparable services of acceptable cost.

National Association of
Social Workers (1996)

1.02 Self-Determination

Social workers respect
and promote the right of
clients to self-
determination and assist
clients in their efforts to
identify and clarify their
goals. Social workers
may limit clients' right to
self-determination when,
in the social worker's
professional judgment,
clients' actions or
potential actions pose a
serious, foreseeable, and
imminent risk to
themselves or others.

1.01 Commitment to
Clients

Social workers' primary
responsibility is to
promote the well-being of
clients. In general,
clients' interests are
primary. However, social
workers' responsibility to
the larger society or
specific legal obligations
may on limited occasions
supercede the loyalty
owed clients, and clients
should be so advised.

1.06 Conflicts of Interest
(b) Social workers should
not take unfair advantage
of any professional
relationship or exploit
others to further their
personal, religious,
political, or business
interests.

4.02 Discrimination

Social workers should not
practice, condone,
facilitate, or collaborate
with any form of
discrimination on the
basis of race, ethnicity,
national origin, color, sex,
sexual orientation, age,
marital status, political
belief, religion, or mental
or physical disability.

4.04 Dishonesty, Fraud,
and Deception

Social workers should not
participate in, condone, or
be associated with
dishonesty, fraud, or
deception.

55

Thus, while each specialty in the helping field may emphasize one or another ethical principle of practice, it is clear that primary to each of these codes is the concern for, and consideration of, the welfare and well-being of the client (see Exercise 3.1).

Each of the values listed above serve to underpin the rationale and intent of the codes of conduct to be discussed within this text. More specifically, each of these core values have taken shape in a common concern and articulated principles that protect and promote the welfare of the client. It is commonly held across the various helping professions that the

---

EXERCISE 3.1
Identifying Core Values of Ethical Conduct

Directions: For each of the following identify the core value (i.e., autonomy, beneficence, nonmaleficence, justice) being demonstrated and whether the helper's actions are in support (s) or in violation(v) of that core value.

Illustration	Core Value	Support? "S"	Violation? "V"
The helper directs the client in terms of what needs to be done and what goals will be set for each session.			
The helper cancels an appointment with a client because she pays on a sliding scale and he has the opportunity to schedule a full-pay client in that time slot.			
The helper explains to the client that the type of things the clients wishes to discuss and the goals he, the client, wishes to achieve require techniques for which the helper is not trained and therefore a referral might be in order.			
The client called in crisis. The client was feeling very hopeless and, while apologetic about calling the counselor, expressed her fear that she may hurt herself. Even though the helper was in middle of a family celebration, she spent the time needed to assess the level of crisis and to insure that the client felt safe and was with someone who could continue to monitor her, offered support, and set up an immediate appointment for the following day.			

helping relationship exists for the client's benefit, for their care and NOT for the personal needs or benefits of the helper. The helper who uses the helping relationship to make herself or himself feel powerful, important, or needed is placing her or his needs before those of the client and is being unethical. It is in placing the rights and needs of the client as primary, that an ethical helper begins to establish the general framework for ethical practice. The ethical helper—regardless of the specific helping profession—demonstrates this primacy of the rights and needs of the client by providing the client with *informed consent*, establishing *confidentiality*, and creating *boundaries* that maintain a *professional, competent* relationship.

Informed Consent

The ethical helper will demonstrate a respect for the rights of the client to be fully informed. Clients need to be provided with information that enables them to make informed choices.

Clearly, this can pose a challenge in that the helper needs to attain a balance of providing the information needed for informed decision making at a time and in a manner that the client can understand and successfully use that information. Too much information, too soon, can prove overwhelming, anxiety provoking, and even destructive to the helping process. The goal of informed consent is to promote cooperation and participation of the client in the helping process. The specifics of such an informing process, in terms of what to present and how to present it, often create delicate situations and ethical dilemmas as presented in Exercise 3.2. These will be more fully explored in Chapter 6.

EXERCISE 3.2
An Issue of Informed Consent

Swift part Termunaly

Directions: Below you will find a number of scenarios involving a helper and a client for whom informed consent is an issue. As you read the scenarios identify what, if anything, you would tell the client.

Scenario 1: Allison has been directed by her employer to go to counseling at their Employee Assistance Program (EAP) because of her "attitude at work." The EAP has been directed to evaluate Allison for drug use and to make a report to the employer. What, if anything, should the EAP counselor tell the client?

Scenario 2: Timothy walked into his high school counselor's office. Timothy says that he is thinking about running away from home. Further, he states that if he is unable to get away from his parents, he will "kill himself." What information should the counselor convey to this client?

Scenario 3: A child psychiatrist is working with an 8-year-old child with severe attention deficit with hyperactivity. The child's parent told him that this was an "allergy doctor" who may give him some "allergy" medicine. What do you feel the psychiatrist should tell the client?

Confidentiality

For helping to be effective, the client must feel free to disclose and share private concerns. For such a sense of freedom to exist, the client needs to feel that the interaction is one that is *confidential*. As with other areas of practice, confidentiality is not absolute nor are decisions to hold in confidence always black and white (see Exercise 3.3). The use of confidentiality requires professional judgment, which at times can be very challenging. Chapter 7 provides a detailed look at the issue of confidentiality, its limitations, and special challenges.

Appropriate Boundaries for Professional Relationship

Finally, it is generally agreed that the client has a right to enter a *professional* relationship with the helper. Relationships in which the helper is using the interaction with the client to meet his or her own personal needs, or situations in which there exists a dual relationship between the helper and the client—such as may be the case when the helper and client have social and personal relationships—threaten this principle of professional contact. As with all of the ethical guidelines, it is not a simple, cut-and-dried matter. Clearly, there are times—situations—when one may be a friend and yet be able to gain the professional objectivity to assist the client. Under these situations it is important for the helper to attempt

---

EXERCISE **3.3**
Confidentiality?

Directions: Along with a classmate or colleague, read each of the following client scenarios. Identify those in which you feel confidentiality should be maintained, and in which, if any, information needs to be disclosed. After reading Chapter 7, review your initial responses to this exercise and see if they change.

1. A school counselor is told by a 13-year-old that she is going to have sex with an older boy.
2. A husband, in marriage counseling with his wife, calls the counselor and informs the counselor that he is currently having an affair with a man but does not want that disclosed in their couple sessions.
3. An irate worker informs a counselor that "if I don't get a raise I'm going to kill Harold" (the worker's boss).
4. A young woman informs her therapist that she has herpes and refuses to tell the man she is about to marry.
5. A 14-year-old student tells his counselor that he is gay and is interested in experiencing a homosexual relationship.
6. A depressed elderly man tells the nursing home social worker that he has been saving his medications and intends to overdose on them.

to define and maintain some control or boundaries on the types of information being discussed or on the nature of the relationship as it may be appropriate to each of the varied roles (e.g., friend or helper) (see Case Illustration 3.3). The issues of boundaries and the ethical use of power is discussed in detail in Chapter 8.

CASE ILLUSTRATION **3.3**
Maintaining Boundaries and Clarifying Roles

Alex is a school counselor working at Mt. Helena High School. Alex was asked to work with a female student, Nguyen, who was new to the school, and for whom the teacher, Mr. E had some "serious concerns." Alex liked to consult with teachers whenever possible, so before meeting with the student, he went to talk with Mr. E. In conversation with Mr. E he discovered that Mr. E was concerned that this girl "looked just like his girlfriend Kim" and he just recently discovered that his girlfriend "was a liar and cheat." When asked directly as to the relevance, Mr. E became very upset—started to cry and said, "It's not Nguyen who needs the help, it's me—I can't get over her, I can't believe she was cheating on me. I feel like such an idiot."

Alex asked Mr. E to come down to his office. Alex felt that he needed to reach out to his colleague in crisis and attempt to assist him in calming down and maybe make a plan for dealing with his own emotional upset. The following dialogue insued:

ALEX: It is clear that what has happened with you and Kim has been very upsetting to you. It even seems to be carrying over into your work?

MR. E (crying): It is. I can't sleep. I haven't eaten in the last two days. I don't care any more.

ALEX: It can certainly feel crushing when you lose someone you cared about.

MR. E (gaining some composure): Alex, I feel like such a fool, she and I were talking about getting married. But apparently she thought there was something wrong with me sexually or I couldn't . . . .

ALEX (Interrupting): Joe, it sounds like you have a lot of questions that need to be answered. Questions about your relationships, maybe even questions about yourself and the types of relationships you find yourself in . . . I know this is a painful time, but sometimes these are the times when, with the help of another, we really can gain some insight and grow.

MR. E: I know. Gads, it hurts. You said, with the help of another, would you work with me?

ALEX: First of all, Joe, I'm honored you've asked. But you and I are colleagues, we need to work together all of the time, plus I am trained as a school counselor and really not able to provide you the counseling that would be best for you. I do know people who are excellent for these kinds of experiences and I could give you their names and maybe even help you make a connection, if you would like.

MR. E: Yeah . . . think I really need to do this. Thanks, Alex. I would appreciate those names. And (smiling) you don't have to call Nguyen down, she'll be fine.

C A S E   I L L U S T R A T I O N   **3.4**
Knowing Limits of Competence

Lewis is a marriage and family therapist certified through AAMFT. Lewis has been in private practice for two years and has already developed a reputation as an ethical, effective helper. A couple called and asked to make an appointment because they were having a lot of problems "communicating." During the intake interview, Lewis discovered that the wife had been sexually abused by both her father and her uncle from the age of 4 through to the age of 17. The woman revealed that, while she had never had counseling or therapy for this issue of abuse, she felt that she had resolved this issue and no longer had any problem with it.

As the interview continued it became clear to Lewis that Elsa (the wife) was severely depressed and gave evidence of problems much deeper than the marital communications problem originally presented. Since Lewis didn't feel competent to diagnose the level of her problems or the possible existence of a personality disorder, he felt that proceeding as the couple requested to investigate communication issues might be a disservice to the couple and might even cause harm to the wife, should it engage her in painful memories. Then, Lewis explained to the couple his concerns and helped them understand the value of the referral he was making.

Through careful, sensitive dialogue with this couple and an awareness of the limits of his own competence, Lewis was able to help this couple, and more specifically, Elsa, get the assistance that they needed.

Helper Competence

A final ethical principle shared across the various helping professions is that a helper must be aware of the limitations of his or her own professional competence and not exceed those limitations in the delivery of his or her service.

It is all too easy for a helper to find himself or herself alone in an office or in the field of practice without teachers, mentors, or supervisors looking over her or his shoulder and assume that she or he can try this or that new technique or approach or deal with any and all problems or situations presented. Such is not the case. New techniques and new approaches need to be learned and practiced under the appropriate supervision. Similarly, we cannot be everything to everybody (see Case Illustration 3.4).

Knowing the limits to our competence, being willing to seek ongoing training and supervision, and knowing when to seek consultation from a colleague or make referral to another helper are all characteristics of an ethical helper and are all discussed in detail in Chapter 9.

From Professional Behavior to Personal Being

It is clear that to be an ethical practitioner one must be fully aware and knowledgeable about the specific codes of conduct governing one's profession. However, as suggested previously, these codes of ethics reflect the ever-changing demands and needs of the members of that profession and the experiences of competing rights and responsibilities arising in the course of professional practice. As such, the codes are continually reviewed and revised. The ethical helper needs to keep current on his or her understanding of the literature reflecting the issues involved in ethical practice. Further, ethical practitioners need to consult with knowledgeable colleagues or members of their associations' boards of ethics anytime they have a concern about the ethical conflict of their practice decisions. This level of awareness and level of knowledge is the minimum for the ethical practitioner.

However, as noted, the goal is not simply to know the ethical principles of one's profession. The call is for each professional to assimilate and incorporate these principles into their decision-making process (e.g., Corey et al., 1993; Forester-Miller & Davis, 1995). An organization's code of conduct and articulated ethical principles represent the collective concern and values of the members of that organization. However, until they are owned by the practitioner, they remain only nice ideas and wishful guidelines. As each helper develops within his or her professional practice, he or she will not only gain increased knowledge and skill but will also begin to formulate internal values and standards of practice. The ethical helper must be willing to reflect on the guidelines provided by their profession as well as relevant dialogue with colleagues, and then continue to formulate his or her own values that will then direct his or her helping interactions. In this way, the codes of ethics move from nice ideas or even meaningful statements to becoming embodied ways of practicing.

The goal is not simply to "know" ethics, but rather to *be* ethical. The remainder of the book is devoted to help you in the process of moving from knowing ethics to being ethical.

Case Illustration

Returning to our ongoing case of Ms. Wicks and Maria, Ms. Wicks has identified a number of values or beliefs that are currently giving shape to Maria's decision making and to the helping relationship that is beginning to take significant shape.

As you read the exchange below, begin to identify explicit or implicit areas of potential ethical conflict. While no specific violations of ethics may have occurred to this point, a number of issues are revealed for which an understanding of the code of professional ethics would be essential as a guide for Ms. Wick's decision making. The questions provided at the end of the exchange are provided to guide you in your reflections.

MARIA: You know I just realized that you got me talking about stuff . . . like sex and stuff that I don't tell nobody.

MS. WICKS: I truly appreciate your willingness to share things about yourself, it really . . .

MARIA: (interrupting) Yeah . . . but you are not going to tell anyone. I mean like you know my aunt.

MS WICKS: Your aunt?

MARIA: Yeah, Gloria Enrique. She was a teacher in Elsewhere High, where you used to work . . . anyway . . . she told me you guys are like a priest and you can't say anything to anybody about what I tell you. Like, now this is just a for instance, but, what if I tell you I'm going to run away and go live with my boyfriend—he's dying of AIDS—you can't tell my mom or my aunt?

MS. WICKS: Your boyfriend has . . .

MARIA: (again, interrupting) Yeah, we talked about it and stuff . . . but this happened before he met me . . . so like I'm the only one who knows and I want to be with him and take care of him.

Reflections

1. Does the fact that Ms. Wicks previously worked with Maria's aunt violate any professional values? Create a possible boundary conflict? *yes*
2. Maria sees the mental health practitioner as protecting her confidentiality the same *No* way a priest may regard material shared in the confessional. What are your feelings about this? What do you think Ms. Wicks should say? Do? *get more information/center saw 2/53*
3. What should Ms. Wicks do about this new information regarding Maria's intent to *wt resident* run away? Is that something she should hold in confidence? How about the information about the boyfriend having AIDS? Should she disclose this information? If so, to whom? If not, why not?
4. Of all the information, both explicit and implied, that Ms. Wicks has gained to this point what, if anything, should be documented and recorded? *Everything needs to be documented*

Cooperative Learning Exercise

The purpose of this chapter was to introduce you to the role and function of professional ethics. But beyond this cognitive purpose the hope was also to stimulate you to begin to value the need for a professional code of ethics and a desire to embrace it for your profession. The following is intended to assist you in this valuing process.

As with all of these cooperative exercises, the benefit that comes from the guided personal reflection is augmented by the sharing of this perspective with others.

Directions: Read each of the following scenarios. Identify areas of ethical concern in which issues of autonomy, beneficence, nonmaleficence, and justice may be operative.

1. In the Case Illustration the client, Maria, shared the possibility that she was having unprotected sex with a boyfriend whom she identified as having AIDS. Since AIDS is a medical condition and sexual activity is a personal decision, should either of these issues be of ethical concern for Ms. Wicks?
2. Given your current level of training and the ethical concern for practicing within one's level of competence, what type of helping or for what type of client or problem do you currently feel competent to assist? What else will you need to do to increase your level of competence to be an ethical professional?
3. If codes of ethics are commonly shared guidelines to be employed by each member of a specific profession, what role and level of responsibility does a member have in monitoring that his or her colleagues practice ethically?

4. Identify two forms of unethical practice that you feel deserve maximum sanctioning by one's profession. What form should the sanctioning take?

Summary

Formal Ethical Standards: The Evolution of a Profession

Ethics, including professional ethics, are articulated values and beliefs that are believed to assist in making sound moral judgments (Bersoff & Koepl, 1993). These professional codes of ethics serve to educate the public and the members of that profession as to the specific responsibilities and expectations of that role and thus provide a mechanism for monitoring professional accountability and providing for improvement of practice.

Across the Professions: A Review of Ethical Standards of Practice

Most counselors, for example, belong to the American Counseling Association (ACA), psychologists, to the American Psychological Association (APA), marriage and family therapists, to the American Association of Marriage and Family Therapists (AAMFT), and Social Workers to the National Association of Social Workers (NASW). These professional organizations provide their members with specific guidelines for ethical practice and help give clarification to the uniqueness of the role and function of that profession.

Common Concerns and Shared Values Across the Professions

There are four fundamental principles that serve to underpin each of these professional codes of conduct (Kitchener, 1984). These are (1) autonomy or the value of self-determination; (2) beneficence, or the promotion of good for others; (3) nonmaleficence, meaning to do no harm; and (4) justice. These appear to take concrete form within the various codes of ethics governing the helping professions in the directives to provide the client with *informed consent*—establishing confidentiality—and boundaries that maintain a *professional, competent* relationship.

From Professional Behavior to Personal Being

The goal is not simply to know the ethical principles of one's profession. The call is for each professional to assimilate and to incorporate these principles into their decision making process.

Ethical helpers must be willing to reflect on the guidelines provided by their professions, dialogue with colleagues around the guidelines, and then continue to formulate and reformulate their own values, which will then direct their helping interactions.

IMPORTANT TERMS

American Association of Marriage and
Family Therapists (AAMFT)
American Counseling Association
(ACA)

American Psychological Association
(APA)
autonomy
beneficence

boundaries
codes of conduct
competent
confidentiality
decision-making process
ethics
informed consent
justice

marriage and family therapist.
National Association of Social Workers
 (NASW)
nonmaleficence
power
professional relationship
sanction

SUGGESTED READINGS

Ahia, C.E., & Martin, D. (1993). *The danger-to-self-or-others exception to confidentiality.* Alexandria, VA:
    American Counseling Association.

Bersoff, D.N. (1994). Explicit ambiguity: The 1992 ethics code as an oxymoron. *Professional Psychology:
    Research and Practice, 25,* 382–87.

Coale, H.W. (1998). *The vulnerable therapist.* New York: The Haworth Press.

Forester-Miller, H., & Davis, T. E. (1995). A practitioner's guide to ethical decision making. Alexandria,
    VA: American Counseling Association.

CHAPTER

4 Ethics and the Law

Mr. Harolds: Hi, Michelle. what's up?

Ms. Wicks: Tom, could I talk to you about some legal concern?

Mr. Harolds: Legal concerns? Certainly, but I'm not a lawyer.

Ms. Wicks: No, I know that—but you seem to stay current with laws and regulations regarding counseling and to tell you the truth, I'm not sure if it is a problem or not.

Mr. Harolds: Well, you certainly sound concerned. What's up?

Most mental health practitioners enter the profession intending to employ their knowledge and skills to assist those in need—not concerning themselves about the legal complications of the issues and the people with whom they work. The reality is that just as there are ethical principles and guidelines that need to be considered when making professional decisions, there are also legal mandates and implications of which the ethical practitioner must be fully aware.

Laws, including legislation, court decisions, and regulations, have grown both in presence and importance in the practice of human service (Dickson, 1998). Issues defining the rights of clients, the rights of the practitioner, the way in which services are selected and provided, and the nature of the relationship between the practitioner and client are all being shaped by the professional codes of conduct and now by extension of those codes into law. Some complain that law has made practitioners more concerned for personal liability than client welfare. Bergantino (1996), for example, states: "In our current psycholitigious world . . . we only have left brains, and . . . only what is 'appropriate' is thought to constitute therapy. Forget 'excellence' . . . Our profession is now defined by those who want to make the world safe for mediocrity!" p. 31).

The sad truth is that practitioners are vulnerable to legal action, and many have opted to play it safe at the expense of providing the best service for their clients. While litigation is a reality that now must be placed within the mix of professional decision making, laws are not meant to make practitioners feel threatened. Quite often the law parallels and further codifies sound ethical practice and, as such, need not induce anxiety or concern within the ethical practitioner. But there are times when the relationship between ethics and legality is not clear or in fact may appear in conflict. At those times, the question becomes, "What's the ethical helper to do?"

The current chapter focuses upon the unique and ever-evolving relationship between professional codes of conduct and the law, in hopes of helping practitioners find an answer to this question.

Chapter Objectives

The relationship of professional ethics and the laws governing professional practice is the focus of the current chapter. After reading this chapter you should be able to do the following:

1. Describe the obligations incurred by a helper who has established a "special relationship" with a client.
2. Explain what is meant by "duty to care" and what defines that obligation.
3. Describe how licensure and/or certification may lend legal power to the professional codes of conduct.
4. Provide examples of ethical practice that may be illegal and legal requirements that may violate professional codes of ethics.
5. Describe one model for identifying and resolving conflict between ethics and legality.

The Helping Process as a Legal Contract

As a result of malpractice suits and legal actions, it is generally recognized that a professional relationship, or even the perception that the relationship is a professional one, constitutes the basis of the existence of legal duty to provide appropriate care for a client. The professional help giver, by the very nature of holding himself or herself out in practice, implies that he or she will conduct himself or herself in a skillful and responsible manner and will follow the dictates of that profession's code of ethics.

The issue of whether helping is contractual and thus a minimum duty of care is established rests with the courts' decision as to whether a "special relationship" existed that would be sufficient to create a "duty of care." Such a special relationship can certainly be created with the use of formal treatment contracts in which the "duties" of each party are specified (see Exercise 4.1). However, the establishment of a formal contract articulating the relationship between client and practitioner or the rendering of a bill and exchange of money for services is not necessary in order to provide evidence of a special relationship and a duty to care.

A special relationship between helper and client can be established as a result of implicit acts. Courts, for example, may determine that a special relationship and thus a duty to care was established by the helper's action of taking notes, scheduling formal appointments and even advertising as one who can provide unique, helping services. These actions can be interpreted as reflecting an intent to render service and thus constitute a basis of establishing the intent to form a special relationship and thus a contract to provide the care. As with many areas of law and ethics, there is no singular court case or clear directive that determines what actions, beyond a formal contract, can be used to demonstrate an intent to form a special relationship and thus a duty to provide care.

While there has not been a single court definition and ruling that provides a universal standard regarding implicit contract or duty to care, numerous state rulings have begun to give shape to this contract of professional service. For example, in a case resolved in the Supreme Court of Wisconsin (*Bogust v. Iverson*, 1960), the court ruled against the parents

---

EXERCISE **4.1**
The Use of Contracts: Formal–Informal

Many mental health practitioners, as a reflection of their concern to assist clients to be fully informed, have begun to provide clients with "contracts" of service. These contracts can be more or less formalized, ranging from simple information sheets with identified fees, cancellation policies, etc., to a formal statement requiring signatures and witnesses from all parties involved.

Directions: Contact each of the following: (1) a residential treatment program or hospital, (2) a free clinic, (3) a private practitioner, (4) a university counseling center, (5) an elementary or high school counseling center, and (6) a local church. For each of these service providers identify each of the following:

a. Do they employ some form of agreement or contract when providing services (counseling, mental health) to their clients? If so, why? And what is included? If not, why not?
b. Do they provide informational brochures or materials? Do these describe any special services that are offered and any requirements or responsibilities of the clients?
c. When they see a client do they maintain records? Collect a fee? Schedule appointments (versus simply walk in service)?
d. Do they feel that their clients perceive that the services they offer are professional in nature, even if no fees are collected?

Share your data with you colleagues or classmates. Discuss which of the service providers appear to employ contracts or actions that would characterize them as establishing "special relationships" with their client and therefore incurring a duty to care.

---

of a student, Jane Dunn, who filed suit against the director of student personnel services at Stout State College. The parents alleged there was negligence because the director failed to provide proper guidance or protection for the student, who committed suicide. In the ruling against the parents, the Wisconsin Supreme Court referred to the defendant as a teacher and not a counselor and as such reported that no special relationship had been established. "To hold that a teacher who has no training, education, or experience in medical fields is required to recognize in a student a condition the diagnosis of which is in a specialized and technical medical field, would require a duty beyond reason" (*Bogust v. Iverson*, 1960). Another court ruling that seemed to suggest that specialized training and credentialing was needed prior to the establishment of a special helping relationship and the duty to care was *Nally v. Grace Community Church*. In *Nally v. Grace Community Church* (1988), the parents of a 24-year-old, Kenneth Nally, sued the Grace Community Church and its pastors for negligence when their son committed suicide after receiving several years of informal counseling. Kenneth also saw secular psychologists and psychiatrists during these years and, following an unsuccessful attempt at suicide in 1979, his parents rejected the recommendations of a psychiatrist to have him committed. This recommendation was also made by one of the pastors of the church and similarly rejected. The California Supreme Court ruled in favor of the church and its pastors because it found that there was no duty of care that was breached by them and no special relationship that would create such duty. In this case, the California court made a distinction between nontherapists, counselors, and professional therapists such as psychiatrists or certified psychologists and counselors. Since the pastors were non-therapists without the requisite special relationship, the court did not find, nor impose the duty of care. These two rulings appear to point to the essential need to be recognized as a professional helper as defined by one's credentials, such as licensure as the basis for a special relationship, and to identify that thus duty to care has been established. However, in *Eisel v. Board of Education of Montgomery County* (1991) new legal precedent was set.

As noted, previously the courts did not find a duty of care in situations in which a non-professional attempted to provide help to a client. This was true even in situations in which an outpatient client who may have been suicidal was seen by a school counselor. However, in *Eisel*, the court noted a special relationship sufficient to create a duty of care when an adolescent in a school setting expresses an intention to commit suicide and the counselor becomes aware of such intention. In Eisel, the court noted that the school as a result of standing in loco parentis does have a special duty to exercise reasonable care to protect a pupil from harm. Further, the relationship of school counselor and pupil is not devoid of therapeutic overtones, as suggested by the counselor's job description. Thus, in addition to pointing to special training, licensing, and certification, the existence of a special relationship and the duty to care can be established based simply on the job definition from which one provides service.

Another approach to the definition of a special relationship between helper and client bases it on the principle of fiduciary responsibility. Any time an individual places his or her trust in a party who has the potential to influence his or her action, a fiduciary relationship exists (Black, 1991). Given this definition, it could be reasonably argued that all professional helping relationships have this fiduciary potential and thus bring with it a duty to act to the benefit of the other individual in any matters related to an undertaking between them (Black, 1991).

While there is an inherent logic in using this fiduciary argument to demonstrate that helping has a contracted special relationship, the courts have not made de facto rulings to the fiduciary nature of each professional relationship but noted that it was up to the specific nature of each relationship to determine that (*Hodgkinson v. Simms*, 1994; *M.(K.) v.M. (H.)*, 1992; *McInerney v. MacDonald*, 1992). When a fiduciary relationship exists, a practitioner has these obligations:

a. To act with good faith and loyalty toward a client (*McInerney v. MacDonald, 1992*)
b. Not abuse the power imbalance by exploiting the client (*Norberg v. Wynrib, 1992*)
c. Act in the best interest of the client (*Hodgkinson v. Simms*, 1994; M.(K.) v. M.(H.)., 1992)

While the anxiety surrounding the possibility of litigation may serve as a motive for practitioners to be more fully aware of the law applicable to their practice, knowledge and awareness of the law is a professional responsibility regardless of anxiety. Professional codes of conduct direct practitioners to know and practice in ways consistent with the law. For example, psychologists are directed to "plan and conduct research in a manner consistent with federal and state law. . . ."(APA, 1992, 6.08).

The Legal Foundation of Ethical Practice

The process and relationship between health and human service professionals and their clients is increasingly shaped by law (Dickson, 1998). Issues such as informed consent, confidentiality, and competency as well as mandates, such as mandated reporting of child abuse and duty to warn, are significant influences on the practice of human service (see Case Illustration 4.1). In addition, courts of law can employ regulatory and ethical standards for health and human services professionals, as ways of identifying negligence, malpractice, and liability.

CASE ILLUSTRATION **4.1**
The Changing Face of School Counseling

The following was the result of an interview with Mr. L, an elementary school counselor. Legal precedents relative to Mr. L's comments have been inserted:

> *Well, I've been a elementary school counselor now for over 23 years and I can tell you my job and my strategies in working with children have changed dramatically as a result of litigation. I mean there was a time when I first started that if a kid was acting out or a real disruption in a classroom we could simply have him removed, suspended, as a way of providing a "wake up call." Try that now and you will find yourself sued. Everything requires DUE PROCESS now.*
>
> In 1975, the Supreme Court ruled in *Goss v. Lopez*: "Due process requires, in connection with a suspension of 10 days or less, that the student be given oral or written notice of the charges against him and, if he denies them, an explanation of the evidence the authorities have and an opportunity to present his side of the story" (581).
>
> *This even gets to the point that you start to worry about using "time out" procedures because it may be argued that you are excluding a child from his right to have an education. I don't know, I feel like I should have become a lawyer rather than a counselor.*
>
> *Goss v. Lopez* focused on exclusion from an education, and while it did not define or give examples of de minimus punishments that would not require due process, they probably would include practices like after school detentions or "time outs" or even temporary exclusion from extracurricular activities.
>
> *And another area that you have to be supercautious about is record keeping. I mean it used to be that my records were confidential—no one had access. Now I feel like any one can waltz in and see my files, since they are school files. Where's the privacy? A lot of the counselors in our district, simply keep special files or school-only files that parents simply don't have access to.*
>
> The Family Educational Rights and Privacy Act (FERPA) provides parents and students 18 and older with certain rights with regards to the inspection and dissemination of "education records." As a federal law, it applies to school districts and schools that receive federal financial assistance through the U.S. Department of Education. FERPA makes clear that all education records, no matter where they are stored or how they are identified (i.e., "School only") must be made available. However, not all information obtained by a counselor need be disclosed. The legislative history of FERPA clarifies that education records do not include the "personal files of psychologists, counselors, or professors if these files are entirely private and not available to other individuals" (120 Cong.Rec. 27, 36533 (1974)).

Codes of ethics provide guidelines for practice decisions; however, they are not binding unless they are otherwise codified or incorporated into law. Granted, professional associations have the power to sanction their members for unethical practice, via admonishment, suspension or expulsion. But the extent of the sanctions is limited and such sanctioning does not automatically imply legal action. The professions' codes of conduct, however, do often provide the basis, or at a minimum a standard, for developing laws and regulations that govern the practice of that profession. In most states the ethical principles and standards of practice have been incorporated into laws or regulations that not only govern requirements for certification or licensure, but serve as consumer laws governing the practice of mental health services (Bennett et al., 1990). For example, in Pennsylvania the code of ethics for psychologists has the force of law in that licensed psychologists who practice in Pennsylvania are legally responsible for adhering to this code (Bricklin, 1993) (see Exercise 4.2).

While the professional codes of conduct have been incorporated into laws, in some cases the reverse has been true; that is, the legal system has stimulated mental health professions to develop and enhance their ethical standards. Mental health professionals employ sensitive, and careful ethical practices to ensure that clients will not hurt themself or others. The steps taken to warn and protect potential victims of dangerous clients are clearly integrated into all professional standards of conduct and were stimulated by the landmark decision surrounding the *Tarasoff v. The Regents of the University of California* court case (see Chapter 7). An illustration of how case law has given shape to ethical principles of practice can be found in Case Illustration 4.2.

EXERCISE 4.2
State Laws Codifying Professional Ethics

Directions: Licensed psychologists who violate the State Board of Psychology Code of Ethics in Pennsylvania not only run the risk of facing sanction of the Board but also may be prosecuted by the Commonwealth of Pennsylvania. The Pennsylvania Code of Ethics for Psychologists has the force of law in Pennsylvania. Licensed psychologists who practice in Pennsylvania are legally responsible for adhering to this Code (Bricklin, 1993).

Contact the department of state, the attorney general's office or the department of license and measurements for your state and do the following:

1. Inquire if your state licenses mental health professionals. If so, which professions? What does the law say about the practice of those within that profession who are not licensed? Or, for those from other profession who practice within that state?
2. Request a copy of the licensing law within your state.
3. Inquire if the code of ethics for your profession has the force of law within your state.

p x [illegible]

CASE ILLUSTRATION 4.2
The Issue of Duty to Warn

Jonathan was referred to Dr. Ranklin, a licensed psychologist who provided services to employees of company L as part of its Employment Assistance Program. In the initial session, Dr. Ranklin explained his role and the fact that he was contracted by Company L. to provide employees with brief, solution-focused counseling and referral. Dr. Ranklin also described the conditions of confidentiality and provided Jonathan with an information sheet about the services available.

During the initial session, Jonathan revealed his intent to "get even with Alex" (his immediate supervisor). When asked what "get even" meant, Jonathan stated:

> Alex has been on my case ever since he became a supervisor. He thinks he's hot stuff, better than the rest of us. He keeps calling me lazy and asks if I've seen the shrink yet—he told me he made the referral to you. Anyway, he does this stuff in front of the other guys and I have had it. I'm just going to wait for him one night this winter, when it's dark, and get him out in the parking lot.

When asked if he could provide more information about what it was he was planning, Jonathan went into great detail:

> I know where he parks and he always leaves just around 5:45, after most of the guys have cleared out of the lot. I'm going to be waiting for him. I'll just hide in the dark and when he goes to get into the car I will whip him terribly. I've got an ax handle with his name all over it. I crack that dumb head of his and then we'll see who's crazy. If he dies, that's his problem.

Throughout the session, Dr. Ranklin attempted to gain a guarantee that Jonathan really wouldn't do what he was saying, but each time Jonathan insisted that he would and that Alex deserved it. When reminded of the "limits of confidentiality" that Dr. Ranklin explained and that were listed in the handout, Jonathan said "I don't care." "You can tell him or anyone. He deserves it and I'm going to give it to him."

Since all attempts to persuade Jonathan to commit to not harming Alex were unsuccessful, Dr. Ranklin felt duty bound to protect his client (Jonathan) from legal action and his identified victim (Alex) from potential harm. Thus, he made an appointment to meet with Alex to disclose this information.

Dr. Ranklin's actions were stimulated by the now famous Tarasoff case and subsequent state case laws in Nebraska where he practiced. Dr. Ranklin knew that while confidentiality was an ethical directive, in Nebraska therapists are required to initiate whatever precautions are necessary to protect the potential victims of the patient (*Lipari v. Sears, Roebuck & Co.*, 1980).

Many of the ethical principles to be discussed and illustrated within the upcoming chapters have strong legal foundations. Thus in addition to providing a review of the principles, some of the laws and court decisions that tint or give further shape to the application of these principles will be discussed. Table 4.1 provides a thumbnail view of a couple of these legal decisions and their impact on professional practice.

TABLE 4.1   **Examples of Laws as Foundation for Ethical Practice**

Boundary violations	A number of rulings (e.g., *Mazza v. Huffaker*, 300 S.E. 2d 833, (1983); *Horak v. Biris* 474 N. E. 2d 13 (1985)) argue that due to the power differentials within the relationship and the potential for abuse of power, sexual relationships between client and practitioner are actionable as malpractice.
Competence	The foundation for negligence as based, in part, on the failure to use knowledge, skill, and care ordinarily exercised in similar localities was established in *Wilson v. Corbin*, 41 N.W. 2d 702.
Confidentiality	Duty to break confidence in service of the duty to warn was established in *Tarasoff v. The Regents of the University of California*.

Ethical Does Not Always Equal Legal

While codes of ethics most often overlap with legal requirements, they are distinct from them and in some cases may be in conflict. The potential for conflict has been recognized within the American Psychological Association Code of Ethics (1992), which states:

> Psychologists accord appropriate respect to the fundamental rights, dignity, and worth of all people. They respect the rights of individuals to privacy, confidentiality, self-determination, and autonomy, mindful that legal and other obligations may lead to inconsistency and conflict with the exercise of these rights. (Principle D).

Unethical, Yet Legal

Conflict can occur when a practitioner's decisions are unethical and yet remain legal. For example, in most states it is not legally mandated that a practitioner inform a client of the limitations to confidentiality or how confidential information may be used, but many professional codes of ethics require that such limitations be clearly described to the client (see Table 4.2).

Ethical, Yet Illegal

There are times when a practitioner's actions may be considered illegal yet fall within the codes of ethical conduct. Consider the situation in which a client with AIDS refuses to inform an identified sexual partner about the AIDS or take steps to protect that partner. Although disclosure of a client's status as having AIDS or being HIV positive without that client's permission is illegal in many states, the ethical duty to protect third parties from harm may direct the practitioner to disclose this information to the current sexual partner.

TABLE 4.2　Notification of Limits to Confidentiality

Professional Ethical Standards	Statement of Notification
American Psychological Association (1995)	5.01 Psychologists discuss . . . (1) the relevant limitations on confidentiality, including limitations where applicable in group, marital and family therapy, or in organizational consulting; and (2) the foreseeable uses of the information generated by their services. Unless it is not feasible or is contraindicated, the discussion or confidentiality occurs at the outset of the relationship and thereafter as new circumstances may warrant.
National Association of Social Workers (1996)	1.07 Privacy and Confidentiality
	Social workers should inform clients, to the extent possible, about disclosure of confidential information and the potential consequences, when feasible before the disclosure is made. This applies whether social workers disclose confidential information on the basis of a legal requirement or client consent.
	Social workers should discuss with clients and other interested parties the nature of confidentiality and the limitations of clients' right of confidentiality. Social workers should review with clients circumstances where confidential information may be requested and where disclosure of confidential information may be legally required. This discussion should occur as soon as possible in the social worker–client relationship and as needed throughout the course of the relationship.
American Counseling Association (1995)	A.3.a Client Rights
	Disclosure to Clients. When counseling is initiated, and throughout the counseling process as necessary, counselors inform clients of the purposes, goals, techniques, procedures, limitations, potential risks, and benefits of services to be performed and other pertinent information. Counselors take steps to ensure that clients understand the implications of diagnosis, the intended use of tests and reports, fees, and billing arrangements. Clients have the right to expect confidentiality and to be provided with an explanation of its limitations, including supervision and/or treatment team professionals; to obtain clear information about their case records; to participate in the ongoing counseling plans; and to refuse any recommended services and be advised of the consequences of such refusal.
	B.3. Minor or Incompetent Clients
	When counseling clients who are minors or individuals who are unable to give voluntary, informed consent, parents or guardians may be included in the counseling process as appropriate. Counselors act in the best interest of clients and take measures to safeguard confidentiality.

(*continued*)

TABLE 4.2   Continued

Professional Ethical Standards	Limitations to Confidentiality
American Psychological Association (1995)	5.05 Psychologists disclose confidential information without the consent of the individual only as mandated by law, or where permitted by law for the valid purpose, such as (1) to provide needed professional services to the patient or the individual or organizational client, (2) to obtain appropriate professional consultations, (3) to protect the patient or client or others from harm, or (4) to obtain payment for services, in which instance disclosure is limited to the minimum that is necessary to achieve that purpose.
National Association of Social Workers (1996)	1.07 Privacy and Confidentiality (c) Social workers should protect the confidentiality of all information obtained in the course of professional service, except for compelling professional reasons. The general expectation that social workers will keep information confidential does not apply when disclosure is necessary to prevent serious, foreseeable, and imminent harm to a client or other identifiable person. In all instances, social workers should disclose the least amount of confidential information necessary to achieve the desired purpose; only information that is directly relevant to the purpose for which the disclosure is made should be revealed.
American Counseling Association (1995)	B.1. Right to Privacy c. Exceptions. The general requirement that counselors keep information does not apply when disclosure is required to prevent clear and imminent danger to the client or others when legal requirements demand that confidential information be revealed. Counselors consult with other professionals when in doubt as to the validity of an exception.
American Association of Marriage and Family Therapists (1998)	2.1 Marriage and family therapists may not disclose client confidences except: (a) mandated by law; (b) to prevent clear and immediate danger to a person or persons; (c) where the therapist is a defendant in a civil, criminal, or disciplinary action arising from the therapy(in which case client confidences may be disclosed only in the course of that action): or (d) if there is a waiver previously obtained in writing, and then such information may be revealed only in accordance with the terms of the waiver. In circumstances where more than one person in a family receives therapy, each such family member who is legally competent to execute a waiver must agree to the waiver required by subparagraph (d). Without such waiver from each family member legally competent to execute a waiver, a therapist cannot disclose information received from a family member.

TABLE 4.3   Interaction Between Ethics and the Law

Interaction	Description	Illustration
Ethical and legal	Professional follows a just law	Keeping client disclosures confidential when such is also protected by law
Ethical and illegal	Professional disobeys an unjust law	Refusal to breach confidence even when court ordered
Ethical and alegal	Professional decision to do good in the absence of law	Providing pro bono (free service) to poor clients
Unethical and illegal	Following an unjust law that conflicts with professional ethic	Employing testimonials in advertisement that is allowed by the Federal Trade commission but is viewed by ethical principles as unethical
Unethical and illegal	Failing to abide by a just law	Sharing confidential information when such information is legally protected and ethically required
Unethical and alegal	Making a harmful decision that is not prohibited by law	Fostering client dependency as a way of enhancing one's own feeling of power

Note: Adapted from *Guide to Ethical Practice in Psychotherapy* by A. Thompson, 1990, New York: John Wiley & Sons. Copyrighted 1990 by John Wiley & Sons. Adapted by permission.

It is clear that the relationship between law and ethics is not always clear-cut. Thompson (1990) identified six ways in which law and ethics may interact. These, along with examples of each, are presented in Table 4.3.

Ethical and legal standards are by their very nature broad in spirit and language, thus open to situational interpretation. As a result, practitioners must remain informed about the legal interpretations of the applications and misapplication of the ethics of practice and practice decisions as they continue to unfold through legislation and court decisions.

When Ethics and Legalities Collide

When ethics and law collide, the practitioner will need to use his or her own sense of judgment about the issues and directions to be taken. Such judgment should be formed on accurate understanding of the specific ethical principles involved and the laws governing practice decisions. While the mental health practitioner is not called upon to be a legal expert, it is important that the practitioner have some knowledge of court rulings (local, state, and federal), since such rulings provide the precedents for future actions by the courts. Clearly, the better informed a practioner is, the more likely conflicts between legal and ethical principles can be resolved.

It is generally believed that mental health professions have an obligation to abide by the legal requirements of the situation. This obligation is most often considered as prima facie, meaning that the legal obligation needs to be considered in every case and only set aside when ethical and/or legal reasons of greater importance compel such action. However, the uniqueness of each situation and the characteristics of each client complicates the decision to be made.

There may be situations in which even with the greatest understanding of both the law and the ethical principles, a clear path resolving the conflict cannot be found. It is possible that the action mandated by law may not appear to be in the best ethical interest of the client. Such a conflict places the mental health practitioner in quite a moral and professional dilemma. Under these situations it is the responsibility of the professional to review all of the pertinent information, discerning which avenue both upholds the intent of the law and essence of the professions ethics while providing the maximum benefit to the client.

Remley (1996, p. 288) provides four steps for counselors to take when confronted by an apparent conflict between ethics and the law. These steps have been adapted and are listed below:

1. The practitioner should identify all of the forces that are impacting issues regarding the professional decision and behavior. That is, while the conflict may certainly be the result of an ethical principle or a legal mandate, other forces such as policies and procedures within a specific workplace, accreditation rules or requirements and even parameters for funding may be the source of the conflict, rather than the law.

2. When the question is one of law, legal advice should be obtained. Quite often the state or national associations may provide legal consultants who are trained in both the mental health field and the legal profession. Another source of legal advice may be obtained through one's liability insurance company.

3. If there is a problem in applying an ethical standard or in understanding the requirements of an ethical standard, the practitioner should consult with a colleague and those perceived as experts within the field. Again, it is also useful to contact the local, state, or national associations and speak to members of the ethics board.

4. If a force other than law or ethics (for example, employment requirements) is suggesting that a practitioner take some action he or she perceives as illegal, the counselor should obtain legal advice to determine whether such action is indeed illegal and what form of recourse or protection is available should the counselor refuse to follow the directive to perform this illegal act (see Chapter 5).

The need for ethical practitioners to remain informed as evolving ethics receive the force of the law through court decisions and/or evolving law gives new shape to codes of conduct cannot be overemphasized. Fortunately, practitioners are not alone in their concern and their quest. State and national associations, along with liability insurance companies, provide continuing education programs to update the practitioner's knowledge and may even provide consultation services in case of conflict. The final exercise (Exercise 4.3) is provided to help increase your awareness of the supports available to assist you in becoming both an ethical and legal practitioner.

EXERCISE 4.3
Resources in Support of the Ethical-Legal Practitioner

Directions: It is essential to remain informed about the changing face of law and codes of professional conduct as you continue to develop and practice as a helper. Ongoing information and continuing education programs are often provided by state and national associations along with the various companies providing liability insurance for your profession. Similarly, these same resources oftentimes provide "hotline" consultation for their members who may feel conflicted about a practice decision.

1. Contact your state organization and inquire about its web site or ways that you can be informed about state legal decisions that may impact your own professional practice. Ask if you can be placed on a mailing list announcing continuing education programs geared to updating practitioners on relevant law and ethical principles of practice.
2. Contact your national organization and inquire about its web site or ways that you can be informed about recent legal decisions impacting your practice and continuing education programs geared to updating practitioners on relevant laws and ethical principles of practice.
3. Contact your liability insurance carrier and inquire whether it provides continuing education program on issues of ethics and legality and if it provides a discount for those who attend.
4. Contact each of the above and inquire about the availability of legal assistance or ethical-legal consultation should you have a question or conflict. Identify the process for connecting with this service as well as any fees that may be involved.

Case Illustration

Returning to the scene with which we opened the chapter, we find Ms. Wicks (Maria's counselor) sharing concerns with a colleague. As you read the exchange, look for issues of an ethical nature, issues or concerns that may, in your opinion, have legal foundation and/or implications, and the existence of conflict between Ms. Wicks' ethical standards and the law.

MR. HAROLDS: Hi, Michelle. What's up?

MS. WICKS: Tom, could I talk to you about some legal concerns?

MR. HAROLDS: Legal concerns? Certainly, but I'm not a lawyer.

MS. WICKS: No, I know that—but you seem to stay current with laws and regulations regarding counseling and to tell you the truth, I'm not sure if it is a problem or not.

MR. HAROLDS: Well, you certainly sound concerned. What's up?

MS. WICKS: Well, I'm not sure actually. I've been counseling a student who shared with me that she is currently dating and having unprotected sex with a boy whom she reports as having AIDS. She's 18 and the information was revealed to me in my role of counselor. I am not sure if I am legally responsible to report this.

MR. HAROLDS: Did you share your concern with your client?

MS. WICKS: Yes, and she simply states that she doesn't care. You know this is love and God wouldn't punish her by letting her get AIDS.

MR. HAROLDS: Wow, that's sad. Michelle, when you first met with her, what instructions did you give her regarding the limits to confidentiality?

MS. WICKS: Tom, I know I explained about disclosing information if she informed me of her intent to harm her herself—but I'm not sure how this fits.

MR. HAROLDS: This is tough. After all, she's your client, not the boy. I know individuals with AIDS have a right to privacy, but she is placing herself in harm's way. I don't really know. Why don't we call the state board and ask to speak to one their ethical-legal consultants? Remember, I told you I wasn't a lawyer!

MS. WICKS: Tom, I just appreciate you hearing me out and confirming for me that this is not so clear-cut. I agree that calling may be the thing to do.

Reflections:
1. Do you feel that Ms.Wicks should have gotten Maria's consent to speak with Tom?
2. Do you feel that the specific information shared with Tom was a violation of Maria's right to confidentiality?
3. Do you feel that the potential for conflict be between law and ethics exists in this case? If so, where? If not, why not?
4. How do you feel about the fact that Ms. Wicks contacted a colleague in a situation like this? Is there anything else she should have done instead? Or in addition to?

Cooperative Learning Exercise

The purpose of the chapter was to familiarize you with the unique and sometimes conflictual relationship between law and professional codes of ethics. Because they are broadly stated, both ethical and legal standards are open to situational interpretation. The remaining chapters provide more detailed information about specific ethical principles and laws applying to those guidelines.

Below you will find three scenarios. Along with your colleagues read each scenario and identify whether you feel they present issues that are free of conflict or represent a conflict of law and ethics. Where conflict exists, identify the nature of the conflict. Is it legal and unethical, illegal and ethical, or unethical and illegal? Next, contact a professional practitioner in your area and ask him or her for an opinion about the nature of the situation. Finally, as you read more about specific ethical principles in the upcoming chapters, return to these scenarios to see if your initial opinions change.

Scenario 1: A girl, age 13, comes to a school counselor and asks for advice and direction on where and how to go about securing an abortion. The school counselor gives her the names and numbers of a number of agencies that counsel women seeking an abortion. The school counselor also promises the student not to inform her parents. Was the decision a conflict of law and ethics? If so what was the nature of the conflict? Which part of the counselor's behaviors or decisions were conflictual?

Scenario 2: A Vietnam war veteran voluntarily contracted for counseling with a licensed social worker for what was determined to be posttraumatic stress disorder. In the process of therapy the vet reported his intention to kill some college students who, according to the vet, prolonged the war through their protests. When asked to identify the specific students, the client simply said, "It doesn't matter as long as they are in college." The therapist did not take steps to inform anyone about this threat. Should he? Is there a conflict of law with ethics? If so, what is the nature of that conflict?

Scenario 3: Dr. Ortez works in the counseling center at a local university. Dr. Ortez had provided career counseling for a graduate student named Liz. It has been a year since Liz has graduated and over 15 months since her last session with Dr. Ortez. Dr. Ortez calls Liz to inquire how she is doing and while on the phone, asks her on a date. Did Dr. Ortez violate any ethical principles? Any laws?

Summary

The Helping Process as a Legal Contract
In performing one's practice, the helper provides implicit agreement of his or her duty to the client. The issue of whether helping is contractual and thus a minimum duty of care is established rests with the court's decision as to whether a "special relationship" existed that would be sufficient to create a duty of care.

Further, any time an individual places his or her trust in a party who has the potential to influence his or her action, a fiduciary relationship exists (Black, 1991). Given this definition, it could be reasonably argued that all professional helping relationships have this fiduciary potential and thus bring with them a duty to act to the benefit of the other individual in any matters related to an undertaking between them (Black, 1991).

The Legal Foundation of Ethical Practice
Codes of ethics provide guidelines for practice decisions; however, they are not binding unless they are otherwise codified or incorporated into law. In most states, the ethical principles and standards of practice have been incorporated into laws or regulations that not only govern requirements for certification or licensure, but also serve as consumer laws governing the practice of mental health services. While the professional codes of conduct have been incorporated into laws, in some cases the reverse has been true; that is, the legal system has stimulated mental health professions to develop and enhance their ethical standards.

Ethical Does Not Always Equal Legal
While codes of ethics most often overlap with legal requirements, they are distinct from them and in some cases may be in conflict. Thompson (1990) identified six ways law and ethics may interact, (1) legal and ethical, (2) legal and unethical, (3) alegal and ethical, (4) alegal and unethical, (5) illegal and ethical, (6) illegal and unethical.

When Ethics and Legalities Collide

When ethics and law collide, the practitioner will need to use his or her own sense of judgment about the issues and directions to be taken. Such judgment should be formed on accurate understanding of the specific ethical principles involved and the laws governing practice decisions. Remley (1996) provided four steps that counselors should take when confronted by an apparent conflict between ethics and the law: (1) Identify the forces that are at issue, (2) obtain legal advice, (3) consult with colleagues or experts in the field of professional ethics, and (4) seek legal advice, when forces other than law and ethics are at the core, in order to understand available options.

IMPORTANT TERMS

Bogust v. Iverson   implicit acts
contractual   legal precedent
duty beyond reason   *Nally v. Grace Community Church*
duty to care   prima facie
Eisel v. Board of Education   principle of fiduciary responsibility
ethical, yet illegal   unethical, yet legal

SUGGESTED READINGS

Fischer, L. & Sorenson-Paulus, G.(1996). *School law for counselors, psychologists and social workers, (3rd ed.).* White Plains, NY: Longman Publishers.

Swenson, L.C. (1997). *Psychology and law for the helping professions.* Pacific Grove, CA: Brooks/Cole.

Woody, R.H. (1997). *Legally safe mental health practice: Psycholegal questions and answers.* Madison, CT: Psychosocial Press.

PART THREE

The Nature of the
Helping Relationship

5 Ethical Conflicts: The System and the Interests of Others

Ms. Wicks: Hi, Tom it is me again.

Mr. Harolds: Hey, how are you? Did you get that information from the state association?

Ms.Wicks: Not yet. They are supposed to call me. But, things are getting more confusing. . . .

Mr. Harolds: Really?

Ms. Wicks: Ms. Armstrong, the principal at the school, informed me that it is understood in the district that we are not to counsel students regarding sexual issues. She said it is not a formal policy, just something that "we" all know not to do. So now I'm not sure if I broke a law or violated a code of ethics or may have stepped over the line in terms of my job definition. I am so confused!

When working with a client, a helper needs to be aware and sensitive to the many individual issues and concerns presented by the client. In addition, the helper also needs to be fully cognizant of the ethical and legal implications of his or her own professional decisions in relationship to these client concerns. Now, to complicate matters even more for those practitioners working within an organization or a system, be it a school, a hospital, an agency or a company—individual practice decisions must also reflect and be congruent with policies, procedures, and informal standards and values operating within that system.

The current chapter looks at the ethical culture of social systems and the influence it exerts on the practice decisions of those helpers working within that system. The chapter will discuss the impact of working for and within an organization. Further, in this chapter we will look at situations in which conflicts arise when what the professionals feel is best for the individual client falls outside of or even runs contrary to policies, procedures, or values of the organization. Under these conditions, what's a practitioner to do?

Chapter Objectives

The chapter will review the process and implications of making ethical practice decisions within an organizational or system context. Attempting to balance the needs of the individual client with the requirements of the employing organization and other interested parties (e.g., managed care organizations) is not an easy or clear-cut process. After reading this chapter you should be able to do the following:

1. Define what is meant by "system culture."
2. Discuss the impact of system culture on ethical decision making.
3. Identify possible points of ethical conflict when working in a managed care environment.
4. Identify possible points of ethical conflict when working with third-party payees.

Serving the Individual Within a System

Professional practice does not occur within a vacuum. At a minimum, professional practice occurs within the social context of a client and a helper. But for those working within an organization, professional practice and ethical decision making occurs not only within this dyadic system, but also within the context of the larger system or organization in which the helper works. Ethical problems in professional practice are often the result of the confluence of context, setting, and standards of practice.

Practitioners who work in schools, clinics, hospitals, and/ or those who serve as providers for managed care can find themselves in conflict with these competing client systems (see Case Illustration 5.1).

Certainly the school psychologist presented in Case Illustration 5.1 is confronted with a serious ethical and potentially legal dilemma. As in this case, practice decisions must

---

CASE ILLUSTRATION 5.1
A Diagnostic Dilemma

Linda Alfreds is a new school psychologist, the first ever employed by the Hallstead School District. Linda's job involves performing all psycho-educational assessments, especially those required for special education placement. Linda was informed, however, that with the exception of a few "slower" children, the district really didn't have children with special needs, which according to the superintendent was a blessing since they have very limited monies for providing such services.

Linda was asked to see Marquis, a transfer student, who was reported as having difficulty keeping up with the work in a number of his classes. The test data presented Marquis as an impulsive child, with a significant receptive language problem. From her work at a previous school district, Linda knew that Marquis would benefit from placement in either a learning disabilities room or a resource room with a special education teacher trained in learning disabilities and language disorders.

Linda discussed the situation with her department chairperson and was told that the District did not have a LD class nor resource room personnel. However, the other middle school in the district did provide a classroom for "slow learners." The chair person directed Linda to record Marquis as being retarded rather than as having a language disability since this would at least get him some special services. It was clear to Linda that the data would not support this diagnosis, but identifying the child as LD might fail to provide any special learning assistance to Marquis.

clearly reflect not only the needs of the client as well as the characteristics and orientation of the helper, but also the unique characteristics and demands of the context or organization in which the helping occurs. Balancing all of these unique needs is not always easy nor clear-cut. The ethical practitioner needs to be aware of the system and the subtle and oftentimes not so subtle influences that a system can exert. Such an awareness begins with an understanding of the nature of systems.

A system is "an entity made up of interconnected parts with recognizable relationships that are systematically arranged to serve a perceived purpose" (Kurpius, 1985, p. 369). The specific nature of these parts and the type of relationships they have, along with the specific purpose for which the system exists, all need to be viewed as exerting pressure on the decision making of those within that system, including the professional helper. As Beauchamp and Childress (1994) suggested, a professional role, as well as the expectations of professional behavior, are shaped in response to the organization's expectations and needs and, therefore, incorporate these expectations as standards and guides for practice decision. Therefore, understanding this context—which includes not only the people involved (i.e., clients, families, professionals), but also the values, meaning, and standards of the specific and global milieu in which the services are being delivered—is essential if one is to function as an ethical practitioner.

It would appear that divided loyalties could be the problem especially in situations such as Employee Assistance Programs in which the professional is under contract with the organization. Under these conditions information regarding the client's treatment as related to job performance may be within the need to know and thus conflicts with the client's right of privacy and confidentiality. The practitioner, while respecting the confidentiality of the information gathered needs to be sensitive to the obligations agreed to in contracts with the organization. The EAP counselor described in Case Illustration 5.2 appears to have developed a plan for balancing the needs of the organization with the rights of the client.

Ethical Culture of Social Systems

Organizations or, for that matter, any social system develop their own values or standards that guide decision making and practice within that system. These values present that system's view of the importance of certain goals, activities, relationships, and feelings (Kuh & Whitt, 1988) and serve as the basis for what has been described as a system's culture (Schein 1990). Schein (1990) described system culture as (1) a pattern of basic assumptions, (2) invented, discovered or developed by a given group, (3) as it learns to cope with its problems of external adaptation and internal integration, (4) that has worked well enough to be considered valid and, therefore, (5) is to be taught to new members as the (6) correct way to perceive, think, and feel, in relationship to those problems (p. 111). The assumptions which serve as the base for the development and maintenance of a system's culture form the unquestioned, nondebatable truths and reality of people within the system. These develop when a solution or procedure works repeatedly. As a result those involved begin to take it for granted to the point where what was once only a hunch or possibility starts to get viewed and treated as a reality. These basic assumptions then serve as the foundation from

CASE ILLUSTRATION **5.2**
Balancing the Needs of the System and the Client
A Case of Confidentiality

Hanna Johannson was a private practicing mental health counselor who was certified as an EAP (Employee Assistance Program) counselor. In addition to seeing clients for a fee, Hanna provided EAP services to the members of a local school district. In this EAP capacity, Hanna received a contracted fee and was to provide three to five sessions free of charge to any school district employee who desired such counseling. In addition, should additional counseling be desired or required, Hanna would make a referral to another provider, and the employee would then be responsible to continue on a fee-for-service basis.

As part of the contract with the school superintendent, the EAP counselor was to provide monthly reports that included (1) the number of people seen, (2) the specific school in which the employee worked, (3) the job class (i.e. teacher, administrator , staff, etc.), (4) the type of problem presented, (5) the number of sessions utilized, and (6) and evaluation of the outcome. While the specific names of clients and any details of the nature of the problem presented were not to be disclosed, Hanna felt that the information requested was such that it could jeopardize the confidentiality of those who utilized this EAP service.

Hanna worked out a compromise with school administration so that all first sessions could be made completely confidential. In that first session, as part of setting the boundaries of confidentiality, Hanna explained to each client the types of data she would reveal to the superintendent and asked the client for their informed consent before making additional appointments. If the client would not give that consent, Hanna would provide a referral list and no information about the contact would be shared with the central office.

which the system defines structures and processes to guide its operations. This is an important concept for the ethical practitioner to grasp because when members of an organization embrace these assumptions, they in turn shape what the members value and the form these values take (see Exercise 5.1).

The cultural values of a system become enacted in the way members prioritize and function—shaping policies, decision making, and other operations. Practice decisions, therefore, may begin to reflect institutional values and organizational ethics more than they represent "best practice" or codes of professional conduct. While it is possible that organizational ethics can parallel those of the profession, in view of the fact that the purpose of an organization may be different than the purpose of any one helping relationship, the organizational ethics may not only be conflictual but may act to undermine the values and ethics of the practitioner (see Exercise 5.2).

While it is clear that the ethical practitioner must be aware of the oftentimes subtle influence of a system's culture on his or her practice decision, the question remains: "If enculturated, how does one identify the operating assumptions, values, and culture?"

EXERCISE **5.1**
Making Culturally Compatible Choices

Directions: Below is a table that provides a social context, a focus for a practitioner, and two practice decision options. Along with a colleague, select the options which you feel would most likely be encouraged and/or supported by that particular social context and provide your rationale for your selection

Social-Organizational Cultural Context	Focus for Practice Decision	Practice Decision Options	Selection and Rationale
(sample) Catholic High School	Increased evidence of student pregnancy	1. Guidance unit on sexual behavior, safe sex, and sexually transmitted diseases 2. Guidance unit on self-esteem and value of abstinence	Option 2, given the school's belief that sex outside of marriage is unacceptable and immoral
A free-standing clinic that is funded primarily through managed care contracts	A client diagnosed as depressed, with the possibility of having an early history of sexual abuse	1. Referral for anti-depressant medication 2. Contract for long-term, "recovered memories" therapy	
A military industrial complex, making "sensitive" technical equipment	A personnel director who is approached by an upper-level manager experiencing extreme financial pressures and who has had fantasies of "selling technology" to other governments	1. Respect the confidentiality of the relationship and work with the employee on stress reduction 2. Report the fantasies to his supervisor	
A public school, with limited special education facilities and funding	A school psychologist who believes a student is in serious need of ongoing individual psychotherapy	1. Recommend therapy to his family as part of an Individual Education Program . 2. Suggest that his family may find it useful to contact an outside therapist	

EXERCISE 5.2
Goals—Values and Decisions

Directions: As noted within the chapter, decisions are made that not only reflect the values held, but the goals desired. Below you will find a scenario, system and practitioner goals, and decision options. Your task is to identify the decisions preferred by system along with those preferred by the practitioner. Next identify the situations in which these are parallel and/or conflict.

Scenario	System Goals	Practitioner Goal	Decision Preferred by System	Decision Preferred by Practitioner	Parallel or Conflict
1. (sample) Star football player has a very bad sprained ankle	Win the big game	Rest the ankle	Allow the student to play	Sideline the student for one game	Conflict
2. The top salesman for a corporation has embraced his alcoholism and is committed to a treatment program	Maintain sales	Maintain salesman's health	Adjust sales region to allow salesman to attend meetings while continuing sales	Encourage and support in attending meetings	
3. A social worker noted that a Fifth grade teacher who is approaching retirement has a number of physical problems, has been falling asleep in class, and often verbally abuses the children for making noise	Educate children in fulfillment of the schools mission	Protect children from verbal abuse and show concern for an aging teacher with ill health	Try not to make too public for the remainder of the semester and then provide the teacher with an early retirement package	Work with the teacher in developing some cooperative learning units while providing supportive counseling around the benefits of retirement	

Scenario	System Goals	Practitioner Goal	Decision Preferred by System	Decision Preferred by Practitioner	Parallel or Conflict
4. A residential setting for individuals with severe emotional problems	To provide therapy while at the same time reducing patient disruption	To provide therapy geared at empowering individuals to take responsibility for their own actions	Reliance on medication including sedatives	Using the minimum amount of medication in order to support the client's development of cognitive/ behavioral methods of control	

It has been suggested that the use of interpretation of the artifacts and values reveals basic assumptions (Finney & Mitroff, 1986; Schein, 1991). Artifacts would include the visible, tangible, or concrete manifestations, be they the physical surroundings and their appointments, the stories or oral histories still shared and even the rituals and ceremonies practiced whereas a system's values are revealed in what the system views as important in terms of goals, activities, relationships, and feelings (Kuh & Whitt, 1988). By reviewing the way those within the system traditionally and continually address specific problems posed by the situations they face in common, the ethical practitioner can begin to understand the system's values (Parsons, 1996; Van Maanen & Barley, 1985).

Who Is the Client?

One seminal question that needs to be addressed when working within an organization is "Who is the client?" While this at first may appear to be a simple question to answer, balancing a practitioner's responsibility to the employing organization while at the same time servicing the individual helper seeker is not always that clear-cut or easy. The various professional organizations are aware of this potential confusion and area of conflict and have attempted to provide practitioners with guidelines for their practice decisions (see Table 5.1).

Although the various professional organizations address the issue of serving individuals and organizations, it is still for the individual practitioner to resolve questions such as: Does the ethical practitioner, when working with individual members of an organization, make decisions that are best suited for the goals and objectives of the institution even if not in the best interest of the individual care seeker? Or does the individual and the individual's well-being take primacy? (see Case Illustration 5.3)

TABLE 5.1   Ethics of Practice Serving Client and Organization

Professional Ethical Standards	Statement on Serving Client and Organization
American Counseling Association (1996)	D.1.a: Counselors define and describe for their employers and employees the parameters and level of their professional roles. D.1. c.: Counselors alert their employers to conditions that may be potentially disruptive or damaging to the counselors' professional responsibilities or that may limit their effectiveness.
American Psychological Association (1995)	8:03 If the demands of an organization with which psychologists are affiliated conflict with this Ethics Code, psychologists clarify the nature of the conflict, make known their commitment to the Ethics Code, and to the extent feasible, seek to resolve the conflict in a way that permits the fullest adherence to the Ethics Code.
National Association of Social Workers (1996)	3.09 a: Social workers generally should adhere to commitments made to employers and employing organizations. 3.09.b: Social workers should work to improve employing agencies' policies and procedures and the efficiency and effectiveness of their services. 3.09 c: Social workers should take reasonable steps to ensure that employers are aware of social workers' ethical obligations as set forth in the NASW Code of Ethics and of the implications of those obligations for social work practice. 3.09.d: Social workers should not allow an employing organization's policies, procedures, regulations or administrative orders to interfere with their ethical practice of social work.

For Col. Wipps (see Case Illustration 5.3), questions existed about whether individual confidentiality should be respected or whether this individual posed a significant security risk and thus should be identified to appropriate personnel. In part, the answer to this question rested on who Col. Wipps identified as his client, D.L. Kingsley or the U. S. Army.

Most guidelines, like that of the American Counseling Association (see Table 5.1) indicate that the client is the primary concern for the ethical helper and the institution secondary. But it could be argued that accepting a position within an organization is a tacit agreement to serve as its agent and to embrace its values and standards of practice. In fact, the American Counseling Association Code of Ethics advised that acceptance of employment is essentially an agreement with the principles and policies of the institution. Counselors are also admonished that if there is a conflict between the institution's practices and those standards established by the code, resignation from employment should be strongly considered. In a somewhat more conciliatory tone, the American Psychological Association states: "If the demands of an organization with which psychologists are affiliated conflict

---

CASE ILLUSTRATION **5.3**
Who Is the Client?

Col. R.J Wipps was a clinical psychologist working in service of the U.S. Army's Special Service Division. Col. Wipps provided testing and individual counseling to those involved with Special Services.

Col. Wipps was approached by D. L. Kingsley, an officer in charge of a highly sensitive military project. D.L. came to Col.Wipps because of what he reported to be extreme stress as a result of financial difficulties that he was currently experiencing. D.L. noted that he was concerned that his wife would leave him if something didn't happen soon to improve their lifestyle. When asked what he was attempting to do to resolve the financial problems, D.L. was quick to note that "nothing short of something illegal" could help. When confronted directly about whether he had considered illegal activities, D.L. stated: "Of course not . . . but I've been drinking a lot lately and God only knows what I could do if I get drunk!"

Col. Wipps recommended that D.L. take a medical leave while he went into a treatment program for the alcohol and also received some individual and marital counseling. D.L. said he would think about it, but really did not feel that was necessary. D.L. asked if he would be able to see Col.Wipps for some counseling during this really stressful time. D.L. also wanted to be sure that the relationship would be confidential.

---

with this Ethics code, psychologists clarify the nature of the conflict in a way that permits the fullest adherence to the Ethics Code" (APA, 1992).

It would appear, therefore, that the ethical practitioner needs to be accountable and responsive to both the system of employment and the individual clients served within that system. As such it is essential that the practitioner not only understand but also commit the mission of the organization, as well as the specific values underlying that mission and the ways it becomes manifested in the procedures, policies and decision making processes.

This does not mean to suggest a blind allegiance to the organization at the cost of the individual. In fact it can be argued that the ethical helper will attempt to change organizational policies and procedures that are not healthy for those within the system. For example, the American Counseling Association Code of ethics states : "Members must alert their employers to conditions that may be potentially disruptive or damaging" (ACA, 1995, D.1.c).

Similarly, it does not mean absolute and blind protection of the individual care seeker. Thus, while some practitioners find themselves feeling responsible for championing the client's right to confidentiality in the face of the organization's rules and regulations, in some situations this is neither legal nor ethical. For example, in the military, confidentiality is guided by federal statutes, Department of Defense regulations, and the specific service (i.e., Army, Navy, Air Force) regulations, a point that needs to be considered by Col. Wipps (see Case Illustration 5.3). While supporting respect for the privacy of the individuals, these directives also mandate access to confidential materials by federal employees on a "need to know" basis (Jeffrey, Rankin, & Jeffrey, 1992).

An ethical practitioner attempts to resolve conflicts between organizational need and individual need in a way that not only reflects the desire of the practitioner to be supportive of his or her organization, but also upholds the professional code of ethics. Thus, when confronted by the desire to protect the care seeker's privacy while abiding by the rules and regulations of the organization in which one is employed, the use of advanced warning on the limits of confidentiality would be essential as a means of serving both the organization of employment and the care seeker.

When There Are Multiple Masters

Ethical practitioners will not only know the mission, objectives, and values of the organizations within which they work but will also make known to their employers the nature of their own professional ethical commitments. Beyond this, it appears that an ethical practitioner will also share with his or her clients the obligations of fidelity and conditions of employment and how these may flavor the helping relationships and the practitioner's decisions. This is especially important when an organization's disclosure policy places additional limits on the confidentiality between client and helper (see Case Illustration 5.2).

Recently, the issue of multiple clients, or conflicts between the needs of an employing organization with those of the client, has taken on a new dimension with the introduction of managed care. Managed care is a term applied to a widespread set of attempts to contain health care costs. The term has been used to describe "any type of intervention in the delivery and financing of health care that is intended to eliminate unnecessary and inappropriate care and to reduce costs" (Langwell, 1992, p. 22). Under managed care, third-party payers review requests for the initial delivery of services, determine the volume of services to be provided, and review any subsequent requests for service continuations. Given the level of involvement in the professional decision process, it could be argued that in managed care situations the practitioner has in fact two clients, the primary client being the person seeking assistance and the secondary client being the managed care company. The potential for conflict arises in that the needs and goals of these two clients may not always be congruent.

Managed care is essentially an economic strategy designed to provide care of equal or better quality for less money. While the concept of cost containment is noble, the reality is that often the goals of managed care are in conflict with those of the practitioner (Blum, 1992). Shore (1996) critically suggests that "[m]anaged care favors clinicians who generate a profit and cause no trouble. Skill, training, and ethics matter less than compliance with managed care procedures" (p. 324). The question becomes at what point does the focus on cost containment interfere with the client's needs and the helper's ethical practice?

Managed care may challenge the practitioner's ability to provide ethical practice. Managed care stresses time-limited interventions, cost-effective treatment, and a move toward preventive rather than remedial processes (Cummings, 1990). Professional literature raises several concerns about the impact of managed care on the effectiveness of treatment provided (Denkers & Clifford, 1994; Hipp, Atkinson, & Pelac, 1994; Miller, 1996). As noted by Miller (1996), managed care could result in clients' receiving undertreatment in that they may go underdiagnosed, experience restricted referral, and have insufficient follow-up. Thus, the policies of managed care may conflict with the decisions of an ethical practitioner, especially when utilization review decisions are contrary to professional judgment, or when short-term or limited interventions are inadequate forms of treatments (Reamer, 1997). Ethical rules and standards are often incongruent with the realities of treatment situations. Many of the standards of care promulgated by professions incorporate procedures that require long-term contact for implementation (Coale, 1998). In a managed care environment with restrictions to the number of sessions allowed, adhering to professional guidelines for risk management and standard of care service may simply be unrealistic.

In addition to potentially restricting treatment choice, the third party review can also compromise client privacy (Alperin, 1994; Brown, 1994; Schlesinger, 1995; and Wells, 1995). For example, Edwards (1995) reported that the number of individuals within the managed care system who have access to records has increased dramatically, a point that threatens the fundamental concept of confidentiality.

Given these potential areas of conflict what is the ethical practitioner to do? At a minimum, the ethical practitioner needs to inform clients how their delivery of services may be influenced by managed care policies and restrictions. Reamer (1997) noted that clients should be fully informed about the potential invasion of their privacy by the review process employed by many managed care agents. Further, practitioners may need to be willing to balance the requirements of managed care's cost containment principle with the ethical concern of providing quality of care (Newman & Bricklin, 1991). How it is accomplished is truly the dilemma faced by all managed care providers. Do therapists continue pro bono? Do they challenge the managed care gatekeepers about artificial limits to needed care?

While the limitations to the number of sessions to be paid by insurance may make good economic and business sense for the insuring body, the question remains: What happens to the client once these limits are reached? Should the client continue to need care, the helper is ethically bound not to abandon him or her. The helper could refer the client needing additional treatment or provide pro bono services. Both strategies invite complication. How does one refer if referral sources are limited? How does one provide pro bono services to so many and survive financially? The answer may lie in the decisions an ethical practitioner makes before engaging in managed care service. Haas and Cummings (1995) advise therapists to consider the question of how to provide service to the client and how to avoid abandoning clients without going bankrupt before one joins a managed care plan. Understanding the nature of the managed care contract and resolving areas of professional standards of practice and care with those of economic necessity is a must for the ethical helper (see Exercise 5.3).

Beyond Professional Standards:
A Personal Moral Response

While it is easy to grasp and comprehend the dilemmas one may face as the varying demands, needs, and responsibilities of client, profession, and system of employment converge on a practitioner, positioning oneself to make the ethical decision may be quite another story. The existence and potential impact of these forces is not a simple intellectual or academic issue. It is a real-life dilemma that has the potential to impair not only the client but the practitioner, a point poignantly described by Doherty (1995):

EXERCISE **5.3**
Serving Clients in a Managed Care Environment

Directions: Contact two private practitioners who provide clinical services and are part of a managed care organization. Ask the practitioner each of the following questions:

1. What are the limits to the types and/ or length of services you can provide to your managed care clients?
2. Are there are any unique limitations to the confidentiality of your records when working with managed care clients?
3. What, if any, avenues of appeal do you have regarding the decisions made by the managed care utilization review boards?
4. How do you inform your clients of the special conditions regarding type and length of service, utilization review, confidentiality, etc. that may exist by the nature of providing managed care services?
5. Have you turned down any opportunities to join a particular managed care group because you found it too restrictive?
6. Have you been able to change any policies, procedures, or requirements in the managed care organization of which you are a part as a way of better servicing your clients.
7. As a provider in managed care, what do you find to be the most challenging factor to your ability to provide ethical, professional care for your clients?

Unsupportive and alienating work settings inevitably affect therapists' ability to care, especially for difficult clients at the end of a long workday or workweek. Having our work undermined by other professionals in positions of greater institutional power erodes motivation and investment in clinical care. Seeing too many clients during a workweek does the same, as does having to fit the client's needs to the rigidly enforced restrictions of managed care contracts. Therapists start to go through the motion, it shows, and we know it. We become negative about our clients, we hope for no-shows and cancellations, our natural caring declines, and our ethical caring begins to feel like martyrdom.

Doherty (1995) suggests that under these conditions the ethical practitioner is left with few options: either to change the context or get out, since one cannot sustain the fundamental virtue of caring. This author concurs. Acceptance of employment is essentially an agreement with the principles and policies of the institution. When conflict exists between the institution's practices and the standards established by the code, ethical practitioners need to clarify and resolve conflicts in a way that maximizes adherence to ethical dictates of their profession. This can be facilitated by establishing a pre-plan of resolving potential conflicts between organization and professional ethics and values, including adjusting contracts and contract demands so that they are in line with system goals AND professional standards. When this is not possible, then it is this author's contention that the ethical practitioner should consider resignation. Exercise 5.4 is provided as a stimulus for your own development of such a pre-plan.

EXERCISE 5.4
Recontracting or Resigning

Directions: Part 1: Below you will find a number of organizational policies or procedures that a practitioner would need to follow. Identify those you find objectionable. How would you attempt to rework these policies/procedures before you would resign your post?

Organizational Directive (Policies/Procedures)	Rework or Recontract	Resign?
1. All clinical records, including notes, are open to inspection by anyone identified as an executive administrator within the organization.	1. Attempt to specify the specific types of data open for review and tie each level of data to a specific administrator with a "need to know." Further, all clients would be informed as to the access to records.	Yes, if not modified
2. Allowed only to utilize a brief therapy form of service. Therapy restricted to eight sessions maximum.		
3. Prior to providing service all intake information must be shared with a review board in order to achieve permission to continue. Further, a specific treatment plan and progress reports must be completed after every four sessions.		
4. As an employee you are required to provide service, in-house for all the clients you see, regardless of their needs and your level of training.		
5. You are required to acquire a minimum of thirty continuing education credits in your professional field every two years.		

Part 2: Ask an individual care provider who is a member of a managed care program to show you his or her contract and statement of responsibilities, policies, and procedures governing service delivery. Review this contract and identify areas that you feel may potentially compromise your ability to provide ethical practice.

Case Illustration

Returning to the scene with which we opened the chapter, we find Ms. Wicks (Maria's counselor) expressing her felt conflict among the informal values and rules of conduct held within the system in which she works, her concern for her client, and her understanding of her professional code of ethics. As you read the continuing dialogue, try to identify some of the values and/or underlying assumptions existing within that school's culture and begin to identify where and how these may conflict with this particular counselor's understanding of her professional code of conduct. The questions in the reflection section that follows the exchange should help you in this process.

MS. WICKS: Hi, Tom, it is me again.

MR. HAROLDS: Hey, how are you . . . did you get that information from the state association?

MS.WICKS: Not yet—they are supposed to call me. But, things are getting more confusing. . . .

MR. HAROLDS: Really?

MS. WICKS: Ms. Armstrong, the principal at the school, informed me that it is understood in the district that we are not to counsel students regarding sexual issues. She said it is not a formal policy, just something that "we" all know not to do. So now I'm not sure if I broke a law, or violated a code of ethics, or may have stepped over the line in terms of my job definition. I am so confused!

MR. HAROLDS: Well, Michelle, this is a very conservative community, and the truth is that with so many of our students having Latino backgrounds, we really don't want to impose mainstream cultural values where they don't belong.

MS. WICKS: But, Tom, it is not like I'm going to promote a particular position here—I am just very concerned that she is making some decisions that could prove harmful and even potentially lethal to her.

MR. HAROLDS: It is clear you are concerned about your client but you need to understand something. In the past we attempted to help the students make what we thought were value decisions. In fact, in health class we used to have a unit on sexuality and sexually transmitted diseases. Well, five years ago a parent group took the health teacher, the principal and the school superintendent all to court for supposedly "imposing moral values" on their children. As a result, we removed health from our curriculum, replaced it with something on career choices, and created a parent supervisor board for the school who reviews curriculum decisions.

So the superintendent is like extremely sensitive about anything that may be interpreted as promoting a set of values or beliefs. I guess Ms. Armstrong is simply trying to avoid pressure from the central office. No sense rocking the boat.

Reflections

1. Assuming that Mr. Harold's depiction of the way the system operates is accurate, what would be the primary value or motive driving decisions around controversial topics?

2. When it comes to decision making, which of the following would you suspect takes primacy in the culture of that school? Do what's expedient? Avoid conflict at all costs? Be politically correct? Do what is best for the students?
3. Could you identify an artifact that reflects the operating values and assumptions within that school?
4. What do you feel Ms. Wicks should do? In relationship to her client? Future clients? Her principal? Her job definition and contract?

Cooperative Learning Exercise

Directions: With a colleague review each of the following scenarios and
1. Identify potential areas of conflict
2. Decide if the behavior of the practitioner is ethical
3. Identify decision options available for the practitioner
4. Discuss possible pre-plan options that could have been implemented to reduce the potential of conflict.

Scenario 1: High School Counselor

A high school counselor has been working with a student who was self-referred because of his concern about his tendency to steal and his desire to risk experimenting with drugs. The student expressed genuine concern over both of these tendencies and appeared willing to work with the counselor in order to curtail both the desires and the actions. Working throughout the first part of the school year, the student made significant gains as defined by the reduction of the number of times he had taken something that was not his. Prior to the Christmas break the student was asked by the school nurse to volunteer as her "messenger" during his study hall. Part of the role of messenger would be to watch the office, take phone calls, and record students' names who came in when the nurse was out of the office. As with many schools, the nurse's office is where many of the children's medications are kept—including stimulants used for children diagnosed with ADHD. The counselor feels that he should warn the nurse about the student's tendencies toward taking things and experimenting with drugs.

Scenario 2: An EAP Provider

Dr. Livingston is a licensed social worker working in private practice. Dr. Livingston also provides short-term counseling to employees of a local manufacturing plant. In this capacity as an Employee Assistance Counselor, she has agreed to provide short term (maximum of five visits) counseling to all employees and offer referral services for those needing more extended care. Further, her contract calls for her to consult with managers in order to increase their effectiveness when working with their employees.

In working with Helen, Dr. Livingston discovered that Helen and her coworkers have been punching in and out for each other and, as a result, have developed a system where they can cut approximately eight hours a week off their actual work while recording and receiving pay for a full forty-hour week. Helen is a little troubled by this procedure but reports that is what everybody does. Dr. Livingston feels that she should report this information to Mr. Hansen, the owner of the company, since it is he with whom she has a contract.

Summary

Serving the Individual Within a System

Practice decisions made must clearly reflect not only the needs of the client and character-istics and orientation of the helper, but also the unique characteristics and demands of the context or organization in which the helping occurs.

A professional role, as well as the expectations of professional behavior, are shaped in response to the organization's expectations and needs; therefore, these expectations are incorporated as standards and guides for practice decision.

Ethical Culture of Social Systems

System culture is a pattern of basic assumptions invented, discovered, or developed by a given group as it learns to cope with its problems of external adaptation and internal integra-tion. The pattern has worked well enough to be considered valid and is taught to new mem-bers as the correct way to perceive, think, and feel, in relationship to those problems.

Once enculturated within a system it is easy for the cultural values to become enacted in the way members prioritize and function—shaping policies, decision making and other operations. As such, practice decisions may begin to reflect institutional values, and orga-nizational ethics more than they represent "best practice" or codes of professional conduct.

Who Is the Client?

Most guidelines, like that of the American Counseling Association, indicate that the client is the primary concern for the ethical helper and the institution secondary. But it could be argued that accepting a position within an organization is a tacit agreement to serve as its agent and to embrace its values and standards of practice.

The ethical practitioner needs to be accountable and responsive to both the system of employment and the individual clients served within that system.

When There Are Multiple Masters

Ethical practitioners will share with their clients the obligations of fidelity, conditions of employment, and how these may flavor the helping relationships and the practitioners' decisions. One special situation in which it is clear there may be more than one client is in the case of managed care.

Managed care is essentially an economic strategy designed to provide care of equal or better quality for less money. The policies of managed care may conflict with the deci-sions of an ethical practitioner, especially when utilization review decisions are contrary to professional judgment or when short-term or limited interventions are inadequate forms of treatments

Understanding the nature of the managed care contract and resolving areas of pro-fessional standards of practice and care with those of economic necessity is a must for the ethical helper.

Beyond Professional Standards: A Personal Moral Decision

Acceptance of employment is essentially an agreement with the principles and policies of the institution. When conflict exists between the institution's practices and the standards established by the code, the ethical practitioner needs to clarify and resolve conflicts in a way that maximizes adherences to ethical dictates of his or her profession. This can be facilitated by establishing a pre-plan of resolving potential conflicts between organization and professional ethics and values, including adjusting contracts and contract demands so that they are in line with system goals AND professional standards. When this is not possible, then it is this author's contention that the ethical practitioner will consider resignation.

IMPORTANT TERMS

artifacts	managed care
basic assumptions	need to know
client	organizational ethics
cultural values	pre-plan
ethical culture of social systems	system
limits of confidentiality	utilization review

SUGGESTED READINGS

Bersoff, D.N. (Ed.). (1995). *Ethical conflict in psychology*. Washington, DC: American Psychological Association.

Clark, R. W., & Lattal, A.D. (1993). *Winning the integrity revolution*. Lanham, MD: Rowman & Littlefield.

Weinberger, L.E., & Screenivasan, S. (1994). Ethical and professional conflicts in correctional psychology. *Professional Psychology: Research and Practice, 25*, 161–167.

CHAPTER

6 Informed Consent

Ms. Wicks: Hi, Maria, have a seat. I really appreciate you coming down to see me. I need to
share some things with you and ask you for a favor.

Maria: A favor?

Ms. Wicks: Well, not really a favor, just your permission to do something.

Ms. Wicks is apparently about to speak to Maria about her desire to do something about which she feels Maria should be fully informed. While we are not clear what it is that Ms.Wicks is going to seek permission for, it is clear that she respects Maria's right to be a full participant in those helping decisions that may impact her. Seeking informed consent is an ethical imperative and requires that a helper be fully versed and skilled in establishing the conditions that will allow a client to provide fully informed consent.

Chapter Objectives

The chapter will discuss the rationale for seeking clients' informed consent for the implementation of one's helping decisions. Further, the chapter will discuss the conditions under which such informed consent is not required and the conditions that may make obtaining informed consent difficult. Finally, the chapter will review specific issues related to the format and content of informed consent procedures. After reading this chapter you should be able to do the following:

1. Define informed consent as applied to a helping relationship.
2. Explain the rationale and utility of gaining informed consent while working with a client.
3. Identify the essential elements required to ensure informed consent.
4. Discuss the special considerations and difficulties incurred while gaining informed consent working with minor and cognitively impaired clients.

The Rationale for Informed Consent

Informed consent refers to the client's right to agree (and/or disagree) to participate in the various forms of helping and the specific procedures and services to be applied. The practice of gaining informed consent for treatment has its origins both ethically and legally in the medical profession. According to Dickson (1998), the term *informed consent* did not appear in an American court decision until 1957 (*Salgo v. Leland Stanford Jr. Board of Trustees*, 317P.2d 170). In this case a California court found that a physician had a duty to disclose the facts required for a patient to make an intelligent choice. Vesper and Brock (1991) noted: "The doctrine of informed consent was originally designed to require physicians and surgeons to explain medical procedures to patients and to warn them of any risks or dangers that could result from treatment. The intent of the doctrine was to permit the patient to make an intelligent, informed choice as to whether to undergo the proposed treatment or procedure" (p. 50).

The doctrine of informed consent involves the right of the client to both consent to and refuse the procedure(s) that are contemplated (Winick, 1991). Implied within this practice is the assumption that such consent is provided freely, without coercion of any form from the participating professional. The freedom to choose to participate in these helping procedures requires that the client understand the nature of the procedures, the potential benefits and detriments of these procedures, and the training and competency of the treating professional.

Ethically, the concept of informed consent is grounded in the belief in a client's right to self-determination and the right to benefit from treatment. In addition to reflecting ethical obligations, informed consent is generally viewed as good clinical practice. The concept of informed consent reflects the profession's belief that the client has the right to be supported in autonomous decision making regarding his or her own treatment. Stromberg, Stone, and Claiborn (1993) noted that "viewing informed consent as a means of sharing power with the client can have clinical significance, especially for clients who have been previously victimized. For such clients, issues of power and control can be of central concern" (p. 159).

The assumed value of a client's informed consent has been supported in the research. The use of proper informed consent procedures have been reported to decrease a client's anxiety, an increase in client compliance with treatment and ultimately more rapid recovery (Pope & Vasquez, 1991). Further, Sullivan, Martin, and Handelsman (1993) found that clients "may be more favorably disposed to therapists who take the time and effort to provide informed consent information" (p. 162).

Informed Consent Across the Profession

While the concept of informed consent has traditionally been applied to issues in making medical decisions, it can occur in any place that a patient or client is asked to make a major decision (e.g., consent for treatment, voluntary participation in a treatment or research program etc.). All mental health professionals recognize the importance of informed consent and require practitioners to disclose to clients the various risks, benefits, and alternatives to the proposed treatment (see Table 6.1)

The provision of information upon which a client can make informed decisions starts with the initial contact. In fact, helpers should begin the informed consent process at the initial intake, almost as a "pre-helping" screening and information session. During this initial contact, basic information about the process of helping, the policies and procedures typi-

TABLE 6.1 Informed Consent

Professional Ethical Standards	Statement Confidentiality
National Association of Social Workers (1996)	1.03 Informed Consent (a) Social workers should provide services to clients only in the context of a professional relationship based, when appropriate, on valid informed consent.
American Counseling Association (1995)	A.1. c Counselors and their clients work jointly in devising integrated, individual counseling plans that offer reasonable promise of success and are consistent with abilities and circumstances of clients. Counselors and clients regularly review counseling plans to ensure their continued viability and effectiveness, respecting clients freedom of choice.
American Association of Marriage and Family Therapists (1998)	1.8 Marriage and family therapists obtain written consent from clients before videotaping, audiotaping, audiorecording, or permitting third-party observation. 2.2 Marriage and family therapists use client and/or clinical materials in teaching, writing, and public presentations only if a written waiver has been obtained in accordance with 2.1(d), or when appropriate subprinciple steps have been taken to protect client identity and confidentiality.
American Psychological Association (1995)	4.02 Psychologist must obtain informed consent to therapy or related procedures in understandable language.

cally employed (e.g., billing, scheduling, and canceling appointments, limits to confidentiality, etc.) helper competency, and the initial client issues and objectives can be identified. But the issue of informed consent is not something restricted to the beginning of the professional contact. It continues throughout the professional relationship. Any time a significant change in the treatment or procedure being carried out is contemplated, it is imperative to obtain informed consent for the change (Anderson, 1996; Crawford, 1994). From this perspective informed consent is an ongoing dialogue regarding treatment and treatment issues.

The specific content and the manner and timing of presentation (e.g., written or oral, early, pre-, etc.) may vary as a function of legal requirements, agency policies, the unique characteristics of the client, and/or the setting in which services are provided. However, the conditions or elements essential to informed consent appear to hold across the professions or clients. Most agree that informed consent requires that the client be competent, have knowledge of what will occur, and engage in treatment voluntarily (Anderson, 1996; Bennett et al., 1990; Crawford, 1994; Stromberg and Colleagues in Law Firm, 1993). Each of these components is discussed in some detail below.

Competence

Implicit in any discussion of informed consent is the assumption of a client's competency to make informed decisions that are in his or her own best interests. Competency refers to the client's ability to make decisions for himself or herself (Beauchamp & Childress, 1989). A client judged to be competent to make these judgments is then also viewed as having a right to be fully informed about the nature of the treatment, the alternatives available, possible risks and benefits of each, and the practitioner's competency to provide service.

This sense of competency is not an all-or-none proposition. The identification of competence will fluctuate as a function of the context or the decision criteria defining competence (see Case Illustration 6.1). Clearly, while George lacks the competency to make business decisions, he appears able to understand the nature of the relationship and to consent to the process.

Competency may also be temporarily impaired as a result of psychological and or physical trauma, or could be more permanently impaired as a result of a degenerative

---

CASE ILLUSTRATION **6.1**
A Limited Competence

George is a 43-year-old who has been a successful owner of a mid-sized manufacturing company. Over the course of the past month, George has gone on a spending spree that has not only jeopardized his own financial well-being but has actually placed his company on the brink of bankruptcy.

In addition to purchasing a new foreign sports car and refurbishing his house and office with expensive European furniture, George has recently placed an order for an executive jet plane. The truth is that George's business does not require him to travel nor can his business afford the multimillion-dollar expenditure. In addition to the spending spree, George has not been sleeping, exhibits a general restlessness, and has been developing plans to expand his company to the level of an international conglomerate.

In response to a confrontation by his wife and the chair of his board of directors, George agreed to go for a psychiatric evaluation. Following general introductions the following exchange occurred:

DR. WINCOCK: George, I can understand that you feel that people are overreacting to your recent purchases and behavior, but it does appear that you are not sleeping well and that a number of the decisions, for example, placing a down payment on a company jet, may not reflect the best of your business and personal decisions.

GEORGE: Well, it may look like the business can't afford it, but I have plans for that as well. We are going to grow the business—significantly! I know I can get the business to be an international concern within the next year and can probably triple our bottom line. I am even thinking about writing up my business plan and publishing it. I think it can revolutionize the way business is done.

DR. WINCOCK: Well, perhaps that is something we could talk about. But for the time being, I would like to thank you for coming and explain a little about what I do and what I hope we can do during the session. Would that be okay?

GEORGE: I really don't think I need to do this, but if it helps ease the minds of my family and friends, then I am willing to give it a try—hell, maybe I'll decide to even change my career—this seems to be a pretty cushy job.

DR. WINCOCK: Well, as you know I am a psychiatrist, and in addition to seeing patients here in the professional building, I am also on staff at the hospital here and teach in the university. I have been working in the field of psychiatry for over fifteen years, and while I am able and do often prescribe medication to my clients who may benefit from it, I also am trained in a type of therapy called cognitive-behavioral therapy.

GEORGE: I am little familiar with that type of therapy . . . I mean I read a book by . . . I can't remember his name . . . it was a little yellow book on depression. . . .

DR. WINCOCK: Was the book *Feeling Good* by David Burns?

GEORGE: Yeah—I think that was the title. I liked the concept—you know none of that laying down stuff and talking about your childhood . . . just get to the point. . . .

DR. WINCOCK: Well, I'm glad you are somewhat familiar with cognitive therapy. As we go along I would like to explain a little more about the approach and the possible benefit of combining it with some medication.

GEORGE: Well, no meds for me, Doc, that stuff slows you down . . . and they are for whackos.

DR. WINCOCK: Well, before we talk about the pros and cons of medication in your case, let me explain that I would like to spend the remainder of our time together, which is about 50 minutes, to find out about some of the decisions and plans you've been making as well as how you've been in general.

Now, I know that you read my little brochure, "Welcome to my practice" that describes my fees, length of sessions, policies regarding cancellations, insurance, etc. Did you have any questions about that information?

GEORGE: No—it was real clear, in fact, I'm going to make something like that up for my own business . . . great idea. . . .

DR. WINCOCK: Okay. Now I do know that pamphlet talked about the fact that the information you share with me will be held in confidence, and if you look here on page 3 it points out a number of exceptions to that principle of confidentiality. In general, if you share information with me that seems to suggest that you are jeopardizing your own life or intend to harm someone else then I may have to share that information as a way of protecting yourself or anyone you may seek to harm. Do you understand that?

Do you have any questions about what I just shared or what is the brochure?

GEORGE: No, I got it—it makes sense . . . no fear I'm not gonna hurt myself or anyone else unless you consider the fact that my business is going to wipe out my competitors . . . "doing harm to others." Hell, maybe you should warn them! Only kidding, Doc. Actually I've been through this before so I think I know the routine and I'm okay with it.

DR. WINCOCK: Well, that's good but if there is any question now or as we proceed about what we are doing or why we are doing it, I really want you to ask. The more you and I work together the better it will be. You mentioned that you were familiar with this information since you've been through it before. Would you tell me about that?

disease or irreversible brain damage (see Case Illustration 6.2). When an individual is judged not to be competent enough to understand the nature of the helping relationship or to fully consent to participation in the helping, a legal guardian or parent should be identified and provide consent.

Comprehension

In addition to having the general cognitive competency and ability to process information, the client must be able to comprehend the information being presented. The form in which such information is transmitted is truly open to the discretion of the helper and the needs and abilities of the client. Information could be presented in writing and if one has real concern that such disclosure is documented, acknowledgment of understanding could be documented by way of a client's signature. Regardless of the specific format, the guiding principle is that this information needs to be provided in a clear, comprehensible form that is presented at a level that the client can understand (Handelsman, Kemper, Kesson-Craig, McLain, & Johnsrud, 1986). Interestingly, Handelsman and colleagues (1986) found that the readability of many consent forms employed in therapy were at the college level of reading equivalency, similar to that found within an academically oriented periodical. Clearly, such a level of writing could restrict the ability of clients to fully comprehend and, therefore, consent to the information provided.

It is essential that a helper present information in a way that maximizes the client comprehension of both what is being suggested and the possible impacts of these decisions. The standard is that the practitioner share the information in a way that a reasonable individual in the client's position would be able to understand and make a reasonably informed decision (Simon, 1992a). The information should be provided in simple, declarative sentences that avoid jargon (Everstein, Everstein, Hegmann, True, Frey, et al., 1995; Stanley, 1987). The ethical helper must be sure that the form of the information (e.g., oral, written) is comprehensible to the client, that the language is one in which the client is fully literate, and that the timing is sensitive to the client's fatigue, emotional state, or level of distractibility (see Exercise 6.1).

As a measure of ensuring comprehension, the ethical helper will ask questions that elicit evidence of the client's comprehension (see Case Illustration 6.2).

In deciding what type of information should be provided, the common position is that as much information is required as would be needed by a "reasonable patient or client" to make this decision. But when the practitioner believes that the disclosure of information would be harmful to the client, it may be restricted. Such nondisclosure has found some support in the courts (see *Canterbury v. Spence*, 464 F.2d772, 1972), which recognized that sometimes disclosure can cause such emotional distress that it could complicate or hinder the treatment or even pose psychological damage to the client. In this case the court allowed for restricted disclosure.

Voluntariness

As noted in the various codes of ethics, consent is to be given and solicited freely and without undue influence (see, for example, APA 4.02 a, Table 6.1). While in most cases in

EXERCISE 6.1
Was the Client Informed?

Directions: After reading the following scenarios, discuss the cases with a colleague and identify if you feel the duty to inform and gain informed consent was achieved. If not, what else do you feel should have been done?

Scenario 1:

An individual is referred by his employer because of what his employer suspected was a drinking problem. At the first meeting the counselor informed the client that one of the purposes for them coming together was for the counselor to make an assessment of the client for possible alcohol abuse. The counselor informed the client that he was asked by the employer to assess the employee and to determine if he had an alcohol problem and if so to determine the degree to which it would it impair his work performance. The counselor noted that he was expected to give this information in a written report to the employer as a condition of the employee's return to work. The counselor suggested that any specific information gathered in their interview would not be shared with the employer but that his clinical impressions regarding the existence of a possible drinking problem and the degree to which that, should it exist, could impair the employee's work performance would be shared with his employer. The clinician presented the steps he would take in writing and asked the client if he understood and if he would sign the paper as evidence of his informed consent to release that information to his employer.

Scenario 2:

Enrique is a 14-year-old freshman who asked to see his school counselor. The counselor met with Enrique and in the process of the initial interview found out the following: Enrique described himself as feeling very sad and lonely and that while he had never entertained thoughts of hurting himself, he just wished his "down feelings" would disappear. Enrique said that he started feeling this way a long time ago. He was very concerned that maybe he is "strange," not like the other boys and that maybe he's "gay." The counselor asked Enrique if he would like to talk again, especially about his feelings of being gay and feeling so sad. Enrique agreed. Following the initial interview the counselor consulted his chairperson and shared the information he received from Enrique. The chair suggested that the counselor call Enrique's parents and inform them of his sexual-orientation concerns. The counselor calls and sets up an appointment to meet with the parents.

---

which clients are seeking treatment on their own initiative, the condition of voluntariness is easy to ensure, there may be situations in which the client is "sent" to treatment or mandated to participate in assessment or therapy. Under these conditions consent—without any coercion, undue influence, misrepresentation, fraud, or duress being applied to the person's decision making (Simon, 1992b; Stanley 1987)—may be hard to obtain. Under these conditions voluntariness, while perhaps difficult to ensure, is still an essential component of informed consent (Case Illustration 6.3). However, even when court ordered a helper needs to inform the client that he or she is free to withdraw from treatment or evaluation at any time, while explaining the potential consequences of such a decision.

CASE ILLUSTRATION **6.2**
Ensuring Comprehension

Dr. Federico is a marriage and family therapist in private practice. She was about to meet Anthony and Carol for an initial session. About 10 minutes before the session was scheduled to begin, Dr. Federico went out to greet the couple. She introduced herself and informed the couple that she would be with them in about five minutes. In the meantime, she provided them with a little brochure that described her practice. She invited them to review the brochure prior to their session. She explained that this would help them understand her practice and that it provided answers to some of the typical questions often asked by clients.

At the scheduled time, Dr. Federico came out to invite the couple into the office. After some initial chatting, Dr. Federico asked the couple if they were able to review the brochure and if they had any questions.

> CAROL: Yes, we both looked at it. It is very clear. We are both a little nervous because we've never done this kind of thing before.
>
> DR. FEDERICO: Well, I am glad you reviewed the brochure and I can understand how this may be a little anxiety provoking. How about if we just take a few minutes to try to relax and get some general information as well as answer any questions you may have about me or the practice?
>
> CAROL: That would be fine, but I don't think we have any questions.
>
> DR. FEDERICO: Anthony, I can see you nodding in agreement? As outlined in the brochure, you understand I am certified as a marriage counselor and have been in private practice for nine years. Our session will be 50 minutes and my fee is $110 per session. Do you have any questions about the fee or about the possibility of insurance reimbursement?
>
> ANTHONY: Carol and I talked about it before even coming and we checked with our insurance carrier. They don't cover marriage counseling but luckily we can afford this, and we both think it is important enough to do even without insurance.
>
> DR. FEDERICO: That's a good start, with both of you valuing yourselves and your marriage enough to commit to counseling. The other issue that some people are often concerned about is whether the information we talk about is going to be private.
>
> ANTHONY: We are not ashamed about coming here.
>
> CAROL: We actually have shared with our family we were doing this and they are thrilled.
>
> DR. FEDERICO: Well, the fact that you come here would be something that would be hard to keep private, given the public nature of the office building. But you certainly have a right to know that what we talk about will be held in confidence with some of the restrictions that were noted in the information I provided.
>
> CAROL: We actually underhand that in order to protect us you may have to disclose information, but we don't see that as a problem (Anthony nodding agreement).
>
> ANTHONY: We also saw in your brochure that sometimes with couple counseling, when it ends in some legal action, that often one spouse may have the records subpoenaed by a lawyer. We really have no intention of going to a divorce—we just

know we have to work on some things to improve our marriage. But—we also understand that if court ordered you will release the records.

DR. FEDERICO: Well, you guys certainly did read the information and appear to understand it. But as we proceed I want to encourage you to ask if something I am doing is unclear or if you have any questions about the process you are experiencing.

CASE ILLUSTRATION 6.3
Compulsory Treatment

Warren was recently arrested for driving while under the influence. As part of the conditions of his sentence, he was required by the judge to attend a 14-week group counseling program. At an individual session scheduled prior to the first group meeting, Warren met with Linda, the drug and alcohol counselor.

WARREN: What do I have to do?

LINDA: I'm not sure what you are asking.

WARREN: Just tell me what to do and I'll do it.

LINDA: Warren, this is a session that we set up for the people going to start our group program. We want to explain to you what we are intending to do with the group, let you know that we are required to make an assessment following your participation in the group program and then provide a written report with recommendations to the court. So we need to be sure that you understand all of this and agree to it before beginning the process.

WARREN: Agree? You gotta be kidding. I have to be here. Look lady, I am here to do what I gotta do.

LINDA: Warren, I am aware that you are here because it was part of your sentencing. But I want you to understand that we really have found that if you understand our program, and have a feel for what you can get out of fully participating, that it really can be beneficial for you. Now—while it may not seem it, you do have options. Even though this was mandated by the judge, you can choose not to come or not to participate. However, you know that decision would result in your incarceration.

WARREN: Yeah, great choice. Do this or go to jail!

LINDA: Well, it is a choice and it is yours. Further, the degree to which you participate in the group or not participate is also your choice. But again, we have found . . . and you will hear from others who have attended that the more you put in the more beneficial it . . . that the more you put in, the more beneficial it is for you. Plus—we will be describing your level of participation in our report to the court.

WARREN: I get it, and yeah, I guess I have choices to make . . . let's just see how things unfold.

LINDA: Well, that sounds a little more open and that's good. After our first group session I want to meet with you again so that we can evaluate your experience. At that time maybe we could find other options or choices available to make the program as beneficial as possible for you. How about that?

WARREN: That sounds like a plan . . . thanks.

TABLE 6.2   Areas of Informed Consent

Nature and Orientation of Helping	It is important to inform the client as to orientation and theory employed by the practitioner. Further, it is important to inform the client of the possible negative experiences one may encounter (e.g., anxiety, depression, etc.) in the process of therapy. Finally, goals and steps anticipated need to be disclosed.
Therapist-Credentials	Details regarding the therapist's specific training, education, experience, and unique credentials should be disclosed to the client. Similarly, any anticipated involvement with consultants and supervisors regarding this case needs to be discussed with the client.
Fees and Insurance	All costs and fees for service should be discussed at the beginning of the relationship. Procedures and processes involved in seeking insurance reimbursement along with limitations of the specific coverage need to be discussed along with an agreed upon plan addressing any and all gaps in coverage. When the helper is part of a managed care process, he or she needs to inform the client (1) that a financial policy may exist to limit the amount or type of service provided (Newman & Bricklin, 1991); (2) about the requirement for disclosure to the managed care agency; and (3) about the limitations on service the agency may impose (Haas & Cummings, 1991).
Record Keeping and Access to Files	Records are kept for the benefit of the client, and clients generally should be provided access as long as the information would not be misleading or detrimental to the client. While the type of information stored as well as the decision to share this information with the client may vary as a function of the setting, the client and the helper, the nature of a practitioner's records and access policies should be clearly explained to the client.
Limits to Confidentiality	All of the professional codes note the importance of providing the client with the limitations of confidentiality from the outset of the relationship. Further, the helper needs to inform the client about the distinction and application of confidentiality, privileged communication, and privacy of files.
Treatment: Benefits, Risks, and Alternatives	Even though research is limited, causing it to be difficult to discuss the benefits and risks of various treatment forms (Bednar, Bednar, Lambert, & Waite, 1991), it is important to discuss what is known in the research and what has been experienced by the helper.

EXERCISE 6.2
Comprehensibility?

Directions: Below you will find descriptions of the form, timing, and language used in providing a client with information needed to gain informed consent. Review the details of each scenario and identify what may be modified to increase the comprehensibility of the information.

Scenario 1: Mrs. Lewis, an elementary school counselor, is sitting with Mrs. Robinson, mother of Tommie, a third grader who recently wrote in his journal: "I wish I died!"

> **MRS. LEWIS:** Mrs. Robinson, I'm glad you could come right in.
>
> **MRS. ROBINSON:** Yes, I left work immediately after you called. What's up? It sounded serious.
>
> **MRS. LEWIS:** Well, as you are aware we have a policy in the district which requires that we inform parents anytime we (counselors) wish to work with a child. We feel it is important that parents know that we are counseling their children and understand how we would like to handle issues such as confidentiality.
>
> **MRS. ROBINSON:** Counsel Tommie? Why? What happened (anxiously)?
>
> **MRS. LEWIS:** Well, Tommie has given some evidence of having suicidal ideation and I would like to begin working with him immediately.
>
> **MRS. ROBINSON:** WHAT? Suicide?

Scenario 2: R.L. Linquist is a social worker providing community service to a group of migrant farm workers. Juan is a 38-year-old farm worker who came to the community mental health center because of his concern about possibly having a drinking problem. Prior to meeting with Juan, the social worker went to the waiting room and handed Juan a five-page booklet explaining the policies and processes employed at the center. The social worker asked Juan to read the document and to sign before they began their session.

Scenario 3: Rene is a psychiatric nurse assigned to do intake at a residential treatment center. Tony and Harriet Bledshoe brought their 83-year-old father in because, according to the Bledshoes, he seems to be drifting off, has become incommunicative and has been twice found wondering outside the house without his shoes and/or pants. Rene met with Mr. Bledshoe (the client) and the following dialogue occurred:

> **RENE:** Hello, Mr. Bledshoe, have a seat.
>
> **MR. BLEDSHOE:** Hi, Harriet.
>
> **RENE:** Mr. Bledshoe, my name is Rene and I am a nurse here at Taylor Manor.
>
> **MR. BLEDSHOE:** Yes, dear. Where is your mother?
>
> **RENE:** Mr. Bledshoe, this is Taylor Manor and you were brought here by your son and his wife. They are concerned about you.
>
> **MR. BLEDSHOE:** Is Tony coming to lunch?
>
> **RENE:** Mr. Bledshoe, I would like to ask you some questions and then have you meet with our psychiatrist. It may be a good idea for you to stay with us for a while.
>
> **MR. BLEDSHOE:** Of course . . . anything you say.
>
> **RENE:** So you understand and are willing to sign yourself into our hospital?
>
> **MR. BLEDSHOE:** Of course . . . Harriet. Is Tony going to be here with us for lunch?

Special Challenges to Informing for Consent

Most agree that all information relevant to the understanding of the nature of the treatment process should be provided to the client. However, while providing the client with needed information, it is important not to overwhelm the client with too much information. Finding the balance and the timing of information is an important consideration for all mental health professionals. Further, without full understanding, the process of helping should not proceed. This last point demands that the clinician present the material in a manner that is understandable to the client so that the client's choices are free and noncoerced.

Working with Minors

Competency, as noted above, refers to the ability to make a rational decision. The client must have the cognitive capacity to make a competent decision concerning the proposed relationship and/or the procedure(s) contemplated (Everstein et al., 1995; Simon, 1992b; Winick, 1991). When a client is not competent to make the decision, another person able to make substitute consent on behalf of the client is required (Everstein et al., 1995).

With the exception of emancipated minors, most states recognize that minors generally lack the capacity to give informed consent. When this is the case, the capacity for informed consent goes to the parents or guardian. Emancipation is defined differently in various states, but in general it refers to an individual living independently and supporting himself (see *Smith v. Seilby*, 72 Wash.2d 16, 1967). However, there are exceptions to this. In some states, minors are allowed to seek birth control counseling and counseling related to venereal disease, pregnancy/abortion, and substance abuse without consent of a legal guardian or parents.

For the practitioner who feels that client participation and autonomy are important, providing appropriate information to clients—even minors—to encourage their voluntary participation in the helping process is good therapeutic practice. This includes discussing the limits to confidentiality in a way that they can fully understand. It is important to understand the state laws governing such service to minors as they may impact your decisions regarding provision of service. Thus, while it is good therapeutic practice, it must be remembered that in most cases it is not required and may not be sufficient. It is up to the practitioner to understand the policies and mandates of the organization in which he or she is employed as well as any state or federal laws governing the need for parental consent in working with minors.

Third-Party Involvement

A second area in which the issue of informed consent can be complicated is in the case of third-party referral. A client may be directed to therapy by a third party, which under some situations could have taken place involuntarily or compulsorily (e.g., court ordered). Even in these cases of compulsory treatment, a client has the right to refuse service. However, it is important for the practitioner to fully inform the client of the process and the procedures that will be enacted should he continue and/or terminate the treatment. In court situations or legal proceedings the client also has the right to know the helper's role—that is, will the helper disclose information? Testify? If so, the client needs to know these consequences before accepting treatment.

An interesting variation on the theme of "voluntarism" comes when informed consent is viewed within the context of managed care. Managed care requires the exchange of information and disclosure of information for initial and continued care to be approved. There is a potential problem with maintaining helper–client confidentiality that needs to be understood and agreed upon by the client. This limitation of a helper's ability to retain confidentiality needs to be fully disclosed and consented to before the establishment of a helping relationship.

Working with the Cognitively Impaired or the Elderly

A final population for whom informed consent is sometimes difficult to acquire is the elderly and/or cognitively impaired (Pepper-Smith, Harvey, Silberfeld, Stein, & Rutman, 1992). The elderly with diminished cognitive capacities may be considered legally competent but still have difficulty understanding the nuance of treatment. Often it is important to gain a consent to inform and consult with family members so that appropriate treatment can be monitored (see Case Illustration 6.4).

CASE ILLUSTRATION **6.4**
Competent Yet Cognitively Impaired

Maryellen is a social worker specializing in gerontology. Maryellen has been asked to work with Louise, a 74-year-old woman who recently lost her husband and who is presenting as depressed. Louise was brought to the session by her daughter who also accompanied her into the office. Maryellen asked Louise if it would be all right if just she and Maryellen met, without the presence of her daughter. Louise said that would be fine, but noted that she has problems with remembering things and that if Maryellen needs some information, her daughter may need to provide it. According to her daughter, Louise has been diagnosed by a neurologists as giving evidence of mild dementia, a condition that in the last month has worsened following the death of her husband.

Maryellen began the interview with Louise and noted that Louise was unable to provide her daughter's address or phone (where she has been living for the past month) or the names of her current physician or neurologists. Throughout the interview, Louise would often drift off and have to ask Maryellen to repeat a question or to tell her again what she just said. While it was clear that Louise had a diminished cognitive ability, when asked where she was and why she was there, Louise was very clear that she came to a counselor because, as she noted, she was having a difficult time feeling okay after her husband's death. Because she understood both the need and nature of the reason she was with Maryellen, Maryellen decided to explain the process and policies she would be using . In the course of describing how she would like to proceed, Maryellen asked Louise for permission to contact her neurologist. Louise said: "That would be fine . . . I can't remember who he is, you should ask my daughter, she'll know." Maryellen thanked her and said that at the end of the session she would invite Louise's daughter in and ask her for some information, like her home address, phone number, and doctor's names if that would be okay. Louise, responded positively, stating, "Actually—I appreciate you letting my daughter give you the information. It sometimes gets me upset when I can't remember."

Beyond Professional Standards: A Personal Moral Response

Gaining client informed consent is clearly an ethical and legal mandate. However, gaining informed consent is more than a process of practice. It is a reflection of the nature of the helping relationship that is respectful of the client' autonomy and valuing of a client's full participation. Moving from the mandates of law and ethical codes to this type of relationship is the hallmark of the ethical practitioner. It demonstrates that for this practitioner, informed consent has moved from an ethical principle to a personal moral value and response in relationship with the client.

Moving beyond professional standards to a personal moral response may take a conscious effort on the part of the practitioner. The following checklist is a list of reminders for the ethical helper. The information presented has been adapted from materials presented by Bertram and Wheeler (1994) in their workshop "Legal Aspects of Counseling: Avoiding Lawsuits and Legal Problems," Alexandria, VA: American Counseling Association. These items are useful both in developing informed written consent procedures and, more importantly, in reinforcing the basic trust and fundamental valuing of the client that characterizes ethical helping. They are presented here as a mechanism to be used by a practitioner with each client and in so doing will facilitate elevation of informed consent to a personal value and a moral response.

1. *Voluntary participation*: Assisting clients to commit to treatment voluntarily with knowledge that termination can occur at any time without penalty.
2. *Client involvement:* Identify the level and type of involvement expected and desired from the client.
3. *Helper involvement:* Describe the level and type of involvement to be given by the helper along with information regarding the hows and whys for contacting the helper, especially in the case of emergencies.
4. *Model and approach:* Describe the helper's particular model and/or orientation and how this will affect treatment.
5. *Risks and benefits associated with helping:* Identify potential beneficial outcomes as well as possible risks, if any, associated with a particular approach to helping.
6. *Confidentiality, privilege, and limitations:* Specify how confidentiality will be handled and maintained along with the conditions under which confidential and privileged information will be released.
7. *Helper credentials:* Disclose training and experience relevant to this case along with special credentials, certifications, and licenses held.
8. *Fees and reimbursements:* Identify all fees and charges, describe how these are collected, and what involvement the helper will take in terms of insurance and insurance filings.
9. *Cancellations:* Inform client as to cancellation policies and whether a fee is charged.
10. *Consultation and supervision:* Describe any required supervisory or consultative relationships in which the helper is engaged, along with the specific impact of such a relationship on the current client–helper relationship.

11. *Disputes and complaints:* Inform the client of the address and phone number of state credentialing departments (certification, licensing) should complaints about fee or service result.

Case Illustration

We began the chapter with a brief dialogue between Ms. Wicks and Maria. As you read the continuation of the dialogue, which is presented below, observe Ms. Wicks' behavior as it reflects or fails to reflect the principles discussed within this chapter. Further, a number of brief questions for your reflection are offered following the case to stimulate your application of your knowledge on informed consent.

MS. WICKS: Hi, Maria, have a seat. I really appreciate you coming down to see me. I need to share some things with you and ask you for a favor.

MARIA: A favor?

MS. WICKS: Well, not really a favor, just your permission to do something.

MARIA: I don't understand.

MS.WICKS: Well, after we met last time, I was very concerned about the possibility that you may be engaging in dangerous behavior, something that could harm you. So I went to Mr. Harolds, the chairperson for the counseling department to ask him for some advice.

MARIA: Wait—what are you saying? You're blabbing everything I tell you to other people?

MS. WICKS: No, that's not what happened and in fact that's what I wanted to talk with you about. In speaking with Mr. Harolds, I didn't let him know who the student was, and I was careful not to disclose any information with which he could identify you. But I asked him if I needed to contact anyone or call your mom about the risk you are running by having unprotected sex with a boy who has AIDS.

MARIA: Okay—so you didn't call my mom or anything, right? And Mr. Harolds doesn't know you are talking about me?

MS. WICKS: That's correct, but the truth is I don't feel real comfortable with what you are doing. I care about you and I feel you are really endangering yourself by having unprotected sex with a person with AIDS. Maria, I would like to share some information about this situation with Ms. Armstrong. I will not tell her who you are by name and I will try not to share any identifying information. But I want her permission to refer you to a clinic for some blood work, as well as some information on safe sex. I would be willing even to go with you, if you would like . . . but I need Ms. Armstrong's permission to give that type of information out.

MARIA: I think you are overreacting—but I would be willing to go to some clinic—if you would come with me.

> MS. WICKS: I will if it is permitted as part of my work here, but for that I need to talk to Ms. Armstrong. I outlined the type of information I would like to share with Ms. Armstrong as a way of convincing her of the importance of allowing me to do this. Let's go over this list so that I can explain each item and make sure it is okay with you. Okay?
>
> MARIA: Okay!

Reflections:
1. Do you feel this discussion was even necessary or could/should Ms. Wicks simply have discussed this issue with Ms. Armstrong, the principal?
2. Ms. Wicks spoke with Mr. Harolds without receiving Maria's informed consent. Did she violate confidentiality? Did she need Maria's consent?
3. Ms. Wicks is going to discuss a list of points that she wishes to convey to Ms. Armstrong. Is there anything in addition to that which you feel she should do?
4. Should Ms. Wicks have Maria sign a formal consent form?
5. What is the rule for providing information to a minor regarding family planning, safe sex, and venereal disease in your state?

Cooperative Learning Exercise

The purpose of this chapter was to introduce you to the concept of informed consent along with the elements involved in obtaining such consent. As noted throughout the chapter, gaining client informed consent is not always necessary or even possible in some situations. Working with a colleague or classmate, contact a person working as a (1) school counselor, (2) drug and alcohol counselor, (3) court-appointed mental health practitioner, and (4) marriage counselor and ask each of the following questions. Share your information with other colleagues and/or classmates looking for common areas of practice and or concern.

1. Do you gain informed consent from all of your clients? If not, why not and how is that decision determined? If so, when and where within the helping process do you seek informed consent?
2. When you seek informed consent, how do you ensure (a) capacity/competency, (b) comprehension, and (c) voluntarism?
3. How do you document that you have gained informed consent?
4. What value, if any, do you find in gaining informed consent?

Summary

The Rationale for Informed Consent
The doctrine of informed consent involves the right of the client to both consent to and to refuse the procedure(s) that are contemplated. Ethically, the concept of informed consent is grounded in the belief of a client's right to self-determination and right to benefit from treatment.

Informed Consent Across the Profession

Most agree that informed consent requires that the client be competent, have knowledge of what will occur, and engage in treatment voluntarily.

The identification of competence will fluctuate as a function of context or decision criteria defining competence. In ensuring comprehension the practitioner needs to share the information in a way that a reasonable individual in the client's position would be able to understand and make a reasonably informed decision. Finally, consent is to be given and solicited freely and without undue influence.

Special Challenges to Informing for Consent

Working with minors presents a challenge to the principle of competency. With the exception of emancipated minors, most states recognize that minors generally lack the capacity to give informed consent. When this is the case, the capacity for informed consent goes to the parents or guardian. In some states, minors are allowed to seek birth control counseling, and counseling related to venereal disease, pregnancy/abortion, and substance abuse without consent of a legal guardian or parents.

The issue of voluntary consent is potentially compromised when a client may be directed to therapy by a third party, which can take place involuntarily or compulsorily (e.g., court ordered). Even in these cases of compulsory treatment, a client has the right to refuse service.

Comprehension can be challenged in situations in which a practitioner is working with a client with diminished cognitive capacities. It is possible that the client may be considered legally competent but still have difficulty understanding the nuances of treatment. Often it is important to gain a consent to inform and consult with family members so that appropriate treatment can be monitored.

IMPORTANT TERMS

client compliance
competency
comprehension
context
decision criteria
emancipated minors
impaired
informed consent

legal guardian
mondisclosure
pre-helping screening
power
self-determination
third party
voluntariness

SUGGESTED READINGS

Handelsman, M.M., Martinez, A., Geisendorfer, S., & Jordon, L. (1995). Does legally mandated consent to psychotherapy ensure ethical appropriateness? The Colorado experience. *Ethics and Behavior, 5,* 119–129.

Koocher, G.P., & Keith-Spiegel, P.C. (1990). *Children, ethics and the law: Professional issues and cases.* Lincoln, NE: University of Nebraska Press.

Melton, G.B., Koocher, G.P., & Saks, M. (Eds). (1983). *Children's competence to consent.* New York: Plenum.

White, M.D., & White, C.A. (1981). Involuntarily committed patients' constitutional right to refuse treatment: A challenge to psychology. *American Psychologist, 36,* 953–962.

CHAPTER

7   Confidentiality

Maria: It's okay. You can talk to Ms. Armstrong as long as you don't tell her who I am. I don't want anyone knowing what I told you. Besides, I thought talking to you was like talking to a priest in confession . . . you know, a major secret?

Maria understands the fundamental nature of the helping relationship. It is one in which the individual's right to privacy is respected. However, as with most things in this profession the issue of privacy or confidentiality is not simply yes or no.

While confidentiality is a value held and practiced by all ethical practitioners, the extent of such confidentiality can and will vary as a result of the context, client characteristics, and the nature of the information shared. The concept and ethical principal of confidentiality, along with those conditions that define the extent and limits of confidentiality, will serve as the focus for the current chapter.

Chapter Objectives

After reading this chapter you should be able to do the following:

1. Describe what is meant by the terms confidentiality and privilege
2. Identify the conditions under which confidentiality and privilege should be breached.
3. Discuss the conditions that need to exist for the Duty to Warn to be implemented.
4. Describe the special challenges facing practitioners working with both minors and those with HIV/AIDS in regards to confidentiality.

Confidentiality: What and When Warranted?

Privacy and the right to decide for oneself the time and circumstances under which to disclose personal beliefs, behaviors, and opinions is a cornerstone to our individual rights under the Constitution of the United States. It is this constitutional right to privacy that serves as the legal basis of privileged communication and the professional concept of confidentiality (Kurpius, 1997).

Confidentiality Is Not Privileged

Confidentiality refers to the ethical principal that conveys that the information discussed within the context of the professional relationship will not be disclosed without a client's informed consent. As defined, confidentiality is "the general standard of professional conduct that obliges a professional not to discuss information about the client with anyone" (Keith-Spiegel & Koocher, 1985, p. 57). Confidentiality is essential to the nature of a helping relationship. The helping relationship requires a client to place his or her trust in the helper, knowing that the information will remain confidential. Research suggests that people are less apt to seek help and to self-disclose if therapy is not confidential (Merluzzi & Brischetto, 1983; Miller & Thelen, 1986).

Confidentiality should not be equated with privileged communication. Privileged communication is a "legal term that describes the quality of certain specific types of relationships that prevent information, acquired from such relationships, from being disclosed in court or other legal proceedings" (Keith-Spiegel & Koocher, 1985, p. 58).

Confidentiality is the broader concept that includes the expectation that material will not be divulged, whereas privileged communications carry a strong admonition that material will not and may not be divulged even in court. While confidential material covers most of what transpires between the client and the practitioner, privilege belongs only to certain defined "protected relationships" such as physician and patient; lawyer and client; psychologist, social worker, and psychiatrist and their clients. The privilege brings with it the necessity to receive permission from the client, the holder of the privilege, prior to disclosure (see Case Illustration 7.1).

CASE ILLUSTRATION 7.1
Release Only with Consent

Dr. Ramerez is a licensed psychiatrist. Dr. Ramerez is currently working with Alfred who has been diagnosed as having a post traumatic stress syndrome as a result of a serious car accident in which thirteen people were killed. Alfred was the only one of four people within his car that survived. The accident, which involved an oil truck and seven cars, was caused by an oil-tank truck driver, who had fallen asleep at the wheel. An insurance company representing one of the other victims in the crash in a lawsuit against the oil company subpoenaed Dr. Ramerez's records reflecting his diagnosis and treatment of Alfred.

Dr. Ramerez, respectfully declined to honor the subpoena, claiming the information to be privileged and stating that he would release this information only when his client would consent to its release. The lawyer representing the complainant in the lawsuit against the truck company explained that the only purpose of the request was to demonstrate the "potential" psychological impact that his client could experience well after her physical wounds had healed and he wanted to use Alfred's case as an illustration of PTSD. Dr. Ramerez explained the request to Alfred, who wanted to sign a consent to release the information form. Dr. Ramerez still felt that releasing the information was neither required nor desired. However, Dr. Ramerez understood that privilege belonged to the client and not to the therapist; since Alfred consented to release the information, he did.

For communication to be privileged it is generally held that the communication must satisfy four criteria (see Wigmore, 1961):

1. The communication must originate in confidence that it will not be disclosed.
2. The confidentiality of information must be essential to the full and satisfactory maintenance of the relationship.
3. The relationship must be one that should be sedulously fostered in the opinion of the community.
4. Injury to the relationship by disclosure of the communication must be greater than the benefit gained by the correct disposal of litigation regarding the information (Schwitzgebel & Schwitzgebel, 1980).

With these criteria as backdrop it would appear that the legal concept of privileged communication does not apply in group situations or even couple therapy, since the presence of the third person makes ensuring the origination of confidence difficult to enforce. Anderson (1996) suggests that therapists inform their clients of the ethical need for confidentiality while highlighting the lack of legal privilege concerning disclosures made in the presence of a third party. Further questions regarding who can claim the privilege, what type of information is privileged, and what the limitations to privilege are can vary extensively state to state. As such, it is imperative for each practitioner to know the answers to these questions as defined within the state in which they practice. Exercise 7.1 is provided to assist in this process.

Confidentiality Across the Professions

The provision of confidentiality is common throughout human service professions and is widely held as a therapeutic necessity. All professional organizations address the issue of confidentiality (see Table 7.1). While the specific wording varies, the intent of the ethical

---

EXERCISE **7.1**
A Question of Privilege?

Directions: As suggested in text, the nature of privileged communication can vary state by state. Contact either your state professional organization or the state board of professional affairs and gather information to the following questions:

1. Who can claim privileged communication, or under what conditions can privilege be claimed?
2. What type of communications are covered by privilege?
3. Which professions and professionals have privilege?
4. What are the limitations to privilege?
5. What constitutes a waiver of privilege?

TABLE 7.1 Confidentiality

Professional Ethical Standards	Statement Confidentiality
American Psychological Association (1995)	5.02 Psychologists have a primary obligation and take reasonable precautions to respect the confidentiality rights of those with whom they work or consult, recognizing that confidentiality may be established by law, institutional rules, or professional or scientific relationships.
National Association of Social Workers (1996)	1.07 Privacy and Confidentiality (c) Social workers should protect the confidentiality of all information obtained in the course of professional service, except for compelling professional reasons. The general expectation that social workers will keep information confidential does not apply when disclosure is necessary to prevent serious, foreseeable, and imminent harm to a client or other identifiable person. In all instances, social workers should disclose the least amount of confidential information necessary to achieve the desired purpose; only information that is directly relevant to the purpose for which the disclosure is made should be revealed.
American Counseling Association (1995)	B.1. Right to Privacy a. Respect for Privacy. Counselors respect their clients right to privacy and avoid illegal and unwarranted disclosures of confidential information.
American Association of Marriage and Family Therapists (1998)	Section 2. Marriage and family therapists have unique confidentiality concerns because the client in a therapeutic relationship may be more than one person. Therapists respect and guard the confidence of each individual client.

principle of confidentiality articulated by the various professional organizations is similar to that presented by the National Association of Social Workers (1996):

Social workers should protect the confidentiality of all information obtained in the course of professional service, except for compelling professional reasons. The general expectation that social workers will keep information confidential does not apply when disclosure is necessary to prevent serious, foreseeable, and imminent harm to a client or other identifiable person or when laws or regulations require disclosure without a client's consent. In all instances, social workers should disclose the least amount of confidential information necessary to achieve the desired purpose; only information that is directly relevant to the purpose for which the disclosure is made should be revealed.

Neither confidentiality nor privilege is an absolute. Since both are in place in support of the protection of the client, not the helper, both can be waived by the client. Beyond client waiver, conditions exists that limit the degree to which communications can be maintained as confidential. Conditions such as those dictated by local laws and organizational regulations, as well as situations in which a client or an identifiable person might be harmed should confidentiality be maintained, necessitate the breaching of confidentiality and privilege. These conditions and other complicating factors are discussed in the next section.

Limits and Special Challenges to Confidentiality

Since confidentiality is not an absolute, in addition to respecting the confidentiality of the client's information, the ethical professional is directed by standards of practice to inform the client, when appropriate, of the limits of confidentiality. The Code of Ethics for Social Workers (1996), for example, states: "Social workers should inform clients, to the extent possible, about the disclosure of confidential information and the potential consequences, when feasible before the disclosure is made." (NASW, 1996, 1.07.d).

It is essential that the professional helper explicate the restrictions on confidentiality and assist the client to understand the unique conditions under which information may be shared in the course of providing service. The American Psychological Association's Code of Ethics states that disclosure of the limits of confidentiality should occur at the outset of a professional relationship: "unless it is not foreseeable or is contraindicated, the discussion of confidentiality occurs at the outset of the relationship and thereafter as new circumstances may warrant" (APA, 1995, Standard 5.01b).

Beyond the client's consent to waive privilege or disclose confidential material, the courts and the various professions have identified a number of conditions under which disclosure of this information may be required. These conditions include sharing for professional support when a client is a danger to self or others, in child abuse situations, and when court ordered.

Since breach of confidentiality may be mandated in these and other circumstances, clients should be adequately informed about the limitations of confidentiality early within the relationship (see Chapter 6). Once informed, it becomes the client's responsibility to share such personal information, knowing that confidence may not be maintained.

The ethical professional will maintain that breach of confidentiality is such a strong issue that the basis needs to be strong and justifiable. Further, because a breach of confidentiality that is outside of these conditions may make the professional susceptible to legal and ethical sanctions, ranging from sanctioning by the professional organization to a malpractice suit, it is essential for the practitioner to be fully versed in the laws and ethical standards existing for one's profession and in one's state of practice.

Professional Support

It is generally accepted that confidential material may be shared with colleagues and supervisors for professional purposes. However, only that material essential to the consultation or supervision should be disclosed. Additionally, the conditions under which the information is shared needs to reflect the respect for client privacy and the attempt to maintain maximum confidentiality. Case Illustration 7.2 demonstrates how in our day-to-day professional interactions we may become somewhat insensitive to the conditions under which we share confidential information.

CASE ILLUSTRATION **7.2**
Faculty Room Chatter

Allison is a secondary school counselor. She has been working with Ricky, a twelfth grade student who has been speaking with Allison about his concern and anxiety over his sexual orientation. Ricky has started to accept the fact that he is homosexual and has been working with the school counselor to determine ways in which he can disclose this information to his parents. Because of the anxiety he has been feeling and the amount of psychic energy he has been giving to this concern, Ricky's academic performance has fallen off quite dramatically.

Ricky is very concerned that his two honors teachers may feel that he has simply stopped caring about their courses, and he would like them to write him a letter of recommendation. Thus he asks Allison if she would explain to the teachers about his personal struggle so that they will better understand his falling grades. Ricky gives permission to disclose the information they have discussed, including his own coming out.

Allison sets up a meeting with Mr. Hansen and Ms. Wallace, the two honors teachers. She explains that she has been working with Ricky and would like to share some information that may better help them understand his current academic difficulty. Both teachers express concern for Ricky and are glad to have the meeting. The three meet at a table in the faculty lounge, where Allison begins to share the information with both teachers with the intent of having them more fully understand Ricky's change in performance. While Allison is fully aware that other teachers are in the room, she feels that if they speak in a conversational tone that no one else will either overhear or care to listen.

Client as Danger to Self or Others

While it may be obvious that the ethical practitioner concerned for the well-being of his or her client will break confidence if doing so can protect a client from self-inflicted harm, what may not be as obvious is that a break in confidence may be required as a way of taking reasonable care to protect others who may be in jeopardy of harm at the hands of a client. The professional obligation to warn a third party of a potential danger has been widely discussed starting with the now famous case of *Tarasoff v. The Regents of the University of California* (1976). In this case, the California Supreme Court found a duty to warn and to protect an identifiable and foreseeable victim. The case focused on Posenjit Poddar, the defendant charged with the 1969 killing of Tatiana Tarasoff. Tarasoff's parents alleged that two months prior to the murder, Poddar confided his intention to kill Tatiana to a psychologist employed by the Cowell Memorial Hospital at the University of California at Berkeley. The psychologist had Poddar detained by the campus police, but Poddar was later released. No one warned Tarasoff of the possible peril to her life. Following the appeal, the court ruled that a duty to warn existed, stating:

> When a therapist determines, or pursuant to the standards of his profession should determine, that his [client] presents a serious danger of violence to another he incurs an obligation to use reasonable care to protect the intended victim against such danger. The discharge of this duty may require the therapist to take one or more of various steps, depending upon

the nature of the case. Thus it may call for him to warn the intended victim or others likely to apprise the victim of the danger, to notify the police, or to take whatever other steps are reasonably necessary under the circumstances. (*Tarasoff*, 131 Cal. Rptr. at 20).

The courts in this situation concluded that:

Public policy favoring protection of the confidential character of [client], psychotherapist communication must yield to the extent to which disclosure is essential to avert dangers to others. The protective privilege ends where the public peril begins (*Tarasoff*, 131 Cal. Rptr. at 27).

This case has served as the foundation for the concept of duty to warn, making mental health professionals responsible for assessing the risk of danger that their clients may present to others and assessing the need to breach confidentiality and to warn. Legal extensions of the Tarasoff case are presented later within this chapter. One special arena in which Tarasoff continues to be debated is in working with clients with HIV/AIDS.

Persons with AIDS

Traditional approaches to client confidentiality have certainly been challenged by the introduction of the issue of AIDS and at-risk behaviors (Erickson, 1993). There are few legal guidelines to help professionals determine when or how to inform a potential victim of the threat of HIV transmission (Erickson, 1993).

The law in most jurisdictions protects the confidentiality of a person with AIDS. There have been exceptions to this rule, including public health reporting and in some cases disclosure to a spouse or sexual partner. There have been attempts at applying the Tarasoff decision to AIDS-related cases (Ahia & Martin, 1993; Cohen, 1997; Knapp & Vande-Creek, 1990; McGuire, Nieri, Abbott, Sheridan, & Fisher, 1995). With Tarasoff as the framework for decision making, it would appear that therapists have a duty to protect under the following conditions (see McGuire et al., 1995; Totten, Lamb, & Reeder, 1990):

- When a special client–therapist relationship exists.
- When there is clear and imminent danger—which would be a function of the client's medical diagnosis, the extent to which the person engages in high-risk behaviors, and the degree to which safe sex procedures are or are not employed.
- When there is an identifiable victim. This is compounded with HIV in that the virus can remain dormant for years and the number of persons with whom the client has sexually engaged is difficult to determine. However, when there is a current, exclusive partner, the identification of the potential victim is easier.

The lack of case law, however, makes clear-cut decisions and rules hard to find. Further, the application of Tarasoff has not been generally accepted as the standard. State laws differ regarding HIV and the limits of confidentiality and vary according to specific professional license. Some states may forbid disclosure of any HIV status to third parties, whereas other states may allow for some disclosure or restrict that freedom to some professions (e.g., physician, psychiatrist). Cohen (1997) suggests that practitioners refer to legal precedent, state statutes and professional codes of ethics when attempting to resolve the HIV disclosure dilemma (see Exercise 7.2).

The American Psychological Association did pass several resolutions regarding clients who are HIV positive (APA, 1992) and concerning Tarasoff confidentiality and protection of others. In summary, the APA suggests that unless there is an identifiable client who refuses to behave in a manner that protects this person, the covenant of confidentiality should not be broken. Specifically, the APA's position is that

1. A legal duty to protect third parties from HIV should not be imposed.
2. If, however, specific legislation is considered, then it should permit disclosure only when the provider knows of an identifiable third party whom the provider has a compelling reason to believe is at significant risk of infection; the provider has a reasonable belief that the third party has no reason to suspect that he or she is at risk; and the client/patient has been urged to inform the third party and has either refused or is considered unreliable in his or her willingness to notify the third party.
3. If such legislation is adopted, it should include immunity from civil and criminal liability for providers who, in good faith, make decisions to disclose or not to disclose information about HIV.

The issue of disclosure and the duty to warn when in relation to working with an HIV/AIDS client are not at all clear-cut. The professional's response certainly is a decision that needs to reflect the current position of her or his profession and the directives of the

---

EXERCISE **7.2**
The Duty to Warn and Clients with AIDS

Directions: The application of Tarasoff to situations involving clients with AIDS clients has not been clarified within the courts.

Part 1: Contact a professional in practice within your local community. Pose the following questions to the professional and share your findings with your classmates/colleagues.

a. Are you familiar with the Tarasoff case?
b. If you had a client who expressed an intention to seriously harm an identifiable victim, what would you do? Has this ever happened in your practice?
c. What would you do if your client, who had AIDS, was actively engaged in unprotected sex with an identifiable partner? Has this ever happened in your practice?

Part 2: Contact your state professional organization and ask for the latest position on applying Tarasoff and the duty to warn in situations involving a client who had AIDS or was HIV positive.

EXERCISE **7.3**
To Disclose or Not to Disclose?

Directions: Given the lack of clarity and directions regarding the issue of disclosure and duty to warn in cases of working with clients with HIV/AIDS, individual decisions and standards of colleagues are important reference points for the practitioner attempting to make an ethical decision. Contact at least two professionals currently working in your particular professional arena and pose to them the following scenarios. Record their responses and share your findings with a colleague or a classmate in an attempt to identify the standard of practice currently enacted within your locale.

Scenario:
Assume you are working with a client who has admitted having AIDS and engaging in unprotected sex. Further assume that the client refused to give you consent to disclose this information.

1. Would you warn the client's spouse?
2. Would you warn the client's current, live-in lover (assuming the client was not married)?
3. Would you warn individuals whom your client identified as recent sexual partners?
4. Would you warn individuals who your client identified as having sex over the past five years?
5. Would you continue to work with the client, if he or she refused to begin to practice safe sex?

---

local and federal courts. Exercise 7.3 is presented to give you a "practitioner's view" of this difficult area of professional decision making.

Child Abuse

The Child Abuse Prevention and Treatment Act of 1974 defined child abuse and neglect and set the standards for state mandatory reporting laws. Since that time the definition has been broadened to include various types of maltreatment. Under these conditions disclosure is mandated. However, resolving the complex conflicts among protecting children, maintaining confidentiality, protecting the integrity of the professional relationship and practice, and abiding by statutes and laws is difficult.

While professional standards direct the practitioner to protect the information disclosed within the helping process, breaking the law by not complying with a legal mandate to report is in itself unethical. The American Psychological Code of Ethics (1995), for example, states that "psychologists disclose confidential information without the consent of the individual only as mandated by law, or where permitted by law for a valid purpose" (Standard 5.05a). The tension and conflict between professional values and standards with legal requirements is not easy to resolve. But, as with any ethical dilemma, addressing the issue of mandated reporting can be approached by consulting with a colleague about the situation. Kalichman and Brosig (1993) reported that over 80 per cent of practicing psychologists discuss cases of suspected child maltreatment with colleagues. Professionals need to have a level of certainty that maltreatment has occurred prior to reporting (Kalischman & Craig, 1991).

Records—Court Ordered

All professional codes of conduct provide for the maintenance and utilization of records as well as the maintenance of privacy of these records (see Chapter 10). Records should be maintained in a secure manner in order to protect the client's confidentiality. Failure to maintain adequate records may be seen as a breach of the standard of care and thus serve as a basis for a malpractice suit (Anderson, 1996).

In the case of educational records, confidentiality is protected under federal law, 20 U.S.C. 1232g, the Family Educational Privacy Act (also referred to as the Buckley Agreement). This law applies to any educational agency (public or private) receiving federal funds. It specifies that parents have access to student education records and that any release of educational records requires parental or student (if over 18) written consent. Without consent, only "director information"—limited to name, address, telephone, date of birth, major, and date of attendance—are released. This is not an open file policy. Some records, such as those maintained by a physician, psychiatrist, psychologist, or other recognized professional or paraprofessional acting in his or her professional and paraprofessional capacity, are made, maintained, or used only in connection with the provision of treatment to the student. These are not available to anyone other than persons providing such treatment (20U.S.C., sec. 1232(a)(4)(B)).

While records, including educational records, may be requested by various agencies or legal professionals, the only request to which the practitioner must respond without client consent is one issued in the form of a court order. Often records are requested by insurance companies or others in legal proceedings, often in the form of a subpoena. And while it is important for a mental health specialist to respond to a subpoena, the response can be in the form of a request. Rather than disclosing the information requested, a helper can request that the agency or individual seeking the information obtain a signed release of information from the client. However, if a practitioner is issued a *duces tecum subpoena*, a court order, then the practitioner must appear in court and bring the client's records. Under this condition a claim of privilege could be offered at the court and would require the court to either honor the privilege or demand a breach.

Another condition in which a breach of confidentiality and privilege may occur is when a client files a lawsuit or ethical grievance against the practitioner. Under these conditions the practitioner has a right to reveal relevant information about the client in his or her own defense.

One final area in which release of information may invite a breach of confidentiality is in the case of providing information for insurance claims. Clients need to be informed that information released to insurance companies for the purpose of third-party payment may remain within their records. Typically, the information required includes the client's name, services provided, dates of services, and a diagnosis. The importance of this fact is that once these data are conveyed to the insurance company, the practitioner will no longer have control over access to these records and thus cannot restrict to whom or how the information is used.

Confidentiality and Working with Minors

Although children and adolescents increasingly have been granted rights to free choice, informed consent and privileged communication in counseling these issues remain complex in practice and often confusing to practitioners. There is a lack of general agreement within the profession (e.g., Anderson, 1996; Hendrix, 1991; Salo & Shumate, 1993) regarding confidentiality when counseling minors, specifically in reference to sharing information with parents. Herlihy and Corey (1996), for example, warned that although the legal right may belong to the parents or guardian, there is an ethical responsibility to obtain the minor's permission before releasing information.

For those working with minors in a school setting, the minors' rights to confidentiality are protected by the Family Educational Rights and Privacy Act, known as the Buckley Amendment (1974). While this act provides for access by parents to student records, it also exempts counselor notes, assuming that they are not considered part of the official school record. Because this final designation of "official school record" is open to the interpretation of each school district, counselors should be aware of their own district's policies regarding counselor notes and minor confidentiality.

In a number of states minors over the ages of 12, 13, and 14 have rights to counseling in the specific area of drug and alcohol abuse and venereal disease without informing parents. Some states have even provided for free choice and informed consent for outpatient counseling without requiring them to inform parents (Corey et al., 1993). The rationale is that such right to privacy and freedom to choose increases the likelihood that children and adolescents needing counseling will seek it.

Recent Legal Decisions: Confidentiality and Privileged Communications

Professionals with Privilege

Psychotherapist–client privilege has been supported by a Supreme Court decision. The case involved the ability of a clinical social worker licensed in Illinois to assert privilege for communications between herself and her client in a lawsuit. The client, Mary Lu Redmon, was a police officer who killed Ricky Allen, Sr. The officer responded to a reported fight and found Mr. Allen allegedly poised to stab another individual. The lawsuit brought against Officer Redmond, the City of Hoffman Estates, and its police department by Carrie Jaffee, the administrator of the Allen estate, alleged that excessive force had been used. In the course of the legal proceedings, the family petitioned to obtain notes made by the therapist in counseling sessions with Officer Redmond after the incident. Redmond refused to provide consent, and the therapist refused to respond by providing notes. The judge in that case informed the jury to assume that the notes were unfavorable, and the jury found for the plaintiff. On appeal in the U.S. Court of Appeals for the 7th circuit, the jury verdict was thrown out and the case was remanded for a new trial with the court opinion stating the trial court had erred by not protecting the confidentiality of the records. Jaffee appealed this decision to the U.S. Supreme Court, which in a ruling in *Jaffee v. Redmond*, upheld a strict standard of privileged communication. The justice wrote: "Effective psychotherapy depends upon an atmosphere of confidence and trust in which the patient is willing to make frank and complete disclosure of facts, emotions, memories and fears" (Seppa, 1996). This decision upheld the ability of licensed psychotherapists to maintain the confidences of their clients in federal court cases.

While the *Jaffee v. Redmond* ruling directly applies only within the federal court system, it does extend psychotherapist privilege to another group of licensed professionals, clinical social workers. Many believe that opens the door to the extension of that privilege to other mental health professionals. Each state has laws that govern the conditions and the relationships under which a communication is considered privileged. As such, each practitioner should check on the specific laws and court rulings defining the conditions of privilege for practitioners within their state of employment.

Extending the Duty to Protect

While the release of educational records under the conditions set forth in the Buckley Amendment generally require the informed consent of the parent or the student, if over 18, the need to breach confidence appears to extend to situations involving school counseling when the client appears to be in danger of harming himself or herself. In a court case, *Eisel v. Board of Education* (1991), the Maryland Court of Appeals applied the duty to violate confidentiality to school counselors if a client is judged to be at risk for self-harm. In this case a child threatened suicide in the presence of schoolmates. These schoolmates told both the parents of the child and the school counselor. The counselor interviewed the child, who denied the threat. The counselor did not follow up or notify the parents or school administration. The father sued the counselors and the school following the child's suicide, alleging breach of duty to intervene to prevent the suicide and the court found in favor of the plaintiff (Anderson, 1996).

Extending Tarasoff

At least fifteen states enacted "Tarasoff statutes," including Alaska, California, Colorado, Florida, Indiana , Kansas, Kentucky, Louisiana, Massachusetts, Minnesota, Montana, New Hampshire, Ohio, Utah, and Washington; at least five other jurisdictions have embraced the theory (Reaves & Ogloff, 1996). More recent court cases have attempted to further clarify the elements of "foreseeable danger" and "identifiable victim." While the specifics of what defines "foreseeable danger" are still being debated, the courts have generally upheld that such foreseeable danger is present when there is a readily identifiable victim and the prediction of danger is based on professional standards such as the existence of death threats, possession of a weapon, and the individual's having a clear plan of action. In *Emerich v. Philadelphia Center for Human Development*, the Pennsylvania Supreme Court held that, based upon the special relationship between a mental health professional and his or her patient, when the patient has communicated to the professional a specific and immediate threat of serious bodily injury against a specifically identified or readily identifiable third party and the professional determines that his or her patient presents a serious danger of violence to the third party, then that professional bears a duty to exercise reasonable care to protect by warning the third party against such a danger (Tepper & Knapp, 1999). Several subsequent court decisions have expanded and clarified the duty to warn and protect from dangerous clients. For example, victims who are not specifically identified by the client but who could be considered foreseeable, likely targets of client violence (such as individuals in close proximity to an identifiable victim) should be warned according the ruling of *Hedlund v. Superior Court of Orange County* (1983) and *Jablonski v. United States* (1983).

Other court cases have extended this duty to warn even when the victim is not clearly identifiable. In *Lipari v. Sears, Roebuck & Co.* (1980), the court ruled that the therapist failed in the duty to protect others by not detaining a potentially violent client who had purchased a gun, even though no identifiable victim was named. And in a Vermont Supreme Court ruling in 1985 (*Peck v. Counseling Services of Addison County*), the Tarasoff duty to warn was extended to cases involving property—and not just personal—injury. In this case, the client was viewed as posing a serious risk of danger in that the client's intent of arson represented a "lethal threat to human beings who may be in the vicinity of the conflagration" (*Peck v. Counseling Services of Addision County*, 146 Vt. 61, 499, A.2d 422, Sup.Ct. 1985, at 424 n.3.)

Protecting the Practitioner

Violations of confidentiality and privilege are determined by statutes, court decisions, and professional codes of ethics. These violations may be responded to with criminal action, civil action, and/or professional sanctioning. However, because of the increasing court support for breach of confidentiality in the protection of others (identified or not), many states (e.g., California, Colorado, Kentucky) have legislation protecting mental health professionals from civil liability if they issue warnings in attempts to protect others from potential harm (Herlihy & Sheeley, 1988). Again, it is essential for the ethical helper to understand the laws existing in his or her state of employment that govern such disclosures and such protection.

Beyond Professional Standards: A Personal Moral Response

As noted, confidentiality is essential to the nature of a helping relationship. Clients need to feel safe within the helping relationship and trust that their disclosures will be held in confidence. The ethical principle of confidentiality is founded on the fundamental respect for a client's privacy and the helper's concern for maintaining client welfare. This underlying respect for privacy and the valuing of the welfare of the client need to be more than simply the rationale for the ethical principle of confidentiality. Both need to be personal values.

The ethical professional, who values client privacy and welfare, will maintain that the breach of confidentiality is such a strong issue that the basis needs to be strong and justifiable. However, even with this as a personal value, balancing client need, professional ethics, and legal mandate is not always easy nor clear. Thus it is essential for each ethical practitioner to keep current on the profession's stance and application of ethical principles and the laws governing practice and practice decisions. Specifically, each practitioner should commit to:

- Knowing state laws mandating reporting or breaching of confidence
- Understanding thresholds and criteria for breach of confidence
- Providing disclosure to clients regarding the limitations to confidentiality
- Keeping thorough and detailed records
- Seeking consultation before disclosure
- Maintaining current knowledge of legal and ethical decisions guiding the disclosure of information
- Seeking ongoing education on the issue of confidentiality and its limits

Finally, fear of litigation or concerns about adhering to legal mandates can serve as the motivation for committing to each of the above. However, the ethical professional, one who has assimilated the ethical principle as personal value, will hold client well-being and welfare as the motive for such a commitment. A similar concern for the client's welfare can serve as the guiding light for all practice decisions regarding disclosure.

Case Illustration

We began the chapter with Maria, the client in our ongoing case, giving Ms. Wicks, the counselor, permission to talk with Ms. Armstrong about her case. As you read the continuation of the dialogue, which is presented below, review Ms. Wicks' behavior as it reflects or fails to reflect the principles discussed within this chapter. Further, a number of brief questions are presented as a stimulus to your application of your knowledge regarding principles guiding confidentiality and its limitations.

MARIA: It's okay. You can talk to Ms. Armstrong as long as you don't tell her who I am. I don't want anyone knowing what I told you. Besides I thought talking to you was like talking to a priest in confession . . . you know, a major secret?

MS. WICKS: Thank you for the permission to speak with Ms. Armstrong. Maria, I certainly don't want to break your confidence or reveal private conversations we may have had, but your welfare and you well-being are my primary concern and I want to do all that I can do to keep you safe.

MARIA: But you gotta promise me you ain't gonna tell her who I am.

MS. WICKS: Remember the first day we met? I know you were angry and really didn't want to speak with me. But after a while you seemed to relax and started to share some of your story. Well, when we had that meeting I told you that things we spoke about would be kept private. In fact, I said I wouldn't share information without your permission.

MARIA: Yeah, I remember that . . . that's what I mean . . . you can't tell no one. . . .

MS.WICKS: I'm glad you remember that. Maybe you also remember me saying that while I will respect your privacy that some things just can't be private or confidential. I said if you are thinking about hurting yourself. . . .

MARIA: I am not going to hurt myself . . . I know you said that but it was no big deal since I knew I wasn't planning on hurting myself. . . .

MS. WICKS: Again, I am glad you remember that and happier that you are not thinking that you would like to hurt yourself. But, I also said that if you were thinking about hurting someone else that I may have to inform that person so that they could be protected and you would be safe, as well. Do you remember that.

MARIA: Yeah. . . . but I'm not sure what this has to do with anything, now?

MS.WICKS: Well, even though you are telling me that you have no intention of hurting yourself, I am very concerned that having unprotected sex with your boyfriend, who has AIDS, is endangering your life. And the truth is I am not sure what I am supposed to do with this information. You know I want you to stop, 'cause I care about you. I'm just not sure if I have to tell someone else for legal reasons.

MARIA: Legal reasons. . . . It's my life. . . .

Reflections:
1. Does Ms. Wicks give evidence of providing Maria with the limits to confidentiality early within the sessions?
2. In addition to discussing with a colleague and the principal what else would you suggest Ms. Wicks do?
3. What would you do? Does Maria's actions constitute a basis for breaching confidence?
4. If Maria refused to refrain from engaging in unprotected sex with her boyfriend, should Ms. Wicks continue to work with her? Would you?

Cooperative Learning Exercise

The purpose of this chapter was not only to introduce you to concepts of confidentiality and privileged communications, but also to introduce you to the many elements complicating decisions to maintain or breach confidentiality. Translating theory to practice is not always an easy process.

Directions: Contact two professionals operating in one of the following roles and ask them the questions that are listed below. Discuss your findings with a supervisor, colleague, or classmate, looking for common approaches shared across professions.

    a. School counselor
    b. Licensed marriage and family therapist in private practice
    c. A mental health counselor

    d. A clinical social worker currently employed with a county agency

    e. A therapist who does custody evaluations in divorce cases

Questions:

1. When meeting with a new client, do you explain the concept of confidentiality? If so, do you also describe the limits to confidentiality or the conditions under which confidentiality may be breached? How do you present these issues?
2. Have you ever had your records subpoenaed? How did you respond?
3. Have you ever had a situation in which you believe a duty to warn existed? If so, what did you do? If not, what do you think you would do?
4. If you work with minors, how do you address the issue of confidentiality with the minor? With their parents?
5. In your professional role do you have privilege? If so, have you ever called on privilege as a basis for not disclosing client information?

Summary

Confidentiality: What and When Warranted?

Confidentiality is the general standard of professional conduct that obligates a professional not to discuss information about the client with anyone. Privileged communication is a legal term that describes the quality of certain specific types of relationships that prevent information acquired from such relationships from being disclosed in court or other legal proceedings.

    Questions about who can claim the privilege, what type of information is privileged, and what the limitations to privileges can vary extensively state to state.

Confidentiality Across the Professions

The provision of confidentiality is common throughout human service professions and is widely held as a therapeutic necessity. Most statements echo the belief that without compelling reasons, confidentiality must be protected. Compelling reasons for breaching confidence include preventing serious, foreseeable, and imminent harm to a client or other identifiable person or when laws or regulations require disclosure without a client's consent.

Limits and Special Challenges to Confidentiality

Neither confidentiality nor privilege is an absolute. Beyond the client's consent to waive privilege or disclose confidential material, the courts and the professions themselves have identified a number of conditions under which disclosure of this information may be required.

Conditions Limiting Confidentiality

    Professional support

    Client as danger to self or others

Child abuse

Records—court ordered

Recent Legal Decisions—Confidentiality and Privileged Communications

The *Jaffee v. Redmond* (1996) ruling extends psychotherapist privilege to another group of licensed professionals, clinical social workers. Many believe that this opens the door to the extension of that privilege to other mental health professionals.

In *Eisel v. Board of Education of Montgomery County* (1991), the Maryland Court of Appeals applied the duty to violate confidentiality to school counselors if a client is judged to be at risk for self-harm.

Several subsequent court decisions have expanded and clarified the duty to warn and protect from dangerous clients (see *Hedlund v. Superior Court*, 1983; *Jablonski v. United States*, 1983; *Lipari v. Sears, Roebuck & Co.*, 1980). *Peck v. Counseling Services of Addison County* expanded Tarasoff duty to warn in cases involving property—not personal—injury.

Beyond Professional Standards: A Personal Moral Response

The ethical principle of confidentiality is founded on the fundamental respect of a client's privacy and the helper's concern for maintaining client welfare. It is essential for each ethical practitioner to embrace a value of client welfare and keep current on the profession's stance on and application of ethical principles and the laws governing practice and practice decisions.

IMPORTANT TERMS

breach	duty to warn
Buckley Amendment	foreseeable danger
Child Abuse Prevention and	identifiable victim
Treatment Act of 1974	imminent danger
client waiver	privilege communications
confidentiality	protected relationships
constitutional right to privacy	subpoena
court order	Tarasoff
duces tecum subpoena	

SUGGESTED READINGS

Boomer, L.W., Harthsorne, T.S. and Robertshaw, C.S. (1995). Confidentiality and student records: A hypothetical case. *Preventing School Failure, 39(3)*, 15–21.

Pope, K.S. (1990). A practitioner's guide to confidentiality and privilege: 20 legal, ethical and clinical pitfalls. *The Independent Practitioner*, 1, 40–45.

Seppa, N. (1996, August). Supreme court protects patient-therapist privilege. *APA Monitor*, 27(8), 39.

Tarasoff v. The Regents of the University of California, 551 P.2d 334 (Cal.Sup.Ct., 1976).

8 Boundaries and the Ethical Use of Power

Ms. Wicks: But Maria—I do care about you. I am worried you are placing yourself in harm's way. If it would be easier for you, I would be willing to let you stay with me for a while.

Certainly Ms. Wicks is a very caring and concerned counselor. Ms. Wicks has consistently demonstrated a real care and concern as well as a desire to help. However, it appears that her level of concern and her felt sense of urgency about the situation may be clouding her professional judgment. Knowing the boundaries of a professional relationship and being able to operate within those boundaries while expressing professional care and concern is not always an easy process. The power of the helping relationship can be quite awesome and oftentimes seductive. When such power is not restricted by the boundaries of the professional relationship, it invites misuse and abuse of the client.

Chapter Objectives

The chapter will introduce you to the concept of professional boundaries and the conditions under which boundary crossing and violation may occur. After reading this chapter you should be able to do the following:

1. Describe what is meant by the concept of professional boundaries
2. Describe the difference between boundary violation and boundary crossing
3. Explain how simple identification and transference can interfere with the maintenance of professional boundaries
4. Describe what is meant by "dual" or "multiple" relationships
5. List questions for reflection that can guide a practitioner's decisions regarding the ethics of dual relationship
6. Explain why sexual intimacy with a client is clearly a boundary violation.

Setting and Maintaining Professional Boundaries

A professional relationship is a special entity. The professional relationship is definable and does require unique dynamic and role definition. However, the intensity of the emotions shared, the isolation provided, and the level of intimacy sometimes experienced can challenge the boundaries of a professional relationship.

Therapy by definition connects the therapist and client in a mutual journey—one that involves compassion, caring, and empathy—which, according to Greenspan (1995), breaks old boundaries of distrust, isolation, suspicion, and despair. Thus, therapy by definition is boundless (Coale, 1998). Under these conditions it is possible for ethical problems to occur as the helper blends professional role and relationship with more personal involvement. The concept of boundaries and boundary violations have received increased attention as a result of the increasing litigation and ethic committee hearings related to violation of boundaries (Gutheil & Gabbard, 1993). Setting and maintaining professional boundaries are essential steps in preventing such personal involvement and the maintenance of an ethical relationship.

Gutheil and Gabbard (1993) suggest a distinction between boundary crossings and boundary violations. In the first situation, boundary crossing, the roles have been changed. Thus, what was once a professional helper–client relationship may now have moved to an investment partnership or friendship. The second situation of boundary violations occurs when exploitation of the client exists. It is a condition in which there is a misuse of practitioner power for personal satisfaction (Lerman & Rigby, 1994).

The position taken here and elsewhere (e.g., Strasburger, Jorgenson, & Sutherland, 1992) is that all boundary crossings (i.e. departure from commonly accepted professional roles and practices) can become problematic and need to be avoided. Any boundary violation in which the practitioner's needs are given primacy at the client's expense is unethical (Peterson, 1992). Whether it is something as subtle as the rearrangement of furniture or seating arrangement in order to bring the helper in closer physical proximity to an attractive client or a pause in the conversation that may be inferred as having sexual innuendo, decisions by practitioners that are directed to satisfy their professional needs at the expense of the client are violations of professional boundaries and need to be avoided (Coale, 1998) (see Case Illustration 8.1).

CASE ILLUSTRATION **8.1**
Changing Seats—Moving Closer

Allison, a 32-year-old recent divorcee has been working with Dr. Manel for the past five weeks. Their sessions have been focusing on Allison's sense of grief and her anxiety about establishing or reestablishing herself as a single woman.

For each of the past five sessions, Allison sat on the sofa and Dr. Manel directly across from her in a large overstuffed chair. Allison has, in each of the previous sessions, disclosed fears that she is not attractive and would often break down in tears when she considered the possibility of being alone. At these times Dr. Manel would allow Allison to cry and when appropriate would challenge her conclusions that she would forever be alone.

Allison entered the current session more upset than she had been in the previous three or four. Allison sat and shared with Dr. Manel that she had just received divorce papers and that she wanted to die. Allison began to sob and stated: "I can't stand this! He doesn't love me. No one could ever love me. . . ." At which point, Dr. Manel moved from his chair and took up a seat on the couch next to Allison. As soon as he sat down, Allison flung her arms about his neck, placing her head on his shoulder. Dr. Manel, wiping her tears, stated: "I think you are lovable."

In reviewing the case of Allison and Dr. Manel (Case Illustration 8.1), one must wonder whether Dr. Manel's change in seating and verbal comment were meant simply to support a client in crisis or were in response to his own interest in physical contact.

All professional codes of ethics (see Table 8.1) attend to the issue of boundaries and the need to assure nonexploitation of the client through boundary crossing and the mixing of multiple relationships.

While much attention has been given to sexual misconduct, a point that is discussed in much detail later, there are other more subtle boundary crossing/violations to which a practitioner needs to be sensitive. Accepting gifts from clients, participating in social activities or events provided by the client, engaging in investment activities or bartering professional services for goods or client service, all blur the boundaries of a professional practice. The question that needs to be posed when entering these various types of relationships with a client is this: "Is this what a therapist does?" (Gutheil & Gappard, 1993, p. 190). Clearly, placing the personal needs of the helper above that of the client invites unethical practice. Identifying whose needs are being met by the decisions and actions of the helpers, be it the helper himself or herself, or the client, will help to identify boundary violation.

TABLE 8.1 Boundaries and Mixing of Multiple Relationships

Professional Ethical Standards	Statement on Multiple Relationships
American Counseling Association (1995)	A.6.a.: Counselors are aware of their influential positions with respect to clients, and they avoid exploiting the trust and dependency of clients. Counselors make every effort to avoid dual relationships with clients that could impair professional judgment or increase the risk of harm to clients. (Examples of such relationships include, but are not limited to, familial, social, financial, business, or close relationships with clients.) When a dual relationship cannot be avoided, counselors take appropriate professional precautions such as informed consent, consultation, supervision, and documentation to ensure that judgment is not impaired and no exploitation occurs.
American Association of Marriage and Family Therapists (1998)	1.2: Marriage and family therapists are aware of their influential position with respect to clients, and they avoid exploiting the trust and dependency of such persons. Therapists, therefore, make every effort to avoid dual relationships with clients that could impair professional judgment or increase the risk of exploitation. When a dual relationship cannot be avoided, therapists take appropriate professional precautions to ensure judgment is not impaired and no exploitation occurs.
American Psychological Association (1992)	1.17.a: In many communities and situations it may not be feasible or reasonable for psychologists to avoid social or other nonprofessional contact with persons such as patients, clients, supervises, or research participants. Psychologists must always be sensitive to the potential harmful effects of other contacts on their work and on those persons with whom they deal.

Professional Objectivity: Essential to Professional Boundaries

The effective, ethical helper places the concerns and needs of the client as top priority. Placing the client's concerns as a priority (i.e., altruism) rather than the concerns of the helper (i.e., narcissism) requires the helper to distinguish his or her personal issues and emotional needs from those presented by the client. The ability to be empathic, while emotionally objective, may be difficult to maintain. However, if the helper's objectivity becomes compromised, the professional nature of the relationship may be threatened. The ethical helper must be aware of the various situations that can compromise professional objectivity and know when referral to another helper, who can maintain objectivity, is indicated.

Professional objectivity can be compromised by a number of situations (see Exercise 8.1).

While some, such as simple identification and transference, reflect a distortion of reality on the part of the helper, a more common form stems from the development of a dual relationship with the client involving both a professional and personal tone. Each of these conditions is discussed in some detail.

Simple Identification

A subtle form of loss of emotional objectivity is simple identification. Simple identification occurs when the helper identifies himself or her self with the client. It typically occurs when some element or characteristic of the client, or the client's experience and story, causes the helper to relate to the client's experience as his or her own. Under these conditions that helper can begin to view the client as himself or herself (see Case Illustration 8.2) and thus

---

EXERCISE **8.1**
Threats to Emotional Objectivity

Directions: After considering each of the following, share your response with your colleagues or classmates in order to identify ways of preventing such loss of objectivity.

1. Identify one person with whom you have a personal relationship and discuss how that relationship could block your emotional objectivity and thus interfere with you being an effective helper.
2. How might your own social roles (e.g., son, daughter, mother, father, ex-boyfriend. girlfriend, struggling student etc.) be the source of interference and loss of objectivity when working with some clients or specific types of problems?
3. Identify a number of themes or issues that arouse an emotional response in you (e.g., themes of emotional dependency, victimization, authority and power, etc.) and which might prove too close to your own emotional experience for you to remain objective while working with a client presenting similar concerns.

fails to discern the important difference between himself or herself experience and that of the client.

Mr. Peepers' (Case Illustration 8.2) objectivity was certainly compromised, and his pursuit of Jamal was a violation of his professional boundaries. The problem was that Mr. Peepers was not "seeing" Jamal as he was, but rather seeing himself in Jamal's experience. Jamal looked like Mr. Peepers. He was small and somewhat frail looking. He wore thick glasses and appeared nonathletic. Because Mr. Peepers "identified" with Jamal on the basis of physical similarity, his emotional objectivity was destroyed, and he assumed that what happened to him as a fifth grader was most likely happening to Jamal.

Clearly, such loss of emotional objectivity needs to be identified and confronted if one is to be an effective, ethical helper. Exercise 8.2 provides you with an opportunity to anticipate the conditions under which you may fall prey to simple identification.

Transference

A more complex distortion occurs with transference. In this case, the helper forces the story of the client to fit some aspect of his or her own life. This is a major distortion of reality and

Element or Characteristics	Helper Experience or Characteristics	Impact on Helper Objectivity
(Example): Client is a freshman in college. His father wants him to be an engineer and join his firm. He wants to be a music major but is afraid to upset dad. He is thinking that he could double major, recognizing that he does like engineering and may be able to use the music as a performance option.	Helper was a star athlete in high school. His father has always prepped him to play in college even though did not want to play in college. The helper still resents the fact that he went to the college his dad wanted and played football there even though he truly did not enjoy it	The helper is extremely confrontational with the client. The helper suggests that compromising and doing a double major is a failure of mature assertiveness. The helper keeps pushing the client to confront his father and simply say NO—it is my time to define my life.
1. Client experiencing a personal loss (via divorce, or death, or break up)		
2. A client who has been teased for being overweight, underweight, an early developer, or a late developer		
3. A client who is in an unhappy relationship or work situation		
4. A client who is the one in the family to whom every one turn when there is a problem		
5. A person who is currently having sexual difficulties (impotence, premature ejaculation, low libido, limited opportunity, etc.)		
6. A person whose beliefs (religious, political, sexual) have brought a sense of isolation		
7. Identify a significant experience in your life and in the space to the left identify a type of client or client condition with which you may identify		

occurs below the conscious level of the person distorting. It often results in the person, in this case the helper, using the context of the helping relationship and presence of the client to express feelings, beliefs, or desires that the helper has buried in his or her unconscious and rightfully should address to some other significant person in his or her life. The ability to be sensitive to the possibility of transference is essential to effective, ethical helping.

While the loss of objectivity as a result of distorting the client's reality as in the case with simple identification and transference may be infrequent, all helpers run the risk of losing emotional objectivity if engaged in direct personal involvement with clients. The possibility of engaging with the client in a relationship outside of the boundaries of helping is a topic that has received a lot of attention within the professional literature. The ethics of such dual relationships with clients has and continues to be debated. It is clear, however, whichever side of the debate one finds himself or herself on, dual relationships may serve as a condition in which one's professional objectivity can be compromised.

Dual Relationships: Crossing and/or Mixing Boundaries

A dual relationship is one in which the helper has two (or more) overlapping roles with the client. Table 8.2 highlights a number of professional and nonprofessional relationships for which boundary complication may exist. The table is an adaptation of that originally presented by Evans and Hearn (1997).

Loss of professional objectivity and boundary violations are possible anytime a professional is engaged in multiple relationships with his or her client. This may occur when the professional helper is also engaged in personal friendships, family, or business relationships or shares social activities with their clients (see Case Illustration 8.3).

TABLE 8.2   A Matrix of Dual Relationships

Additional Relationships	Primary Professional Relationship			
	Therapist/Counselor	*Instructor*	*Supervisor*	*Researcher*
Counselor	———	dual	dual	potential
Instructor	dual	———	potential	dual
Supervisor	dual	potential	———	dual
Researcher	potential	dual	dual	———
Social/Personal	dual	dual	dual	dual
Sexual	dual	dual	dual	dual
Political	dual	dual	dual	dual
Financial/business	dual	dual	dual	dual

Taken from Evans, D.R. & Hearn, M.T. (1997). Sexual and Non-Sexual Dual Relationships Managing to Boundaries. In D.R. Evans (ed.), *The Law Standards of Practice, and Ethics in the Practice of Psychology* (pp. 53–84). Toronto, Canada: Edmond Montogmery Publications, Ltd. Reprinted with permission.

CASE ILLUSTRATION 8.3
Tom and Elaine: Direct Personal Involvement

Tom is a Master's level counselor working in a college career center. Elaine asked Tom to help her with a decision about joining the Peace Corps. Elaine, who is also Tom's girlfriend, explained that she really is unsure if she should move away from their hometown to spend four years in the peace corps or to stay at home and continue in graduate school.

Tom suggested that Elaine employ an actuarial technique in which she would generate all of the costs and benefits to be accrued to both Elaine AND the significant people in her life if she stays or goes into the Peace Corps. This was a technique Tom had found successful with other clients. Typically, he would provide an initial example and then ask the client to complete the process on their own as a "homework." He would then review their matrix at the next session. With Elaine, however, Tom suggested that they do it together. He felt that he could help identify the possible benefits and costs to both Elaine AND certainly to the others in her life.

While Tom (Case Illustration 8.3) may truly want to assist Elaine in making the best decision (for her), he may have difficulty keeping his own strong desire to keep her close to him and at home out of the equation. Thus, his suggestions may be aimed more at meeting his needs for a personal relationship than at Elaine's need to make the best vocational choice. Under this situation the dual nature of their relationship (i.e., love relationship and helping relationship) is contaminating the helping process.

It appears that while all professional codes of conduct warn about the risk of dual relationships (see Table 8.3), not all within the profession are as clear-cut about the evils of dual relationships or about the sanctions that should be applied.

Those who see dual relationships (sexual and/or nonsexual) as problematic (e.g., Pope & Vasquez, 1991), point to the fact that dual relationships

1. Impair the helper's judgment
2. May present conflict of interests
3. Hold a danger of exploitation of the client, since the helper holds a more powerful position
4. Can blur the professional nature of the therapeutic relationship

From this perspective, practitioners are cautioned against engaging in any dual or multiple relationships with a client. Some sources have even suggested that practitioners engaging in dual roles of any kind should be severely sanctioned. In fact, dual relationships are the major cause for disciplinary hearings, ethics complaint and financial losses in malpractice suits against practitioners (Bader, 1994).

However, not all agree with this prohibitive stance. Others suggest that dual roles are often unavoidable and, with the exception of sexual or other exploitive relationships, dual roles can be a useful resource to the helping process (Biaggio & Greene, 1995; Hedges, 1993; Tomm, 1991). For example, counselor educators may serve not only as instructors but may also act as therapeutic agents for their students' personal development (Corey et

TABLE 8.3   Codes Restricting Nonsexual Dual Relationships

Professional Ethical Standards	Statement Regarding Dual Relationship
American Psychological Association (1995)	1.17.a: A psychologist refrains from entering into or promising another personal, scientific, professional, financial, or other relationship with such persons if it appears likely that such a relationship reasonably might impair the psychologist's objectivity or otherwise interfere with the psychologist's effectively performing his or her functions as a psychologist, or might harm or exploit the other party.
National Association of Social Workers (1996)	1.06 Conflicts of Interest (c) Social workers should not engage in dual or multiple relationships with clients or former clients in which there is a risk of exploitation or potential harm to the client. In instances when dual or multiple relationships are unavoidable, social workers should take steps to protect clients and are responsible for setting clear, appropriate, and culturally sensitive boundaries. (Dual or multiple relationships occur when social workers relate to clients in more than one relationship, whether professional, social, or business. Dual or multiple relationships can occur simultaneously or consecutively.)
American Counseling Association (1995)	A.6.a. Counselors make every effort to avoid dual relationships with clients that could impair professional judgment or increase the risk of harm to clients. (Examples of such relationships include, but are not limited to, familial, social, financial, business, or close personal relationships with clients.)
American Association of Marriage and Family Therapists (1998)	1.2: Therapists, therefore, make every effort to avoid dual relationships with clients that could impair professional judgment or increase the risk of exploitation.

al.,1988). As suggested by this example, role blending or dual roles may occur "naturally" within certain contexts such as counselor training and, while possibly presenting ethical dilemmas involving loss of objectivity or conflict of interest, need not by definition be unethical (Herlihy & Corey, 1997).

St. Germaine (1993) suggests that while errors in judgment can occur in dual relationships, that need not be the case. Further, Tomm (1991) argues that the code of ethics that addresses dual relationships may actually create a situation in which the helper actively maintains interpersonal distance, thus promoting objectification of the relationship and the promotion of a vertical hierarchy in the relationship. While caution is advised, it is clear that there is no one directive to which practitioners can turn for guidance in terms of dual relationships. Exercise 8.3 is provided to assist you in gaining the perspective of your local professional community in regards to the ethics of dual relationships.

The position taken here is that it is not the existence of duality that is the problem, but the possibility that such duality will invite exploitation of the client. As such, each case should arouse concern and vigilance on the part of the ethical helper in order to ensure that exploitation does not occur. Gottlieb (1993) suggests that a practitioner assess the potential

EXERCISE **8.3**

The Ethics of Dual Relationships

Directions: Using the questions listed below, assess the perception of the professionals in your area in regards to the ethics of dual relationships. If possible contact a representative from each of the following professions and share your findings with a colleague or classmate. The professions include school counselor, marriage counselor, clinical social worker, licensed psychologis and psychiatrist.

Questions:

1. Have you ever had a professional helping relationship with a friend? A relative? A close professional associate?
2. What are you feelings about the ethics or ethical challenges confronting a professional helper when working with a friend, relative, or colleague?
3. Would you ever engage in a business venture or investment with an active client?
4. What are your feelings about professional helpers who engage in sexual intimacies with a client while still in a helping relationship with that client?
5. What would you do if you were aware that a professional helper, in your locale, was engaged in a sexual relationship with a client?
6. What length of time, if any, needs to pass between the end of a helping relationship and the freedom to date and become emotionally and physically intimate with a previous client?

benefits and problems of a dual relationship in light of (1) the power differential between the practitioner and the client; (2) the duration of the professional relationship; and (3) the clarity of termination in the therapy. With these as guidelines, any long-term therapeutic relationship would mitigate a dual relationship whereas a short-term, clearly articulated and terminated evaluation such as what might occur in a job interview process, may be acceptable (Coale, 1998).

St. Germaine (1993) suggests the following as guidelines for reducing the potential risk involved in dual relationships:

1. Set healthy boundaries from the outset of the relationship.
2. Fully inform clients about any potential risks
3. Discuss with clients any potentially problematic relationship and clarify areas of concern.
4. Consult with other professionals periodically if you are engaged in a dual relationship.
5. Work under supervision in cases where the potential for harm is high.
6. Document discussions about any dual relationships and relevant steps taken.
7. If necessary, refer the client to another professional.

TABLE 8.4   Factors to Consider When Making Decisions About Dual Relationships

Is it a legal or ethical issue?
Are there changes in the vulnerabilities of the client or another party?
What differences in power are there?
What are the risks for the practitioner?
What are the risks for the client?
What are the benefits for the practitioner?
What are the benefits for the client?
What is the impact on professional boundaries?
What is the potential effect on the goal(s) of the professional relationship?
Are alternative resources or solutions available?
What is your decision?

Adapted from Evans & Hearn's (1997) presentation of the work of Valentich & Gripton (1994). (Reprinted with permission.)

Another model for guiding a practitioner in terms of the ethics of dual relationships has been offered by Evans and Hearn (1997). These authors adapted the work originally presented by Valentich and Gripton (1992). Table 8.4 presents the series of questions offered by Evans and Hearn (1997) as a guide to decision making regarding the appropriateness of dual relationships. The table moves the practitioner through a variety of questions and considerations that should help him or her to decide on the appropriate nature of the relationship. Moving from the first question, "Is it a legal or ethical issue?" through consideration of power differential and the identification of the potential risk and benefits for both the client and practitioner, the practitioner is guided to make a decision about dual or multiple relationships. These authors further suggest that the practitioner actually complete the table and place the completed form in the client's file as evidence of the thinking that went into the decision.

Sexual Intimacy: A Clear Violation of Professional Boundaries

The depth of intimacy and the conditions surrounding the interaction found in a helping relationship may stimulate feelings of attraction between the helper and client. For helpers, acting on this attraction is a serious ethical violation. Sexual relationships of any kind are unethical in the helping setting/context. All professional organizations are very clear about prohibition of sexual intimacy between a helper and a client (see Table 8.5).

The inappropriateness of sexual relationship between helper and client rests in the fact that the helping relationship is unbalanced in power and dependency issues. Thus, the reciprocal nature characteristics of a healthy intimate relationship is not possible. When sexual contact becomes part of a therapeutic relationship, the expectation of trust that is fundamental to the process of therapy is violated (Thoreson, Shaughnessy, Heppner, & Cook, 1993).

TABLE 8.5 Intimate Relationships with Clients

Professional Ethical Standards	Statement on Intimate Relationships
American Counseling Association (1995)	A.7.a. Current clients. Counselors do not have any type of sexual intimacies with clients and do not counsel persons with whom they have had a sexual relationship.
American Psychological Association (1995)	1.19 Exploitative Relationships. (a) Psychologists do not exploit persons over whom they have supervisory, evaluative, or other authority such as students, supervises, employees, research participants, and clients or patients.(See also Standards 4.05-4.07 regarding sexual involvement with clients or patients.) (b) Psychologists do not engage in sexual relationships with students or supervises in training over whom the psychologist has evaluative or direct authority, because such relationships are so likely to impair judgment or be exploitative. 4.05 Sexual Intimacies With Current Patients or Clients. Psychologists do not engage in sexual intimacies with current patients or clients. 4.06 Therapy With Former Sexual Partners. Psychologists do not accept as therapy or clients, persons with whom they have engaged in sexual intimacies.
American Association of Marriage and Family Therapists (1998)	1.2: Sexual intimacy with clients is prohibited. Sexual intimacy with former clients for two years following the termination of therapy is prohibited.
National Association of Social Workers (1996)	1.09.a: Social workers should, under no circumstances, engage in sexual activities or sexual contact with current clients, whether such contact is consensual or forced.

In addition to barring intimate sexual contact within a helping context, most codes of behavior also speak to the restriction of sexual behavior between a helper and client after the helping relationship has ended. Some—for example, the APA (1992)—suggest that a period of two years pass before a personal relationship may be entered; other authors (e.g., Gutheil, 1989) suggest that the helping relationship never ends and therefore sexual intimacies are never appropriate.

Recent Legal Decisions

Arguments for the unethical nature of dual relationships usually highlight the fact that a helping relationship is one in which there is a power imbalance and one in which the client may be extremely vulnerable (DeLozier, 1994; *Norberg v. Wynrib*, 1992). The unethical nature of dual relationships reflects the courts' view that the helping relationships (i.e., physician–patient, psychiatrist–patient, and social worker–client) are of a fiduciary nature (Kutchins, 1991; *McInerney v. MacDonald*, 1992; Simon, 1992a), fiduciary meaning that the professional has a duty to act to the benefit of the other individual in any matters related to an undertaking between them (Black, 1991). Since a fiduciary relationship has been defined as occurring when an individual places his or her trust in a party who has the potential to influence his or her actions (Black, 1991), it could be reasonably argued that all professional helping relationships have this fiduciary potential. The courts, however, have not made de facto rulings to the fiduciary nature of each professional relationship. Rather, rulings have suggested that it is the specific nature of each relationship that determines the existence of a fiduciary responsibility (*Hodgkinson v. Simms*, 1994; *M.(K.) v. M. (H.)*, 1992; *McInerney v. MacDonald*, 1992).

If the fiduciary obligation exists, it could be argued that the practitioner is obliged

1. To act with good faith and loyalty toward a client (*McInerney v. MacDonald*, 1992)
2. To not abuse the power imbalance by exploiting the client (*Norberg v. Wynrib*, 1992);
3. Act in the best interest of the client (*Hodgkinson v. Simms*, 1994; *M.(K.) v. M.(H.).,* 1992)

Given the conditions of a fiduciary relationship, it is clear that any sexual contact between a helper and a client is in violation of these conditions. In fact, some states (e.g., Minnesota, California) have enacted statutes that make the therapist–client sexual relations a criminal offense. Further, in these states, the power differential and possible vulnerability of the client to influence makes consent by the client viewed as no defense.

Beyond Professional Standards: A Personal Moral Response

Sexual misconducts, while being one of the most serious ethical violations (Smith & Fitzpatrick, 1995), continue to occur (Olarte, 1997). Thus, while ethical standards are in place that address professional boundaries and ethical use of power, enactment of these standards within the client–helper relationship is less than perfect.

It is clear that more than simply having an awareness of the ethical codes of conduct is needed. Practitioners need to embrace this standard as a personal moral response. As with each of the ethical principles, respect and valuing of the client and client well-being serves as the preventive base for most ethical abuses. Keeping client needs as primary in the relationship can prove invaluable for maintaining appropriate boundaries and use of power within the helping relationship.

In addition to understanding codes of ethics governing the creation and maintenance of professional boundaries, the ethical practitioner needs to continually appraise his or her own personal needs and to monitor how these may impact the nature of their helping relationships. For example, in addressing sexual misconduct, Stake and Oliver (1991) recommended a multifaceted approach highlighting the importance of sensitizing and training therapists to their own sexuality and the power of the helping relationship. Others (e.g., Gutheil, 1989; Holub & Lee, 1990) emphasize the importance of training, not just in the ethical-legal issues surrounding sexual involvement, but also engagement in activities (including personal therapy) aimed at promoting helpers' self-awareness of their own sexuality, sexual needs, and values.

The need to be aware of self and relationships is essential in order to create and maintain appropriate professional boundaries. Ethical practitioners will be aware of their decisions to depart from what is typical and be able to explain the therapeutic reasons for such departures. The question that needs to be answered, especially at times of departure from typical or model procedures is "Whose need is being served?"

It is this type of self-questioning, if assimilated into the practitioner's approach to all clients, that will help move issues of boundaries and power from ethical guidelines to a personal, moral response.

Case Illustration

At the beginning of the chapter we see Ms. Wicks expressing her concern for Maria. The question one needs to ask is "Is this level of concern and type of behavior well within the boundaries of a professional counseling relationship?"

As you read the continuation of the dialogue continually, ask yourself, "Whose needs are being met?" Further, after reading the presentation, use the reflections to begin to conceptualize how you would respond in a situation such as this.

MS. WICKS: But Maria—I do care about you. I am worried you are placing yourself in harm's way. If it would be easier for you—I would be willing to let you stay with me for a while.

MARIA: Stay with you?

MS. WICKS: Well, I mean sometimes it is easier to get away from a guy like Carlos, when you can get out of the area.

MARIA: I don't need to get away from Carlos, I love him.

MS. WICKS: Sometimes, Maria, we romanticize our relationships and we feel like it is love. It is just our way of justifying having sex with somebody. I know . . . I almost ruined my life by quitting school and running away with a high school sweetheart just because I lost my virginity to him. It's real easy to think you love someone when it is only lust.

MARIA: Well—I'm not sure what you are talking about. I love Carlos and he loves me. I don't need to run away from him.

MS. WICKS: I know it seems like love, but trust me, Maria, if you could step back and get away for just a little while, you would see it differently.

MARIA: Ms. Wicks . . . I like you, but . . . you are wrong here. Anyway . . . how did we get talking about this? I thought we were talking about you telling Mrs. Armstrong about me having sex or something?

Reflections
1. What is your feeling about Ms. Wicks' invitation to come and live with her for a while? Why?
2. Do you feel it is appropriate for Ms. Wicks to share her own high school story of romance? Why? Why not?
3. Is Ms. Wicks exhibiting the effects of simple identification or simply demonstrating her real personal understanding of Maria's situation?

Cooperative Learning Exercise

As suggested within this chapter, while the need to create and maintain professional boundaries is essential to an ethical helping relationship, boundary violations do occur. Often boundaries are crossed and inappropriate helper behavior is manifested as a result of the helper's loss of emotional objectivity.

Part 1: Review each of the following scenarios and along with a classmate or colleague, identify where the loss of emotional objectivity may exist and how boundary violations may be manifested.

> Helper 1: A marriage counselor currently going through her own, very painful divorce
>
> Helper 2: A young attractive school counselor working with senior high school honors students
>
> Helper 3: A drug and alcohol counselor who himself has been an addict and who has recently returned to drinking

Part II: Interview three professional helpers, inquiring:

1. During your professional career have you experienced any major life crises (e.g., death of a loved one, loss of a job, divorce?)
2. (For those who have experienced such life crises) During that time what adjustments to your professional work did you make, if any?
3. (For those who have not experienced such a crises) If you had experienced one of these life crises, would you adjust your approach to your professional work during the time of the crisis. If so, how and why? If not, why not?

Share your findings with a colleague and discuss the implications of the responses in light of the content of this chapter.

Summary

Setting and Maintaining Professional Boundaries
All professional codes of ethics attend to the issue of boundaries and the need to assure non-exploitation of the client through boundary crossing and the mixing of multiple relationships.

All boundary crossings (i.e., departure from commonly accepted professional roles and practices) can become problematic and need to be avoided. Any boundary violation in which the practitioner's needs are given primacy at the client's expense is unethical.

Professional Objectivity: Essential to Professional Boundaries

The effective, ethical helper places the concerns and needs of the client as top priority. Placing the client's concerns as a priority (i.e., altruism) rather than the concerns of the helper (i.e., narcissism) requires the helper to distinguish his or her personal issues and emotional needs from those presented by the client.

Professional objectivity can be compromised by a number of situations. While some, such as simple identification and transferences, reflect a distortion of reality on the part of the helper, a more common form stems from the development of a dual relationship with the client, involving both a professional and personal tone.

Dual Relationships: Crossing and/or Mixing Boundaries

A dual relationship is one in which the helper has two (or more) overlapping roles with the client. While all professional codes of conduct warn about the risk of dual relationships, not all within the profession are as clear-cut about the evils of dual relationships or about the sanctions that should be applied.

It is not the existence of duality that is the problem, but the possibility that such duality will invite exploitation of the client. As such, each case should arouse concern and vigilance on the part of the ethical helper in order to ensure that exploitation does not occur.

Sexual Intimacy: A Clear Violation of Professional Boundaries

Sexual relationships of any kind are unethical in the helping setting/context. All professional organizations are very clear about prohibition of sexual intimacy between a helper and a client.

The inappropriateness of a sexual relationship between helper and client rests in the fact that the helping relationship is unbalanced in power and dependency issues. As such, the reciprocal nature of a healthy intimate relationship is not possible. When sexual contact becomes part of a therapeutic relationship, the expectation of trust that is fundamental to the process of therapy is violated.

Recent Legal Decisions

The unethical nature of dual relationships reflects the courts' view that the helping relationships (i.e., physician–patient, psychiatrist–patient, and social worker–client) is of a fiduciary nature (Kutchins, 1991; *McInerney v. MacDonald*, 1992; Simon, 1992a), fiduciary meaning that the professional has a duty to act to the benefit of the other individual in any matters related to an undertaking between them.

If the fiduciary obligation exists, it could be argued that the practitioner is obliged

1. To act with good faith and loyalty toward a client (*McInerney v. MacDonald*, 1992)
2. To not abuse the power imbalance by exploiting the client (*Norberg v. Wynrib*, 1992)
3. Act in the best interest of the client (*Hodgkinson v. Simms*, 1994; *M.(K.) v. M.(H.)*, 1992)

The courts, however, have not made de facto rulings to the fiduciary nature of each professional relationship. Rather, rulings have suggested that it is the specific nature of each relationship that determines the existence of a fiduciary responsibility (*Hodgkinson v. Simms*, 1994; *M.(K.) v.M. (H.),* 1992; *McInerney v. MacDonald*, 1992).

Beyond Professional Standards: A Personal Moral Response

Keeping client needs as primary in the relationship can prove invaluable for maintaining appropriate boundaries and use of power within the helping relationship.

The need to be aware of self and relationships is essential in order to create and maintain appropriate professional boundaries. Ethical practitioners will be aware of their decisions to depart from what is typical and be able to explain the therapeutic reasons for such departure. The question that needs to be answered, especially at times of departure from typical or model procedures is "Whose need is being served?"

IMPORTANT TERMS

altruism	multiple relationships
boundaries	narcissism
boundary crossing	professional objectivity
boundary violations	professional relationship
dual relationships	sexual intimacy
exploitation	simple identification
fiduciary obligation	transference
fiduciary relationship	

SUGGESTED READINGS

Coale, H.W. (1998). *The vulnerable therapist.* New York: The Haworth Press.

Kottler, J.A., Sexton, T.L., & Whiston, S.C. (1994). *The heart of healing: Relationships in therapy.* San Francisco: Jossey Bass.

Noel, B.W., & Watterson, K. (1992). *You must be dreaming.* New York: Poseidon.

Pope, K.S., Sonne, J.L., & Holroyd, J. (1993). *Sexual feelings in psychotherapy.* Washington, DC: American Psychological Association.

PART FOUR

The Process of Helping

9 Efficacy of Treatment

Michelle: Hi, Lynn. Do you have a minute?

Lynn: Sure, Michelle. What's up?

Michelle: I've been working with this girl, Maria, and we have a real good working relationship, but I just don't feel like I have a true grasp of what is going on or that I am approaching this situation the best way. I explained this to Maria, and she has given me written permission to speak with you about the case. I know you are really busy, but I was hoping that you could provide some supervision around this case to see if you feel like I'm on the right track and using the best approach.

While our counselor, Ms. Wicks (Michelle), is certainly skilled and trained professionally, her real interest and concern for her client and her own self-awareness of the limits of her expertise have led her to seek consultation from a colleague. Approaching helping with the essential training and experience is an ethical must. However, beyond this initial training, ongoing professional development, consultation, and supervision are the hallmarks of the ethical professional.

The ethical responsibility to be competent extends beyond the basic credentialing of a helper and includes the helper's ability to employ treatment strategies that are efficacious. It is these issues of treatment efficacy and helper competency that serve as the focus for the current chapter.

Chapter Objectives

The chapter will review the ethics and legality surrounding the issue of competent practice and efficacy of treatment. The value of professional training, action research and referral as elements of competent practice will be highlighted.

After reading this chapter you should be able to understand the following:

1. Describe what is meant by the term competence
2. Discuss the role of continuing education, ongoing supervision, and consultation in the ongoing development of professional competence
3. Describe the value of approaching practice from a reflective, action research orientation
4. Discuss the conditions under which referral would appear to be the most efficacious treatment decision

5. Describe legal considerations and concerns in relation to the issue of helper competence, standard of care, and treatment efficacy

Practicing Within the Realm of Competence

The ethical professional is called upon to accept responsibilities and employment on the basis of competence and professional qualification. Table 9.1 provides the position taken by a select group of professional associations on the issue of professional practice and competency. What should be evident by reviewing Table 9.1 is that each of these organizations supports the notion that one should not engage in practices that require skills beyond those possessed. To be ethical, as a helper, requires that competency be developed and maintained and that the helper's competence level be represented accurately to clients, employers, and the general public.

Competence

Being competent means that the helper has the knowledge, skills, and abilities needed to perform those tasks relevant to that profession. To suggest one is competent implies that the individual is capable of performing a minimum quality of service that is within the limits of his or her training, experience, and practice, as defined in professional standards or regulatory statues.

Competence is defined in relative terms; that is, rather than having one clear, objective standard against which to judge a professional's level of performance as competent or incompetent, competence is most often defined using the conduct of others within the profession as the comparative standard. Often the "reasonable man" standard is applied to evaluate the competence of the professional's behavior. This reasonable man rule simply asks the question, "What would a reasonable person do in a similar situation'"

Professional Development: Knowing the State of the Profession

Competence can be developed from formal training as might be found in graduate training or training for certification and licensure. Further, one's own ongoing continuing education, professional reflective practice, and supervision may serve as additional resources for developing and maintaining competence.

Formal Training

Formal training occurs both at the undergraduate and graduate levels of study. Foundations of general knowledge of helping theory and skills along with research supporting intervention strategies may be acquired through undergraduate and graduate course work. However, in addition to these cognates, the competent practitioner must have guided practice in the application of this knowledge. In many disciplines (e.g., psychology) the doctorate along

TABLE 9.1 Ethical Codes Addressing Helper Competence

Professional Organization	Ethical Principle/Standards
American Counseling Association (1995)	C.2.a: Boundaries of Competence. Counselors practice only within the boundaries of their competence based on their education, training, supervised experience, state and national professional credentials, and appropriate professional experience. Counselors will demonstrate a commitment to gain knowledge, personal awareness, sensitivity and skills pertinent to working with a diverse client population.
American Psychological Association (1995)	Principle A: Competence Psychologists strive to maintain high standards of competence in their work. They recognize the boundaries of their particular competencies and the limitations of their expertise. They provide only those services and use only those techniques for which they are qualified by education, training, or experience. Psychologists are cognizant of the fact that the competencies required in serving, teaching, and/or studying groups of people vary with the distinctive characteristics of those groups. In those areas in which recognized professional standards do not yet exist, psychologists exercise careful judgment and take appropriate precautions to protect the welfare of those with whom they work.
American Association of Marriage and Family Therapists (1998)	3.6: Family therapists do not diagnose, treat, or advise on problems outside the recognized boundaries of their competence.
National Association of Social Workers (1996)	O-1: Social workers should base their practice "upon recognized knowledge relevant to social work" and they should "critically examine, and keep current with, emerging knowledge relevant to social work" (NASW O-1). Ethical Principle: Social workers continually strive to increase their professional knowledge and skills and to apply them in practice. Social workers should aspire to contribute to the knowledge base of the profession. 1.04 Competence (a) Social workers should provide services and represent themselves as competent only within the boundaries of their education, training, license, certification, consultation received, supervised experience, or other relevant professional experience. (b) Social workers should provide services in substantive areas or use intervention techniques or approaches that are new to them only after engaging in appropriate study, training, consultation, and supervision from people who are competent in those interventions or techniques.

with supervised field and intern experiences are considered essential to competent independent practice.

For most of the helping professions, professional organizations and/or certifying and licensing bodies have identified both aspirational levels and mandatory levels of training as a way of defining competence. Each of these levels of governance monitor the development and application of professional practice. Colleges and universities often offer programs of training that have been shaped by the professional standards under the review of professional accrediting organizations. Professional accrediting bodies (e.g., American Psychological Association, Council for the Accreditation of Counseling and Related Educational Programs (CACREP)) qualify educational programs as meeting standards beyond those demanded for colleges or universities to offer degrees and certify that these programs meet high professional standards, thus establishing the foundation for ethical practice. Beyond these school-based programs, professional organizations (e.g., American School Counseling Association, American Rehabilitation Counseling Association, Academy of Certified Social Workers) often develop aspirational codes of ethics, which while not having any internal mandatory enforcement mechanism, call their members to perform at the highest level of professional practice.

Beyond the professional organization level, the professional regulatory bodies at the state and national level promulgate and enforce standards of practice through the establishment of certification and licensure standards. Often these requirements exceed those demanded for entrance into the profession, requiring additional post degree experience and supervision. The definition of minimum professional training for entry level helpers as well as the mandate to remain up-to-date on the state of the profession through continuing education varies from state to state. It is essential for the ethical helper to be knowledgeable about the these standards (see Exercise 9.1).

Being an ethical, competent practitioner requires not only a basic level of initial training, but also the maintenance and development of this knowledge and these skills via continuous professional growth. The ethical helper continually strives for increased com-

---

EXERCISE 9.1
Licensing and Certification Requirements

Directions: Since the requirements defining minimum requirements for competent practice vary from profession to profession and in many instances from state to state, it is helpful for you to be aware of the specific requirements for entrance into your particular field of practice.

Step 1: Identify two arenas for professional practice (e.g., school counselor, psychologist, marriage counselor, clinical social worker, etc.).

Step 2: Identify two states, one in which you intend to practice and a neighboring state.

Step 3: Contact each state's department or bureau of professional license and practice. Often these can be found by simply calling the main number of your state capital.

Step 4: Complete the following grid.

	Profession—Area of Practice		Profession—Area of Practice	
State	*Home State*	*Neighboring State*	*Home State*	*Neighboring State*
Minimum Education (Bachelor's, Master's, Master's+, Doctorate)				
Supervised Experience (internship, practice, etc.)				
Post Degree Requirements (course work, field experience etc.)				
Other requirements				

petence. The ethical helper strives to increase his or her competence by continuing to develop his or her skills and understanding of the helping process.

Continuing Education

All the codes of conduct call for practitioners to be current with emerging knowledge relevant to their profession (see Table 9.2). It is incumbent upon the ethical practitioner to upgrade knowledge and skill by participating in continuing education experiences. Continuing education may be in the form of additional course work at the local university or courses taught through qualified associations and organizations.

While the call for ongoing education and professional development is clear, the specifics are still lacking. Does this suggest a certain number of courses? Credits? Hours of supervision? Many organizations and state licensing and certifying bodies require that a number of continuing education hours be completed within a number of years. For example, the American Association for Marriage and Family Therapists (AAMFT) encourages members to complete 150 hours of continuing education every three years, and the State

TABLE 9.2   **Maintaining Professional Development**

Professional Ethical Standards	Statement on Professional Development
American Association for Marriage and Family Therapy (1998)	3.4: Family therapists remain "abreast of new developments"
American Counseling Association (1995)	C.2.f.: Counselors recognize the need for continuing education to maintain a reasonable level of awareness of current scientific and professional information in their fields of activity. They take steps to maintain competence in the skills they use, are open to new procedures, and keep current with the diverse and/or special populations with whom they work.
American Psychological Association (1995)	General Principle A (Competence) that psychologists "maintain knowledge of relevant scientific and professional information related to the services they render and they recognize the need for ongoing education."
National Association of Social Workers (1996)	4.01.b: Social workers, should strive to become and remain proficient in professional practice and the performance of professional functions. Social workers should critically examine, and keep current with, emerging knowledge relevant to social work. Social workers should routinely review professional literature and participate in continuing education relevant to social work practice and social work ethics.

Board of Licensing for Psychologists in Pennsylvania requires psychologists to complete 30 hours of approved continuing education every two years in order to maintain and/or renew their licenses. However, the specific requirements vary across professions (e.g., marriage counselor, school psychologists, clinical social worker) and from state to state. It is important for each practitioner to be aware of the standards set by his or her own professional organization or those required for relicensing or recertification within the state where they intend to practice.

Supervision and Consultation

Practicing within the realm of competence starts with a practitioner operating within the scope of practice. Practitioners are ethically bound to restrict their professional activities to the profession and specialties for which they have been trained and supervised. When required, they must possess the appropriate certification and licensure. Practicing within the realm of competence also means knowing when it is essential to consult and/or refer to another professional who has more experience and training with this particular type of client and or problem.

The use of peer consultation, in which specific concerns can be shared with an experienced colleague, is a valuable means for maintaining competence. For example, Pope, Tabachnick, and Keith-Spiegel reported in 1987 that psychologists rated informal exchanges among colleagues as the most effective resource for promoting effective and ethical practice.

Peer consultation can provide mutual support for problematic cases. However, when consulting with colleagues regarding a client, the ethical practitioner needs to balance the need for his or her own continued support with the client's right to maintain confidentiality. The American Psychological Association's ethical standards, for example, state:

> When consulting with colleagues, (1) psychologists do not share confidential information that reasonably could lead to the identification of a patient or client with whom they have a confidential relationship unless they have obtained the prior consent of the person or organization or the disclosure cannot be avoided, and (2) they share information only to the extent necessary to achieve the purposes of consultation. (1992, 5.06)

Even with this sensitivity to the requirements of confidentiality, the ethical helper can employ a peer consult to formulate the problem, review the decisions made, and tap a different point of view on the process. Often a colleague with more experience can provide some clarity about the helping process and may even assist the practitioner to develop additional insights or adjustments in the treatment process.

Consulting with a professional peer not only provides the helper a valuable resource for expanding his or her knowledge and skill, but can also serve as a valuable check and balance for the helper when the boundaries of competence may be exceeded. This is especially true when the helper's own objectivity may be blurred (see Chapter 8). Under these conditions the peer consultation can provide a mechanism for examining the ethical and professional issues involved in any one particular case (Lewis, Greenburg, & Hatch, 1988).

For those working within certain clinical settings, formal peer review may be incorporated as a way of maintaining professional competence and standards of care. For those serving in an independent practice, it would be valuable to develop a network of colleagues who can continue to serve as peer consultants.

The Standard of Care: Appropriate Treatment

Most malpractice cases turn on the question of negligence (Bennett et al., 1990). Negligence implies that the practitioner failed to meet the relevant standard of care. According to Bennett and colleagues (1990), the question of negligence will be determined by the debate over the clinical correctness and efficacy of the treatment that was given, along with the practitioner's judgment in choosing it (p. 33).

While there is no single prescribed way to conduct "helping," ethical guidelines establish some standards of care that must be followed. For example, sexual intimacies with clients are prohibited. Further, innovative therapy involving physical contact with clients can be the basis for malpractice suites, particularly when the contact is extreme (e.g., hitting, choking). While these are extreme examples that most mental health providers will not encounter, failure to properly administer and interpret tests and inventories, failure to warn to take appropriate steps in the face of homicide and suicide, and failure to employ appropriate methods and forms of treatment may be areas in which helpers are more likely to fall short of recognized standards of care, failing to provide appropriate treatment.

Defining an Appropriate Treatment

Standards of practice have not specifically been identified. There are no preordained directives for what must be done under each condition of helping. The standard of care and the definition of appropriate treatment are typically determined by comparing the practitioner's performance with that of other professionals in the same community with comparable training and experience.

There is an evolving sense of what should prevail, and it is the standard of what a reasonable and prudent practitioner may do in situations like this that sets the standard of care (see Exercise 9.2)

EXERCISE 9.2
Standard of Care: A Reasonable, Prudent Response

Directions: Below you will find two clinical scenarios. Read each situation and contact a mental health provider in your local community and ask him or her what they would do in this situation.

Situation 1: You are treating an individual diagnosed with AIDS. This individual has informed you that he is in and has been in a long-term relationship. The client also has informed you of the name of his partner, with whom he lives. In your most recent session your client informs you that not only is he engaging in unprotective sex with his lover but that he has not informed his lover that he has AIDS. What do you do? Do you inform the lover?

Situation 2: You have been seeing a couple for marriage counseling. You receive a subpoena for your records on the case from one partner's lawyer. What do you do? Do you respond to the subpoena? How?

Reflections:
1. Did the two practitioners essentially agree on the steps to be taken?
2. Did their responses seem to be in line with what you have read about confidentiality, duty to warn, informed consent, etc.?
3. Share your findings with a classmate/colleague who may have performed the same exercise. Does these seem to be consistency in practitioner response that could be used as a definition of standard of care?

Share your findings with your classmates or colleagues.

Employing Effective Treatments

But beyond a generic standard of what a reasonable and prudent practitioner may do, attention has been drawn to the importance of employing tried and true techniques and strategies of intervention. A number of professionals have called for use of effective treatments as have consumer groups. Klerman (1990), for example, noted: "The psychiatrist has a responsibility to use effective treatment. The patient has a right to the proper treatment. Proper treatment involves those treatments for which there is substantial evidence" (p. 417). Further, the International Association for the Right to Effective Treatment (1996), an educational and advocacy group, was established to ensure that all clients " benefit from the progressive, effective interventions available" (p. 3). Finally, a number of states have introduced bills that would require each psychological treatment procedure to meet legal standards of scientific validity before it can be offered to a client (Cavaliere, 1995). Thus, the ethical helper needs to be aware of the current research on treatment effectiveness and employ these strategies when and where appropriate.

Defining Efficacious

Providing the most effective treatment available requires professionals to keep current on the research on treatment effectiveness for their particular client population (Tutty, 1990). In line with this need to identify and employ effective treatment strategies, the Task Force on Promotion and Dissemination of Psychological Procedures (1995) from the division of clinical psychology within the American Psychological Association, has developed criteria for determining whether a treatment should be considered empirically valid. The task force also established a list of interventions that have been "well established" and a list that are "probably efficacious," citing the literature that supports this claim. Others have enumerated interventions that possess substantial amounts of empirical evidence and support for its efficacy (e.g., Ammerman, Last, & Hersen, 1993; Fischer, 1993; Gorey, 1996; MacDonald, Sheldon, & Gillespie, 1992; Thyer, 1996). These include interpersonal therapy for depression, exposure treatment of agoraphobia and social phobia, stress inoculation training for stress reduction, behavior therapy for female orgasmic dysfunction and male erectile dysfunction, to name a few (Chambless, Sanderson, Shoham, Johnson, Pope, et al., 1996).

As the professions and the research identify specific strategies with demonstrated effectiveness, these interventions become the standard of care. As such, it is essential for the ethical practitioner to not only be aware of this research and these techniques, but to develop the competency required for the ethical application of these strategies. In support of this, the Task Force on Psychological Interventions developed, in addition to its list of effective interventions, references for training manuals that describe the treatment in detail and additional training resources when they were available (see Sanderson & Woody, 1995, pp. 8–11). This task force will update this list annually.

Managed Care: Compounding the Standard of Care Issue

The issue of treatment efficacy is of special consideration when a practitioner is operating with a managed care situation. With managed care pushing for brief, more cost-effective forms of treatment, the ethical practitioner must be able to identify for whom these services are appropriate and which form of service is required. Discerning for whom brief therapy is appropriate and advocating for those clients for whom such an approach may not be appropriate becomes an essential role of the ethical, competent practitioner operating within a managed care environment. Further, competence to perform short-term models of treatment, when appropriate, requires that the practitioner be prepared and able to focus on achievable, specific treatment goals and to be active and more directive in conducting the treatment. Short-term models are not simply long-term therapy models condensed in time. Utilization of these short-term models requires the ethical practitioner to possess unique understanding and skills. Thus, the ethical practitioner will not only know for whom such treatment is appropriate but will also have been trained in this approach.

Employing an Action Research Approach to Practice

In areas for which there is not solid research to direct best practice or in which the standard of the profession is not clearly articulated (e.g., when individual counseling is preferred to groups), service needs to be predicated on theoretical and technical ideas that are held by a substantial portion of the profession (Woody, 1997). Thus, knowing the recognized models, theories, and schools of thought is as essential as having the ability to assess the validity and reliability of a particular strategy for one's own practice. In speaking of psychology, for example, Chambless and colleagues (1996) noted: "Psychology is a science. Seeking to help those in need, clinical psychology draws its strength and uniqueness from the ethic of scientific validation. Whatever interventions that mysticism, authority, commercialism, politics, custom, convenience, or carelessness might dictate, clinical psychologists focus on what works. They bear a fundamental ethical responsibility to use, where possible, interventions that work *and to subject any intervention they use to scientific scrutiny (p. 10, emphasis added)*. This last point suggests subjecting any intervention . . . to scientific scrutiny is a directive to all ethical practitioners and not just those interested in performing large empirical research. The ethical helper will approach his or her practice as a reflective professional, integrating research and practice.

In order to be effective in their practice, human service providers must blend the method and findings of research with the realities of their professional practice. As practitioner–researchers, they will need not only to interact in the moment but also to reflect, inquire, and critique their own interactions. Further, for their observations to provide meaningful data and useful guidance, they must be systematic and valid. *Action research methodology* provides practitioners with the means of acquiring these valid, useful data and results in the development of effective strategies of professional practice.

Action Research Defined

Action research has been broadly defined (e.g., Peters & Robinson, 1984; Shani, 1990). As described by Banister, Burman, Parker, Taylor, and Tindall (1994), action research is simply "a way of trying out changes and seeing what happens (p. 108). As presented here, action research is applied research in which the researcher–investigator is also the practitioner (e.g., a counselor, teacher, social worker) attempting to use research as a methodology for identifying the "what" they do and for making decisions on doing it better. Action research provides practitioners with the method for viewing their professional decisions systematically and deciding on them rationally. It is the opportunity to blend theory with practice, becoming true practitioners–researchers.

Action Research: An Ethical Consideration

Viewed as a frame of mind, action research calls us to a continued interest in serving our constituencies better and providing increased accountability for our service. As such, action research is not simply a good idea, rather it becomes an ethical responsibility for monitoring the effectiveness of our practice and increasing the competency of our service. No one professional can guarantee success in each and every encounter or situation. However, ethical practitioners need to assess the degree to which their practices are both valid and effective. Action research provides a mechanism for monitoring the efficacy and adequacy of practice decisions and methods.

Table 9.3 provides a brief review of one model of action research that has application to the mental health professional. While presented as a linear set of steps to be taken, in practice it is a recurring, recycling process that continually takes and gives shape both in and to practice.

TABLE 9.3   Steps in the Action Research Process

Step	Description
1. Identification of the research question	Three types of questions seem to emerge. First, what are our practice decisions? Second, what specifically about our practice is effective? And finally, what can we do to enhance our effectiveness as practitioners?
2. Problem relevance, problem significance	The goal is to be able to answer questions such as "Why study it?" "What do I expect will happen as a result of this investigation?" "How is the problem and the study significant to my practice?"
3. Definitions	The practitioner–action researcher needs to begin to more concretely identify and define the concepts, the constructs, the variables involved. When and where possible the action research needs to define these by their actions or operations performed (i.e. operational definitions).
4. Review of related literature	Reviewing the professional literature for evidence of similar investigation may prove a valuable step to intervention planning.
5. Developing hypotheses	With action research, it should be remembered that these are truly "working hypotheses." As data is collected and decisions are made, the hypotheses may be reshaped. In fact true, to the qualitative nature of the action research, new hypotheses can emerge from the data as the study progresses.

(Continues)

TABLE 9.3   *(Continued)*

Step	Description
6. Outcome measures	If the action researcher seeks to increase his or her understanding of the operations of his or her professional practice or the impact of specific practice decisions, then measurement of those decisions and their impacts needs to take place. One should employ outcome assessment that measures change from multiple perspectives (i.e., the subject/client, the practitioner–researcher, and others) and through multiple approaches.
7. Methods: Creating a design	As with any study, for our conclusions to be valid we must consider the use of an approach or a design that provides validity of data collection and interpretation.
8. Data collection	The types of data collected and the method of collection will clearly be situation-researcher-and problem specific. But the information gathered needs to be as detailed and as informative as possible so that as an action researcher, you will know what is happening in ways that you previously did not know. The action researcher needs to remember that he or she is a practitioner as well as a researcher and that he or she has a professional responsibility for those involved. There are ethical considerations, especially those regarding informed consent, that need to be considered.
9. Data analysis	At a minimum the data needs to be organized and grouped with themes, with trends and characteristics noted. When appropriate, visual presentation and descriptive and inferential statistics should also be employed.
10. Interpretation	In reviewing the data, the action researcher needs to balance research significance with practical relevance. Having answered the question what happens if . . . , the researcher now needs to answer questions such as: What does knowing what happens if mean for my clients, my students, and whom I service? To me? To my professional decision making? To my current practice decisions?

The Use of Referral

The ethical helper provides only those services for which he or she is trained, experienced, and credentialed (e.g., certified or licensed). Competence refers not only to the degree to which the professional possesses the knowledge, skills, and abilities required to perform the various tasks and procedures relevant to that profession, but also to the ability to discern when it is appropriate to provide the services and when it is desirable to refer.

In the private confines of a helper's office, however, where a practitioner is free from direct supervision or teacher scrutiny, it may be all too easy to be seduced into engaging in problem solving in areas for which one is ill prepared. Consider the following case of Mrs. Robinson (see Case Illustration 9.1).

Even if we assume the best intent on the part of Dr. Hansen, the truth of the matter is that he lacks the training and appropriate experience to work with Mrs. Robinson's clinical depression. Further, his lack of experience and training is more evidenced by his willingness to serve both in the role of Mrs. Robinson's therapist and marital counselor.

CASE ILLUSTRATION **9.1**
Moving from Individual to Couple Counseling

Dr. Hansen received a call from Mrs. Alice Robinson who described herself as "a little down" and unclear about the direction she wanted to go with her career. Dr. Hansen, a certified vocational counselor, scheduled to meet with Mrs. Robinson to begin the process of vocational/career assessment.

Following the initial intake, Dr. Hansen concluded that Mrs. Robinson, while interested in vocational and career counseling, was doing this in reaction to what she "perceived to be a failing marriage." Dr. Hansen saw Mrs. Robinson three more times with the intent of more clearly identifying Mrs. Robinson's goals for counseling. Through these three sessions Dr. Hansen came to realize that Mrs. Robinson was seriously depressed. She revealed a long-standing history of depression and self-medicating alcohol consumption. She also described considering committing suicide on more than three occasions in the past month. Further, Mrs. Robinson noted that she is unable to eat, has lost approximately 20 pounds in a one-month period, and is having difficulty sleeping. The root of this depression, according to Mrs. Robinson, is the fact that "she cannot communicate" with her husband, and she knows unless something is done they will get a divorce. And according to Mrs. Robinson, she simply "would not, could not live without him!"

Mrs. Robinson described how long she has been wanting to seek counseling for herself (her depression) and for she and her husband. But, according to Mrs. Robinson, she just didn't feel comfortable seeking help since there are so many "wacko doctors" out there. Mrs. Robinson expressed her comfort and trust with Dr. Hansen and asked if he would help her and her marriage.

Dr. Hansen, while being trained and supervised in career/vocational counseling, agreed to work both individually with Mrs. Robinson in order to assist her with her depression and also to set up an arrangement to see her and her husband as a couple to start "communications training."

If one were to assume that Dr. Hansen was qualified to work with a depressed client, it might be easy to believe the transition from working with the distraught Mrs. Robinson to couple-marriage counseling was a logical extension of the helping contract. The reality is that marriage and family counseling is grounded in its one unique theoretical framework, which is distinct from that of individual counseling (Cottone, 1992). Simply assuming expertise and competence with a couple, even when competent working with individuals invites unethical behavior and a failure to provide appropriate standard of care. Thus, Dr. Hansen needs to reflect not only on his own training (formal and informal) and supervised experience working with clinically depressed individuals, but also on the extent of his preparation in systemic-relational treatment before proceeding to treat if the couple. This would be essential for ethical, competent practice.

Helpers, regardless of their knowledge and skill, cannot provide every service needed by every client. Ethically, therefore, a helper needs to know not just the when and how of applying helping skills, but also when the situation is beyond his or her capabilities or when the boundaries of his or her competence have been exceeded.

Knowing When to Refer

Knowing when to refer is not always easy. At a minimum, the ethical helper will refer anytime it is determined that she or he is unable to provide the professional, competent services required. The ethical, competent helper needs to be aware of his or her areas of expertise, the kinds of support and supervision available, and an accurate sense of his or her own time, energy, and availability to take on a particular case. When any of these areas are in question, referral should be considered.

If Dr. Hansen (see Case Illustration 9.1) reflected on his own decision making, he might have concluded that a trained, experienced marriage relational counselor might more competently provide the services that Mrs. Robinson and her husband currently need. As such, he would have made a referral rather than attempting to provide those services himself.

Each practitioner can provide competent service, but no one practitioner can be a master of all the knowledge and skills required to competently address the myriad of situations and clients presented. As each profession develops its knowledge base and refines the skills required, it will become increasingly incumbent on the practitioner to recognize the limits of his or her own competency and the richness of resources available through the use of referral.

Knowing Where to Refer

In making a competent referral the practitioner needs to understand the nature of the specific support and services requested. As such, the ethical, competent helper will have a cadre of available referral sources whose character and capacities are known (Bennett et al., 1990). Building a referral system branching through the surrounding geographic area is essential. This referral network should include a variety of professional and indigenous helpers including psychologists, psychiatrists, social workers, ministers, physicians, clinics, social service agencies, hospitals, and so on.

Being fully versed on the resources available not only enables the ethical helper to select the service(s) that most effectively meet the client's needs, but also allows the helper to explain the reason and the process of referral to the client. Being familiar with the services available allows the helper the opportunity to highlight the unique qualifications of the person or program to whom the client is being referred, along with other information needed to make for a smooth and comfortable referral and transition for the client.

While a listing of various human services agencies and providers may be obtained by contacting the local county government or mental health/mental retardation agencies listed in your phone book, more personalized knowledge is required for adequate referral. Exercise 9.3 is offered as a guide for developing this personalized, referral network.

Making the Referral

Recognizing the need or value of referral is only the first step. In addition to recognizing the need and having available resources to whom to refer, the competent helper will also have

---

EXERCISE **9.3**
Developing a Referral Network

Directions: You can begin developing a referral network by contacting local agencies and human service providers by phone or by letter and gathering the following information:

Name:_____

Address: _____

Phone:_____

1. What is the purpose or mission of your professional service or practice?
2. What type of people (age, gender, socioeconomic position, ethnicity, etc.) are best served by your service?
3. What type of difficulty, problem or concern is most often addressed by you/your service?
4. What resources are available (e.g., 24-hour hotlines, medical facilities, educational materials, housing, job placement, etc.?)
5. What is the procedure or process for gaining access, making an appointment, or seeking assistance?
6. What is the general therapeutic theory or model employed?
7. What is (are) the training levels of the helpers who provide these services?
8. Are there fees? How much? Payment plans? Sliding scales? Insurance? etc.
9. Who is the contact person?
10. Is there a waiting list?
11. Other Information: (e.g., special services, general impressions, etc.)

---

the skill to assist the client to accept and embrace this referral. It is not unusual for a client to interpret the suggestion of a referral as a sign of rejection or as evidence of the hopeless nature of his or her condition.

The competent, ethical helper will present the idea of referral in a way that it is seen as a continuing, productive step in the helping process—that, far from being evidence of rejection, it is evidence of the helper's concern. And rather than evidence of the hopelessness of the situation it is evidence of the clarity of the nature of the problem and the reality of the existence of a resource with a record of success in these situations. Consider the dialogue presented in Case Illustration 9.2.

As evident in the exchange (see Case Illustration 9.2), presenting the client with a referral needs to be done as a hopeful, positive step in the helping process. The helper needs to convey to the client that this is not an abandonment, but an extension and refinement of the helping process. In making a referral the helper should

- Be clear and direct about the goal and expectation for seeking referral
- Confront what referral is NOT, that is, it is not a rejection or a statement of hopelessness

CASE ILLUSTRATION 9.2
Preparing Margaret for Referral

Linda is a Master's level mental health counselor working for an Employee Assistance Program (EAP). Her training is in counseling psychology, and she has experience working with individual, solution-focused approaches to counseling. As a counselor in an EAP, she is contracted to provide a maximum of six sessions of direct service, while overseeing and case managing all clients whom she refers for ongoing assistance. Margaret, her client, has come to her because her husband "kicked her out" of their house and is filing for divorce. Margaret, in addition to being depressed about the situation with her marriage, is in crisis over her current living conditions. The exchange occurs near the end of the first session.

LINDA: Margaret, you have certainly been open and honest with me. And I know that speaking about the marriage and your relationship with Tom has at times been very upsetting.

MARGARET: It has been easier than I thought. You are a very kind person and a good listener.

LINDA: Thank you. But as we've talked it has become clear to me that of the things you are concerned about , the one thing that seems to need immediate attention is helping you with your housing problem.

MARGARET: Yeah, I don't have any money to go and get a new apartment right now and last night I slept in the car. I know I have enough money to go to a motel for a night or two but I don't know what I can do . . . (starts to cry). Where can I go?

LINDA: You are correct in saying that you can't continue to sleep in the car, and finding and answer to your question of,"where can you go" should be our primary concern. Do you agree?

MARGARET: Yes (crying).

LINDA: Housing or social service support for displaced women is not something that we provide here at the EAP or that I am very experienced with.

MARGARET: (Interrupting) Oh, NO! You have to help me . . .

LINDA: It going to be all right. I am going to help. Even though I do not work with these type of situations, I know someone who can really help us—who has a lot of experience in these situations. So what I would like to do is call Ms. Anderson over at the Women's Center and see if she has the time to talk with us and see you today. The Women's çenter is right around the corner from here and it provides ongoing counseling for women who are in situations just like yours. They also have resources for temporary housing and even help women find low-cost housing. Plus, once they help you get settled they can help you with some of the job training we started discussing.

MARGARET: But how about you. . . . I like you . . .

LINDA: And I like you. In fact, I really want you to get the best help you can get and I think the Women's Center is the answer. But I can still help, by talking with Ms. Anderson and telling her some of things you have shared with me, especially things about your current concerns and some of your goals. I could also work with you and Ms. Anderson, if that makes sense after talking with her. And, if you want to come

> back to talk with me, or if we want to look into another referral source we could do
> that, as well. So how do you feel about me calling and seeing if we can set up an
> appointment for you?
>
> **MARGARET:**   Okay . . . but I can still call you if I need to?
>
> **LINDA:**   Absolutely . . .and I will call you to see how things are going after you have
> had a hance to work with the Women's Center.

- Share information about the referral source, nature of service, costs, location, etc.
- Discuss the client's feelings and concerns
- Answer all client questions regarding the referral
- Reassure the client about the value of the referral
- Assist the client in making the initial contact.
- Establish a mechanism for follow-up with each other. Encourage the client to let the helper know how the initial visit went

If you are requesting special services for a client from a colleague, it is important to provide the colleague with the information about the case that is necessary to support the goals of the referral. Needless to say, it is essential to gain the client's consent for such collaboration prior to speaking with professional to whom you are referring. Once the referral contract has been established, it is important for the referring helper to back off from case involvement unless specifically requested by the attending professional.

Recent Legal Decisions

Malpractice or professional liability lawsuits are based on negligence theory (Woody, 1997). That is, a client, who in legal proceedings is the plaintiff, would assert that the helper has breached the standard of care. Malpractice requires a demonstrating of injury, however, even when there is no proof of injury complaints to professional ethics committee or regulatory agencies (e.g., licensing boards) can result in sanctions.

The legal concept of negligence is based on the premise that all members of society owe to one another the duty to exercise a certain inherent standard of care. In most cases the courts will look to the profession itself to define which standard should be used. Case law on the standard of care question varies around the country. Some courts will put the emphasis on "accepted" practice, others on what is "customary." In this latter case an attorney will develop evidence to define the customary standard applied by others in the field, with "field" defined in the most specific sense possible (Bennett et al., 1990, p. 37). For example, when a clinical psychologist who has been trained in cognitive techniques and offers this orientation explicitly to his or her clients, comes to the courtroom, the standard for his or her performance is predefined. The cognitive school is recognized by the community of psychologists as a distinct and viable orientation, with well-defined standards for training and clinical guidelines. Should this psychologist be operating without the appropriate training or outside the customary procedures for a cognitive therapist, he or she may be vulnerable to negligence and malpractice. Therefore, not only do helpers need to legally perform within their scope of training, but must perform in ways that are typically or customarily associated with that form of service. Helpers who develop or subscribe to innovative therapies might find themselves having to prove that a "respectable minority" in their profession concurs in their techniques or treatment strategies.

An alternative approach to negligence, malpractice, and the issue of standard of care is that derived not from one's own training but from the clinical imperatives of the client's condition. In *Hammer v. Rosen*, 165N.E. 2d 756 (1960) the court ruled that a therapist's (psychiatrist) decision to beat his patient as part of therapy was a prima facie case of malpractice. The court noted that some acts are so obviously unacceptable that expert testimony is not needed to justify the conclusion of malpractice. If a nontraditional therapy is employed, documentation of the reasons for its choice rather than a more traditional approach, along with expert testimony showing the efficacy of the therapy in a similar situation and/or its theoretical and scientific bases, may be needed should a malpractice action be filed (Dickson, 1998). It could be assumed that the same logic may be applied to the situation in which a practitioner used a traditional, but less than effective strategy of intervention. The theoretical and empirical base for that decision may be essential should a malpractice action be filed.

Beyond Professional Standards: A Personal Moral Response

While the threat of malpractice can certainly motivate one to perform within the boundaries of his or her training, it is not an insurance in and of itself that such ethical, competent performance of duty will occur. As with all of the ethical standards and practice guidelines, directives to provide competently within the standard of care is or can be a mere statement of expectation rather than an operative schema guiding practice decisions.

As ethical practitioners, we need to move the concepts and principles discussed within this chapter from levels of comprehension to incorporation as personal values and moral imperatives. Once assimilated as a personal value and moral response, acting competently will be a simple consequence of being competent— in the broadest sense of the term. The final exercise (Exercise 9.4) is provided to assist you in adding the affective, personal component to this theoretical, conceptual discussion.

Case Illustration

The scenario that opened this chapter not only revealed Ms. Wicks' (Michelle's) deep concern for her client, Maria, but her personal awareness of the possible limitations to her own competence and ability to assist Maria. With these two conditions in place, Michelle sought out a peer for consultation and possible referral.

MICHELLE: Hi, Lynn. Do you have a minute?

LYNN: Sure, Michelle, what's up?

EXERCISE **9.4**
Personalizing the Importance of Competence

Part 1: Below you will find a list of "presenting concerns." As you read the list, place a check mark under the column indicating whether you would work with the person and provide service or refer the person to another helper. If you are currently in a formal degree/training program, answer the question as if you had just completed that training.

Presenting Concerns	Provide Service	Refer to Another Helper
A person with anxiety about making a career decision		
A person grieving the recent death of her parent		
A person thinking about leaving his wife		
A person concerned about the possibility of having a drinking problem		
A person who has questions about her sexual orientation		
A person having academic difficulties in college		
A person who feels extremely depressed		
A person who is experiencing headaches and muscle tensions as a result of job-related stress		
A person who is concerned about his explosive temper		
A person who is having conflict with her adolescent, which at times has exploded into physical confrontations		

Part 2: Now for each of the above, reconsider your decision. This time assume that the client was viewed by you with the same level of care and concern as you would have for someone very close to you (e.g., family member, spouse, best friend, etc.). Once you personalized the level of concern for the client, did you adjust your original decisions? What might this say about your customary standard of care? Consider steps you can take to approach all clients with the same depth of concern and provision of quality, competent service.

Part 3: For those situations in which the decision was to refer, begin to establish referral resources that you would feel comfortable referring all clients to, including a person who was personally very close to you.

MICHELLE: I've been working with this girl, Maria, and we have a real good working relationship, but I just don't feel like I have a true grasp of what is going on or that I am approaching this situation the best way that I might. I explained this to Maria, and she has given me written permission to speak with you about the case. I know you are really busy, but I was hoping that you could provide some supervision around this case to see if you feel like I'm on track and using the best approach.

Following a discussion of case details, their conversation continued:

LYNN: It really does appear that you have gained Maria's trust and, given her recent experience and background, that was not an easy task.

MICHELLE: Oh, thanks . . you are right, it wasn't the easiest—but that's why I want to do the best for her.

LYNN: Well, your specific solution-focused approach really does appear to be effective, especially in helping her with the "life crisis" of finding a place to live, support herself, and essentially stay safe. So I would suggest you continue to strategize with her the way you have been and identify additional resources that she can use. . . .

MICHELLE: I will—but as I said I feel there is much more here than the immediate crisis.

LYNN: I agree . . . It is very clear that Maria has some real issues with her family—especially her father—and I think one of the goals you could try to work on would be to get her to feel safe and crisis-free so that she might be willing to work with her family in some family therapy.

MICHELLE: We touched on that a couple of times but she was resistant. But as you were speaking, I remembered that her resistance did seem to be diminishing. It appears the more she feels comfortable with me and what we are planning, the more she may be willing to risk some family sessions! But I am really not trained in family work—I mean I've had a course, but that's not something I've done. So if she agrees, I would like to refer her. I really respect you and the work you do with families, and I have heard great things about Dr. Hemingway and his work with families. Would it be okay if when we get to that point, I give her your name along with Dr. Hemingway's?

Reflections
1. In reviewing the case, can you see evidence of the helper (Ms. Wicks) placing the client's welfare above her own image and ego?
2. Identify two specific things done by Ms. Wicks that reflect her awareness of the need to provide competent and efficacious service.
3. In addition to having a course in family-systems therapy, what would you suggest is minimally required before one engage in such an intervention?
4. What might you suggest Ms. Wicks do prior to including Dr. Hemingway on a referral list?

5. What might you suggest Ms. Wicks do to prepare Maria for referral? What role could Ms. Wicks continue to play?

Cooperative Learning Exercise

As with all of the previous cooperative learning exercises, the current exercise is designed to help you personalize the material and begin to move your understanding to professional practice. Therefore, before proceeding to the next chapter, read and respond to each of the following. Working with colleagues, classmates, or supervisors, share your insights and develop the comprehensive plan for developing increased levels of competency.

Goal identification: Briefly share your vision or goal in terms of the type of work you would like to do as a practitioner, that is, the type of client you envision working with, the nature/scope of problems, and the setting in which you wish to work.

Legal Requirements: Identify the professional standards and minimal requirements necessary to perform the tasks described in the question above. What are the specific licensing and certification requirements in your state that apply to the practice you envision performing?

Contact: Contact one professional currently practicing in an area similar to the one that you have identified as your professional goal. Identify the level of training, experience, and model this practitioner employs. Identify clients or presenting complaints that this professionals feels are outside the boundaries of his or her competence and gather two resources to whom he or she refers.

Contract: Finally, in discussion with your colleague, classmate, or supervisor, compare your current level of training and experience to the standards established within your state and the level of expertise identified by the professional you contacted. What specific gaps exist and what is your plan to fill those gaps in competency?.

Summary

Practicing Within the Realm of Competence
Being competent means that the helper has the knowledge, skills, and abilities needed to perform those tasks relevant to that profession. Competence is defined in relative terms, most typically using the conduct of others within the profession as the comparative standard.

Professional Development: Knowing the State of the Profession
Competence can be developed from formal training as might be found in graduate training or training for certification and licensure. Further, all the codes of conduct call for practitioners to be current with emerging knowledge relevant to their profession. It is incumbent upon the ethical practitioner to upgrade his or her knowledge and skill through participating in continuing education experiences and peer consultation.

The Standard of Care: Appropriate Treatment

Most malpractice cases turn on the question of negligence, which suggests that the practitioner failed to meet the relevant standard of care. The question of negligence will be determined by the debate over the clinical correctness and efficacy of the treatment that was given, along with the practitioner's judgment in choosing it. The standard of care and the definition of appropriate treatment are typically determined by comparing the practitioner's performance with that of other professionals in the same community with comparable training and experience. However, as the professions and the research identify specific strategies with demonstrated effectiveness, these interventions become the standard of care.

Employing an Action Research Approach to Practice

Practitioners bear a fundamental ethical responsibility to use, when possible, interventions that work and to subject any intervention they use to scientific scrutiny.

In order to be effective in their practice, human service providers must blend the method and findings of research with the realities of their professional practice. As practitioner–researchers, they will need not only to interact in the moment but also to reflect on and critique their own interactions. *Action research* methodology provides practitioners with the means of acquiring these valid, useful data and results in the development of effective strategies of professional practice.

The Use of Referral

Knowing when to refer is not always easy and there are no simple or clear answers.

At a minimum, the ethical helper will refer any time it is determined that he or she is unable to provide the professional, competent services required. In addition to recognizing the need and having available resources to whom to refer, the competent helper will also have the skill to assist the client to accept and embrace this referral.

Recent Legal Decisions

Malpractice or professional liability lawsuits are based on negligence theory—that is, a client would assert that the helper has breached the standard of care. A review of recent court decisions could lead to the assumption that where a practitioner used a traditional, but less than effective strategy of intervention, the theoretical and empirical base for that decision may be essential should a malpractice action be filed.

IMPORTANT TERMS

action research	malpractice
best practice	managed care
brief therapy	negligence
certification	peer consultation
competence	professional development
continuing education	reasonable man standard
customary	referral
efficacy of the treatment	referral network
formal training	regulatory bodies
licensing	standard of care

SUGGESTED READINGS

Bass, L.J., DeMers, S.T., Oglof, J.R., Peterson, C., Pettifor, J.L., Reaves, R.P., Retfalvi, T., Simon, N.P., Sinclair, C., & Tipton, R.M. (1996). *Professional conduct and discipline in psychology*. Washington, DC: American Psychological Association.

Bennett, B.E., Bryant, B.K., VandenBos, G.R., & Greenwood, A. (1990). *Professional liability and risk management*. Washington, DC: American Psychological Association.

Parsons, R.D. (1995). *The skills of helping*. Boston: Allyn and Bacon.

Parsons, R.D., & Brown, K.S. (In press). *Action research*. New York: Addison-Wesley- Longman.

CHAPTER

10 Evaluation and Accountability

Dr. Flournoy: Hello, Ms. Wicks?

Ms. Wicks: Yes.

Dr. Flournoy: I am Dr. Flournoy from Children and Youth Services.

Ms. Wicks: Hello.

Dr. Flournoy: The Ramerez family has been referred to our service, and I understand that you have been working with Maria, here at school. I have requested that your counseling records be subpoenaed, and I simply wanted to let you know ahead of time, so that you could begin to get them in order.

Counseling records? Subpoenas? For some mental health practitioners the idea of maintaining records may be an anathema to the nature of the helping process. Further, the invitation to disclose these records as a result of a simple request, subpoena, or court order can arouse debilitating anxiety.

The need and ethical responsibility of keeping and maintaining records along with the inherent conflict that may exist when disclosure of these records is requested serves as the focus for the current chapter.

Chapter Objectives

The chapter will introduce you to the importance of maintaining records as both a measure of professional accountability and an essential step toward demonstrating ethical practice.

After reading this chapter you should be able to do the following:

1. Describe the benefits of utilizing a system of evaluation within one's practice
2. Define the terms *formative* and *summative* evaluation
3. Describe one approach to measuring outcome and goal achievement
4. Identify the minimal records necessary for demonstrating competent, ethical practice

While it is true that no one professional can guarantee success in each and every encounter, the ethical practitioner will monitor services and adjust as required. Such a monitoring, or evaluation, be it through the informal collection of data or more formal forms can offer direction and serve to demonstrate accountability. However, for some helpers, the concept of "evaluation" may be viewed as superfluous or tangential to the primary function of helping. In fact, Hackney and Cormier (1991) suggest that one of the primary abuses in helping is the failure to monitor and evaluate the effects of the intervention strategies.

Parsons (1995) noted that use of a properly implemented and maintained system of evaluation can

1. Serve as an ongoing reminder that the helping relationship is not one upon which the client can remain dependent; it is terminal
2. Be used as a tool to foster an awareness of the movement of the helping process as well as to anticipate that the helping relationship is coming close to a termination
3. Provide the feedback and criteria needed to decide on an adjustment in treatment approach, a referral or a termination.

The value to the overall planning and decision making of the helper provided by a good evaluation system makes it a practical and worthwhile idea for all helpers. Further, when viewed through the lens of accountability—to the client and the profession—an evaluation system becomes an essential ethical practice (see Table 10.1).

TABLE 10.1 Ethical Positions on Record Keeping

American Counseling Association (1995)	B.4 Records
	(a) Requirements of Records. Counselors maintain records necessary for rendering professional services to their clients and as required by laws, regulations, or agency or institution procedures.
	(b) Confidentiality of Records. Counselors are responsible for securing the safety and confidentiality of any counseling records they create, maintain, transfer, or destroy whether the records are written, taped, computerized, or stored in any other medium.
American Psychological Association (1995)	5.04 Maintenance of Records.
	Psychologists maintain appropriate confidentiality in creating, storing, accessing, transferring, and disposing of records under their control, whether these are written, automated, or in any other medium. Psychologists maintain and dispose of records in accordance with law and in a manner that permits compliance with the requirements of this Ethics Code.
American Association of Marriage and Family Therapy (1998)	2.3: Marriage and family therapists store and dispose of client records in ways that maintain confidentiality.
National Association of Social Workers (1996)	3.04: The National Association of Social Workers (1996) states: (a) Social workers should take reasonable steps to ensure that documentation in records are accurate and reflective of services provided.
	(b) Social workers should include sufficient and timely documentation in records to facilitate the delivery of services and to ensure continuity of service provided to clients in the future.

Monitoring and Evaluating Intervention Effects

Evaluation is often thought of as something that is done at the end of a process. To be pre-scriptive, evaluation of the helping process needs to be both ongoing and "formative," as well as "summative" in form.

Formative Evaluation

Formative evaluation is evaluation that occurs as an ongoing process throughout the help-ing encounter. It is the gathering of feedback and data used to expedite decision making about the current process and the upcoming steps and procedures to be employed. It pro-vides data that give form to the ongoing process. The means of collecting formative data can range in degree of formality. For example, a practitioner may choose to use a structured survey or questionnaire at various points in the helping encounter. Or, more informally, the practitioner may simply set time aside to solicit feedback from the client about his or her experience in the relationship with the helper and the procedures employed up to this par-ticular point (see Case Illustration 10.1).

CASE ILLUSTRATION **10.1**
Formative Evaluation

> **DR. BROWN:** First let me tell you how much I appreciate your openness and willing-ness to share with me some of your concerns about your social relationships and your desire to become more assertive in these. I feel very comfortable working with you and feel that the things we have talked about in this first session have really helped us to clarify your goal and even begin developing a strategy for getting there. I think it may be helpful if we took a moment to share our perceptions on this session as a way of making future sessions more productive. I would be very inter-ested in receiving your feedback about our session today.
>
> **JIM:** To be honest, I was very nervous when I made the appointment. However, I am really surprised how much I shared. I really feel like I can trust you. I feel very com-fortable speaking with you, and that is not my style, usually.
>
> **DR. BROWN:** Well, that is very nice to hear, and I know from what you told me that you tend to be a private person. Jim, as you are aware, we will probably want to talk more about your family background and previous relationships as our sessions go on. How do you feel about that? (Dr. Brown checks Jim's understanding of the help-ing process).
>
> **JIM:** I know that probably needs to be done—it makes me a little anxious—but as I said, I do feel comfortable with you and trust you, especially how you explained the idea of confidentiality. I just may need to go slow.
>
> **DR. BROWN:** That's good feedback for me. The pace of the sessions really will be the one that feels right for you. So if we need to go slow . . . we will. If you want to dive into something, and it seems right to me . . . we will. I think as long as we continue

to "process" how we are doing—we can make sure we stay on track at a pace which is both productive and comfortable. (Dr. Brown checks Jim's comfort level and takes direction.)

JIM: Yeah, me too.

DR. BROWN: So, while overall you are hoping to get some help with developing assertiveness skills, our immediate goal is for you to take notes on two incidents—one in which you felt you were assertive and one in which you felt very unassertive. Are these the goals we agreed on? (Dr. Brown checks agreement on goals.)

JIM: Yes—that's exactly what I want to do . . . get more assertive! And I like the idea of doing some "research work" for our next session.

For this evaluation to truly form and give shape to the decision-making processes, it should begin with the first session. As evident in Illustration 10.1, the helper engaged in formative evaluation within the first session. The approach taken by this helper provided insight into the client's level of comfort with the interaction and his ability to engage collaboratively in the helping process. This evaluation also served as a check on the accuracy of the helper's understanding regarding the desired goals and outcome for the helping process. The use of such a formative evaluation not only provides for helper accountability but provides the data for monitoring and increasing efficacy of treatment.

Summative Evaluation

Summative evaluation is the type of evaluation most typically thought of when considering goal or outcome assessment. The specific purpose of summative evaluation is to demonstrate that the action plan has reached its original objective. Summative evaluation provides the helper and the client data to determine (1) if the original goals were achieved, (2) the factors that contributed to this goal attainment, and (3) maybe even the value of this strategy versus some alternative. The articulation of clear treatment goals, and the employment of summative evaluation strategies, serve as invaluable sources for demonstrating treatment efficacy and helper accountability.

The presence of clearly articulated goals or outcome, is essential for both formative and summative forms of evaluation. Without a clear, shared vision of where the helping process is going, it will be hard to know if it is on track or even if it has arrived. Thus, the establishment of treatment goals and objectives, the identification of outcome measures, and the maintenance of appropriate responsible records serve as keystones to ethical and efficient practice.

Setting Treatment Goals and Objectives

The setting of the goals and objectives for a helping relationship is highly influenced by the values and beliefs of the therapists (Brace, 1997). Research has demonstrated that clients tend to adopt counselor values that, without some forethought, could unduly influence the client to embrace not only the counselor's values but goals and vision for this helping relationship (e.g., Beutler, 1983; Owen, 1982). Because of the potential to influence the client and the client's ability to formulate his or her own goals and objectives, it is important for the practitioner to be sure to engage the client in terminal goal formulation. The development of treatment goals and objectives should be shaped by an overriding concern for the client's welfare and with a desire to facilitate the client's own self-determination and autonomy.

Brace (1997) suggests a set of rules that could guide the development of goals in a helping relationship. These rules reflect a consideration of the ethical concerns for client welfare and best interest, as well as a respect for the client's right to self-determination and autonomy. Table 10.2 reflects a number of these guidelines.

TABLE 10.2   Guidelines for Developing Helping Goals

Guidelines Reflecting Concern from Client Welfare	Guidelines Reflecting Respect for Client's Autonomy
1. Examine goals to be sure they are in the client's best interest.	1. Helpers should explicate their own values as they affect goal development.
2. Goals should be mutually consistent.	2. Changes in the client's values or goals during the course of the helping should happen with the client's conscious volition.
3. There should be adequate reasons for pursuing a chosen end goal (i.e., what the client wishes to accomplish as a result of the helping process) rather than an alternative.	3. Any action taken with the intent to benefit the client, but without the client's consent (e.g., involuntary hospitalization), should be justifiable.
4. The choice of instrumental goals (i.e., the selection of means to accomplish end goals) should be based on adequate reasons; if the ones chosen are found to be ineffective, they should be replaced with others that are effective.	4. The helper should avoid deceiving the client in the development of goals since this violates the client's right to informed consent.
5. Factors that are causal or contributory and pertain to the goal should be assessed.	5. An explicit agreement on the specific goals and their pursuit should be established between the helper and the client.
6. The helper should avoid and/or correct errors in clinical judgment that could adversely affect goal attainment.	
7. Treatment should not harm the client—if harm may result it should be outweighed by the treatment's potential benefit and should have the client's informed consent.	
8. The helper should keep implicit and explicit promises to the client.	

TABLE 10.2 *(Continued)*

Guidelines Reflecting Concern from Client Welfare	Guidelines Reflecting Respect for Client's Autonomy
9. When helping involves more than one person, equal importance should be given to the welfare of each.	
10. Should consider the possible effects of the client's instrumental and end goals on others so as to minimize harm.	

Measuring Outcome and Goal Achievement

The selection of appropriate outcome measures is far from easy. It is, however, one area of helping where the old adage "the more, the better" has application (Sexton, Whiston, Bleuer, & Walz, 1997). Using more than one outcome and outcome measure increases the probability of accurately depicting the experience. At the most fundamental level the practitioner can assume that one outcome reflects the nature of the presenting concern. For example, if a clinician is interested in ameliorating a presenting complaint, the nature of that complaint (e.g., test anxiety, marital dissatisfaction, depression, etc.) provides direction to the outcomes desired. After targeting the general area in which the helper expects to demonstrate impact (i.e., reduce test anxiety, increase achievement level etc.), that particular area needs to be clearly and concretely defined. It is important to realize that while there will be a primary focus for the assessing outcome (e.g., reduce the amount of client depression, or increase student attention etc.), these targets may be manifested in a number of different ways and occur within a unique context. The more perspectives we take on the outcome and the more measures we employ, the greater the chance we have of understanding the nature and depth of impact our practice may have produced. Consider the approach taken by the helper illustrated in the following case (Case Illustration 10.2).

CASE ILLUSTRATION **10.2**

Assessing Outcomes of Treatment with Depressed Client

Alicia came to therapy because of a "constant" feeling of sadness and an inability to get motivated about anything in her life. At the initial meeting with Alicia, Dr. Warrick attempted to identify the various ways in which her feelings of sadness were experienced and were impacting her life.

> **DR. WARRICK:** Alicia, you have mentioned that you are not "doing anything" and you can't get motivated. Could you tell me more about that?

ALICIA: Well, I have a lot of school work that should be done and each time I sit down to do it I think—why bother, nothing is going to come out, and then I walk away from the computer and get something to eat or go to bed.

DR. WARRICK: So it seems that you not only feel sad, at times, but you also have this belief that "nothing is going to work"?

ALICIA: That's right! And it is not just with school stuff. If I get a call from a friend I typically go, why bother going out, it is not going to help. And I stay home.

DR. WARRICK: So one of the things that we may watch as we work together isn't just your feelings of sadness, but also the frequency of this "why bother, it's hopeless" thinking?

ALICIA: I don't want to feel sad anymore, but I also understand what you mean about the thinking.

DR. WARRICK: You also seem to suggest that when you are feeling this way, you avoid your friends and avoid engaging in activities (like school work)?

ALICIA: Yeah, I have not seen my friends in weeks. I'm sure they are annoyed. And I don't even do housework anymore—my place is a mess.

DR. WARRICK: Well, Alicia, I appreciate how open you have been with me today and I truly feel we have taken a good step toward helping you to feel and behave the way you want to. As we continue working together, we will not only keep our eye on your feelings of sadness with the intent of gaining some relief, but we will see if there is an increase in the frequency with which you go out with your friends, or do house chores and school work. Further, we will hopefully as see a change in your thinking. Rather than thinking "why bother" thoughts we will see more productive thoughts. How does that sound?

ALICIA: It sounds like a lot and I'm not sure that we can do this. Yikes, there is that why bother thought again! But if I would start feeling and thinking and acting differently, then I would not need to be here.

DR. WARRICK: That's good—and I like the way you already attacked that thought of yours!

While most individuals recognize depression to be a mood, an affect, or a feeling, depression also manifests itself in a person's behavior, thought processes, and interpersonal interactions. A helper, like Dr. Warrick (see Illustration 10.2), who may be attempting to assess the effectiveness of a particular medication or treatment approach on depression, should assess changes not only in the client's mood but also in the client's behavior (e.g., doing school work), thought processes (e.g., had less frequent thoughts of suicide or thoughts of "why bother"), and interpersonal interactions (e.g., began to reengage with family and friends), along with gathering information about how the client feels about these changes.

Table 10.3 provides one useful way for conceptualizing the various domains in which interventions may impact the client. It is useful to consider gathering data in many, if not all, of these domains in an attempt to accurately evaluate the impact of practice decisions. The listing presented is an adaptation of the work of Arnold Lazarus (1989). The essence of this model is the belief that a person's functioning or dysfunctioning is manifested along

TABLE 10.3 Classification Scheme for Outcome Measures: Using an Example of a Client Experiencing Anxiety in Social Settings

Modality	Manifestation	Sample Methods of Data Collection
Behavior	Withdraws from social contact	Observation
Affect	Anxious	Survey (anxiety checklist)
Sensation	Muscle tension	Self-Report (journal)
Imagery	Dreams about being abandoned	Self-Report (journal)
Cognition	Believes he has no right to say no	Assertiveness questionnaire
Interpersonal	Withdraws and fails to maintain eye contact	Observation, interview peers
Drugs/Biology	Stomach upset/Blood pressure high	Self-report and blood pressure recordings

seven modalities: behavior, affect, sensation, images, cognition, interpersonal relationships, and biology/physiology. Lazarus represented these seven domains with the acronym BASIC ID. Using each of these components as a reference point, the helper can conceptualize the impacts of his or her practice more broadly.

Table 10.3 presents three dimensions for consideration when identifying outcomes to action research. First, *modality* refers to the specific arena in which this construct may be manifested (i.e.,BASIC ID). The second dimension, *manifestation*, is the place where the practitioner identifies the manner or form in which this particular target of the investigation appears. The final column, *data collection techniques*, identifies the types of techniques that can be useful when assessing that domain. It should be noted that while a specific method of data collection has been identified in Table 10.3, other methods may work as well. Exercise 10.1 provides an opportunity to employ to this approach with a problem of your choosing.

EXERCISE 10.1
Identifying Personal Outcomes

Directions: Below are a number of general statements about personal improvement and growth. Select one that may be of interest to you and, using the table below, identify the various manifestations of this goal achievement along with techniques for assessment.

1. Become a better student
2. Become more social
3. Become more spiritual
4. Improve general health

Modality	Definition	Sample Methods of Data Collection
Behavior		
Affect		
Sensations		
Imagery		
Cognition		
Interpersonal		
Drugs		

Record Keeping

Record keeping is important not just to document service, but also to guide and direct the practitioner in his or her practice decisions. Accurate, complete records can, for example, allow a practitioner to review the therapeutic process and thus foster self-monitoring on the part of the practitioner. Thus, implicit within the discussion of evaluation and outcome measurement is the understanding that data will be collected and recorded for later analysis. These data can be of various forms including test scores, clinician observations, and notations. In whatever form they are, these data constitute a client's record and must be handled with sensitivity.

Maintaining thorough records and clinical notes is essential to the planning and monitoring of services as well as to providing data should the interaction ever be questioned as in the case of a lawsuit. In fact, Schaffer (1997) suggests failure to maintain adequate records places a practitioner in great ethical and legal jeopardy. Thus, even with concern about possible requirements to disclose, experiences of inconvenience, or a practitioner's belief in the power of his or her memory, the ethical practitioner will collect and maintain useful professional records. In fact, all of the professional organizations (see Table 10.1) call for the ethical collection, maintenance, and dissemination of client information.

Nature and Extent of Records

Records should document the nature, delivery, and progress of services provided. Additional information may be required by state statute and/or contract as when services are provided as part of a managed care organization. While the specifics of what may be required as part of a client's record varies from state to state, generally it is important to maintain a legible record that includes at a minimum: identifying data; dates of services; types of services; fees; any assessment, plan for intervention, consultation, and/or summary reports as may be appropriate; and any release of information obtained. One example of the types of records one should maintain was developed by the Committee on Professional Practice and Standards of the APA. This committee adopted a set of guidelines (see Canter, Bennett, Jones, & Nagy, 1994), which suggests that a minimum records should contain:

- Intake sheet, including client identifying information
- Documentation of a mental status assessment
- Signed informed consent
- Treatment plans
- Psychological tests
- Documentation of referrals
- Types of services provided
- Appointment dates and times
- Release of information
- Discharge summary

While the above provides some minimal guidelines for identifying the nature and type of records to be collected and maintained, the specific form of each of the above, or the nature and content and style of clinical notes and records, will be determined by the specific regulations of the setting in which the services are provided, state laws, or helper preferences (see Exercise 10.2).

Regardless of the types of data collected, clarity and utility should guide the process. The notes are meant to assist in the treatment (utility), and since records belong to the client and copies could be requested, they should be clearly written in a manner that is honest and nondemeaning.

EXERCISE 10.2
Nature of Records to Be Kept

Directions: Using the questions listed below, interview two professional helpers in each of the following professions.

- Private practitioner
- School counselor
- Criminal justice worker/counselor
- Drug and alcohol counselor
- Marriage therapist

Then ask each helper if he or she keeps client files and if not, why not. If yes, ask him or her:

- What type of information do you keep in your files?
- How long do you maintain your files?
- Does your client have access to these files?
- Have you had your records subpoenaed? If so, what was your response?

Compare and contrast the helpers' responses. Was there commonality within the specific helping profession? What similarities or differences existed across professional groups?

Storage and Access

The collection and maintenance of such sensitive information can conflict with a client's right to personal privacy if not handled professionally and ethically. Violations of appropriate record keeping has been one of the top five areas of legal liability for counselors (Snider, 1987). For example, the American Psychological Association's Ethical Principles of Psychologists and Code of Conduct (1995), principle 5.04 states:

> Psychologists maintain appropriate confidentiality in creating, storing, accessing, transferring and disposing of records under their control, whether these are written, automated, or in any other medium. Psychologists maintain and dispose of records in accordance with the law and in a manner that permits compliance with the requirements of this Ethics Code.

There is, however, no one set of standards that concretely and universally applies across professions and settings. It is incumbent for each professional to understand the ethical principles articulated within his or her profession. In addition to these standards, the practitioner needs to be aware of the legal statutes and practice principles governing the acquisition, storage, and maintenance of records in their own particular setting. For example, practitioners working within a school setting that receives federal funding will be governed by the Family Educational Rights and Privacy Act (FERPA). This act provides rights of access to educational records to students and their parents and defines educational record as any record kept by employees of the educational institution. Since broad access of records is not required of practitioners working within a nonfederally funded setting, it is clear that the decisions regarding the nature of records collected and the forms of storage can vary setting to setting.

In what is now a significant event in the history of educational record keeping, the Russell Sage Foundation, convened a conference in 1969 of representatives from educational and legal institutions, as well as experts in related fields, to address the issue of collecting, maintaining, and disseminating records within the schools. The members concluded that "current practices of schools and school personnel relating to the collection, maintenance, use and dissemination of information about pupils threaten a desirable balance between the individual's right to privacy and the schools stated need to know" (Russell Sage Foundation, 1970). The outcome of this conference was the production of a proposed set of guidelines that, while targeted to pupil records, has value for all practitioners, regardless of the setting, and the population with whom they work. A number of points gleaned from the historic conference are presented in Table 10.4 and serve as a reference point for Exercise 10.3.

Database and Computer Storage

The issue of storage and access takes on special significance when considered within the advances of this technological era and the use of computers for database storage. For example, the American Psychological Association's Ethical Principles describe the situation:

> If confidential information concerning recipients of psychological services is to be entered into databases or systems of records available to persons whose access has not been con-

TABLE 10.4. Summary of Russell Sage Conference

Collection of Data	Consent	No information should be collected without prior informed consent.
		The client should be informed as fully as possible consonant with the practitioner's professional responsibility and the capacity of the client to understand.
		Even when data is collected under conditions of anonymity, the obligation to obtain consent remains.
Maintenance of Data	Levels: Category A	Data included here reflect the minimum personal data necessary (e.g., name, address, date of birth, academic background, etc.).
		For schools, these data should be maintained in perpetuity.
	Category B	Data of clear importance but not absolutely necessary for helping the client or protecting others over time (e.g., scores on standardized testing, family background data, observations and rating scales).
		These data (in regard to school settings) should be eliminated as unnecessary at periodic intervals (e.g., transition points, such as moving from elementary to junior high)
	Category C	Useful information needed for the immediate present (e.g., legal or clinical findings).
		Data should be reviewed at least once a year (in school settings) and destroyed as soon as their usefulness is ended. If usefulness continues and validity of information has been verified, they may be transferred to Category B.
	Confidential, personal files	Any and all data that are considered personal property of the professional should be guarded by the rules given above and dictated by professional ethics, terms of employment, and any special agreements made between the professional and the client.
Dissemination	Releasing without consent	In school setting, category A and B data may be released to other school officials including teachers who have a legitimate educational interest in pupil records.
	With consent/ judicial order	School may not divulge any information to anyone outside of the legitimate school personnel without written consent or compliance with judicial order.
	Nonrelease	Under no conditions, except court order, should school release information in Category C.

Adapted from *Guidelines for the collection, maintaining & dissemination of pupil records.* Russell Sage Foundation, 1970.

EXERCISE 10.3
Assessing School Record Keeping

Directions:

Step 1: Contact your high school or a local high school. Inquire what their policy is regarding the gathering, maintenance, access, and disposal of the following types of records:

1. Student attendance
2. Student course grades
3. Student discipline record
4. Student health records
5. Student standardized test scores
6. Student counseling records (if any)
7. Student IEPs or specialized academic program plans
8. Teacher, counselor, administrator anecdotal notes on students

Step 2: Using the category breakdown listed in Table 10.4 (Russell Sage Foundation, 1970) evaluate the degree to which this school is following the Russell Sage guidelines.

---

sented to by the recipient, then psychologist use coding or other techniques to avoid the inclusion of personal identifiers. (APA, 1996, 5.07)

Recent Legal Decisions

One area of professional practice that has recently been impacted by court decisions, is in regard to a client's right to access psychiatric records. The federal Freedom of Information Act of 1966 and various state patients' rights laws often specify client right to access certain personal records. While mental health records have previously been excepted from this policy, the trend appears to be reversing in favor of client access.

For example, it was initially successfully argued that such free access could result in harm to a client—that sharing technical information with clients who are not equipped to understand or deal with this information may prove counterproductive and/or harmful. This argument found support in the case of *Godkin v. Miller* (1974). Janet Godkin had been a voluntary patient at three different New York hospitals. Later, she and her husband decided to write about the experience and requested access to her records. Her requests were denied. In her lawsuit against the New York State Commissioner of Mental Hygiene and the directors of the hospital, the court ruled that the refusal was warranted in light of the fact that the hospitals stated a preference to release the information to another professional. There are a number of points in the process of record acquisition, storage, maintenance, access, and disposition in which a practitioner may be confronted with ethical and or legal questions. However, the courts have not provided a clear directive covering all of these aspects. As such, it is in the general ethical principles and usual customary practice that a practitioner needs to find direction. Arthur and Swanson (1993) provide a summary of a number of legally relevant points. These authors note:

1. Security of files must be maintained such that unauthorized access is denied.

2. Notes should be written in nontechnical, clear, and objective statements with behavioral descriptions. Subjective or evaluative statements involving professional judgments should be designated as such and written in a separate section clearly set aside from factual content.

3. All client records should be written with the understanding that they might be seen by the client, a court, or some other authorized person.

4. Only information that is necessary and appropriate for the provision of service to the client should be documented.

Case Illustration

The scenario that opened this chapter highlighted the importance of record keeping and the potential that such records may be requested. As we continue the scene, however, we will see that it also raises a number of issues regarding (1) the types of information one collects; (2) the way that records are maintained, and (3) the questions of access to records.

DR. FLOURNOY: Hello, Ms. Wicks?

MS. WICKS: Yes?

DR. FLOURNOY: I am Dr. Flournoy from Children and Youth Services

MS. WICKS: Hello.

DR. FLOURNOY: The Ramerez family has been referred to our service, and I understand that you have been working with Maria, here at school. I have requested that your counseling records be subpoenaed, and I simply wanted to let you know ahead of time, so that you could begin to get them in order.

MS. WICKS: I appreciate your notification. Even though we utilize computerized intake forms, inventories, and counseling notes, it is always nice to have some lead time to get them together. As I am sure you are aware, I will need a copy of the Release of Information and I would like one from Maria, in addition to her parents.

DR. FLOURNOY: I understand that you would like a release and actually I brought copies of both a parent release and the client's signed release. You can keep them for your records. You mentioned that you have intake forms, inventories, and client notes with computer access.

MS. WICKS: Yes.

DR. FLOURNOY: Well, I'm going to ask for all the notes including your professional observations and anecdotal notes.

MS. WICKS: Well, Dr. Flournoy, the school's policy is that counselor records include:

- Intake sheet, including client identifying information
- Signed informed consent
- Documentation of referrals
- Types of services provided
- Standardized test scores and/or inventories employed
- Appointment record
- Release of information
- Summary of contact

So I will be happy to provide these to you.

DR. FLOURNOY: Thank you. But I know as a counselor you probably kept personal notes. I would like to see those as well.

MS. WICKS: The notes that we have are those identified by school policy. I've already listed those and I will be glad to provide them. But first, I do want to speak with Maria, and even though she signed the release, I would like her to know exactly what we will be releasing.

Reflections:
1. What do you think about Ms. Wicks' request for a release of information from both the parents and Maria? Was it legally required? Ethically required?
2. Ms. Wicks outlined the type of information that the school directed counselors to maintain. How adequate do these records appear to be? Is there anything you feel is missing?
3. What concerns would you have with having this data in computer storage?
4. What is your reaction to Ms. Wicks' response in regards to personal, anecdotal notes?
5. Ms. Wicks noted that she wanted to explain to Maria the types of material to be released. Was that necessary? Required? What are your feelings regarding that decision?

Cooperative Learning Exercise

As with all of the previous cooperative learning exercises, the current exercise is designed to help you personalize the material and begin to move your understanding to professional practice. Working with a colleague and/or classmate, identify the types of client information that you feel are needed in the course of your professional practice and that will be retained within a client record. Next,

1. Design samples of the specific forms or data collection tools you will employ.
2. Contact three individuals currently working in the area of professional practice that you envision doing and request copies of their data collection tools and instruments.
3. Finally, contact your state association and inquire about the length of time you will be responsible for maintaining these records.

Summary

Monitoring and Evaluating Intervention Effects
Evaluation of the helping process needs to be both ongoing and formative as well as summative in form. Formative evaluation is evaluation that occurs as an ongoing process throughout the helping encounter. Summative evaluation is the type of evaluation most typically thought of when considering goal or outcome assessment.

Setting Treatment Goals
Because of the potential to influence the client and the client's ability to formulate his or her own goals and objectives, it is important for the practitioner to be sure to engage the client in terminal goal formulation. When articulating treatment goals, the more perspectives we take on the outcome and the more measures we employ, the greater the chance we have of understanding the nature and depth of impact our practice may have produced.

Record Keeping
Record keeping is important not just as a documentation of service but also to guide and direct the practitioner in his or her practice decisions. Maintaining thorough records and clinical notes is essential to the planning and monitoring of services as well as to providing data should the interaction ever be questioned as in the case of a lawsuit. Records should document the nature, delivery, and progress of services provided. The collection and maintenance of such sensitive information can conflict with a client's right to personal privacy if not handled professionally and ethically.

IMPORTANT TERMS

accountability	modality
data collection techniques	outcome measures
evaluation	record keeping
Family Educational Rights and Privacy Act (FERPA)	Russell Sage guidelines
	terminal goal
formative	summative

SUGGESTED READINGS

Coale, H.W. (1998). *The vulnerable therapist.* New York: The Haworth Press.

Crawford, R.L. (1994). *Avoiding counselor malpractice.* Alexandria, VA: American Counseling Association.

Russell Sage Foundation (1970). *Guidelines for the collection, maintenance, and dissemination of pupil records.* Hartford, CT: Russell Sage Foundation.

Schaffer, S.J. (1997). Don't be aloof about record-keeping; it may be your best liability coverage. *The National Psychologist, 6*(1), 21.

Snider, P.D. (1987). Client records: Inexpensive liability protection for mental health counselors. *Journal of Mental Health Counseling, 9,* 134–141.

EPILOGUE

While the text has provided an extensive review of the various professions' codes of conduct and ethical standards, the truth is that relying solely on the ethical codes as a base for practice decision making is insufficient (Treppa, 1998). Throughout this text, a recurrent theme was for the ethical helper to keep the focus of all decisions on the welfare and the well-being of the client. But beyond that focus, it is useful for the helper to continually reflect on the question of "How does who I am impact this process and these decisions?" Asking this question both emotionally and analytically throughout the course of helping can assist helpers in making ethical choices. Ethical codes provide guidelines of practice decision making, however, ethical decisions are at times largely influenced by personal values, biases, cultural mores, and contextual considerations. Thus, it is important that each ethical helper develops a model for ethical decision making that is consistent with their profession's standards of practice while at the same time reflecting their own personal values.

The following decision model is provided as both a conclusion to our text and a beginning of your own long career in ethical decision making. The model, which has been adapted from the work of Hill, Glaser, and Harden (1995), combines the rational-evaluative framework presented in the literature, the emotional and intuitive aspects of the helper's response to the situation. While presented in a linear, stepwise fashion, it needs to be noted that in practice, decision making is less than linear and will weave back and forth across the steps.

1. *Identifying the problem.* A helper becomes aware of a problem either as a direct result of his or her own knowledge of the helping process or ethical codes or via feedback from a supervisor, colleague, or even a client. It is important that the helper identify his or her own reactions to the situation and the role they may play in the continuation of that situation or his or her failure to move in a ethical path.

2. *Defining the problem.* The helper needs to identify what ethical principles, laws or standards of practice and treatment may be at odds. Further, the ethical practitioner needs to consider the specific needs of those people and systems involved. Beyond identifying these elements, the ethical helper needs to also identify the way his or her cultural focus (including gender, race, class, etc.) may affect the situation, as well as the way his or her own feelings and values come to play within the situation.

3. *Identifying a solution.* At this stage the helper needs to generate practice options. While considering the practicality of each solution (i.e., cost-benefit), the guiding principles to this development of a solution is the principle of nonmaleficence ("do not harm") and beneficence ("do the greatest good").

4. *Choosing a solution.* According to Hill, Glaser, and Harden (1995), the questions to be considered when selecting a solution are: "Is this solution the best fit both emotionally and rationally? Does this meet everyones needs, including mine? Can I implement and live with this?"

5. *Reviewing the process.* Once a solution has been chosen, it is important for the helper to consider how his or her own values and personal characteristics may have influenced that choice. Questions to consider include: (1) Would another helper have made a similar or different choice? (2) Is this how I would want to be treated? (3) Is the decision universalizable (Haas & Malouf, 1989)? (4) Does this feel right and would I be comfortable with another's scrutiny of my decision?

6. *Implementing and evaluating the decision.* With implementation comes an ongoing reassessment of both the dilemma and the choice of response. These new data may affirm the decision or require the helper to return and redefine the problem.

7. *Continuing a reflection.* Finally, for this process to become more of a personal moral response rather than a simple rote procedure, the helper needs to reflect on the decision, the process and the impact. It is important to grow through and with each new encounter. Understanding what is learned about one's practice decisions, clients, and most certainly himself or herself, is an important step in the process of becoming an ethical helper.

REFERENCES

Adleman, J., & Barrett, S.E. (1990). Overlapping relationships: Importance of the feminist ethical perspective. In H. Lerman & N. Porter (Eds.), *Feminist ethics in psychotherapy* (pp. 87-91). New York: Springer.

Ahia, C.E., & Martin, D. (1993). *The danger-to-self-or-others exception to confidentiality.* Alexandria, VA: American Counseling Association.

Alperin, R. (1994). Managed care versus psychoanalytic psychotherapy: Conflicting ideologies. *Clinical Social Work Journal, 22,* 137–148.

American Association for Marriage and Family Therapy. (1995). *AAMFT code of ethics.* Washington, DC: Author.

American Association for Marriage and Family Therapy. (1998). *AAMFT code of ethics.* Washington, DC: Author.

American Counseling Association. (1995). *Codes of ethics and standards of practice, American Counseling Association.* Alexandria, VA: Author.

American Counseling Association. (1996). *ACA code of ethics and standards of practice.* Alexandria, VA: Author.

American Psychological Association (1995). *Ethical principles of psychologists and code of conduct.* Washington, DC: Author.

American Psychological Association (1992). Ethical principles of psychologists and code of conduct. *American Psychologist, 47,* 1597–1611.

Ammerman, R.T., Last, C.G., & Hersen, M. (Eds.). (1993). *Handbook of prescriptive treatments for children and adolescents.* Boston: Allyn and Bacon.

Anderson, B.S. (1996). *The counselor and the law* (4th ed.). Alexander, VA: American Counseling Association.

Arbuckle, D.S. (1977). Consumers make mistakes too: An invited response. *Personnel and Guidance Journal, 56,* 226–228.

Arthur, G.L., & Swanson, C.D. (1993). *The ACA legal series: Confidentiality and privileged communication.* Alexandria, VA: American Counseling Association

Atkinson, D.R. (1983). Ethnic similarity in counseling psychology: A review of the research. *The Counseling Psychologist, 11(3),* 73–92.

Bader, E. (1994). Dual relationships: Legal and ethical trends. *Transactional Analysis Journal, 24,* 64–66.

Banister, P. Burman, E.., Parker, I. Taylor, M., & Tindall, C. (1994). *Qualitative methods in psychology: A research guide.* Philadelphia, PA: Open University Press.

Beauchamp, T.L., & Childress, J.F. (1989). *Principles of biomedical ethics.* Oxford: Oxford University Press.

Beck, A.T., Rush, A.J., Shaw, B.F., & Emery, G. (1979). *Cognitive therapy of depression.* New York: Guilford Press.

Bednar, R.L., Bednar, S.C., Lambert, M.J., & Waite, D.R. (1991). *Psychotherapy with high-risk clients: Legal and professional standards.* Pacific Grove, CA: Brooks/Cole.

Bennett, B.E., Bryant, B.K., VandenBos, G.R., & Greenwood, A. (1990). *Professional liability and risk management.* Washington, DC: American Psychological Association.

Benningfield, A.B. (1994). The impaired therapist. In G.W. Brock (Ed.), *American Association for Marriage and Family Therapy ethics casebook* (pp. 131–139). Washington, DC: American Association for Marriage and Family Therapy.

Bergantino, L. (1996). For the defense: Psychotherapy and the law. *Voices* (Fall), 29–33.

Berenson, B.G., & Carkhuff, R.R. (1967) *Source of gain in counseling and psychotherapy.* New York: Holt, Rinehart & Winston.

Bergin, A.E. (1991). Values and religious issues in psychotherapy and mental health. *American Psychology, 46(4),* 393–403.

Bersoff, D.N., & Koeppl, P.M. (1993). The relation between ethical codes and moral principles. *Ethics and Behavior, 3,* 345–357.

Bertram, B., & Wheeler, A.M. (1994). Legal aspects of counseling: Avoiding lawsuits and legal problems. Workshop materials. Alexandria, VA: American Counseling Association.

Beutler, L.E. (1983). *Eclectic psychotherapy: A systematic approach.* New York: Pergamon.

Biaggio, M., & Greene, B. (1995). Overlapping/dual relationships. In E.J. Rave & C.C. Larsen (Eds.), *Ethical decision making in therapy: Feminist perspectives* (pp. 88–123) New York: Guilford Press.

Black, H.C. (1991). *Black's law dictionary* (abridged, 6th ed.). St. Paul, MN: West Publishing.

Blum, S.R. (1992). Ethical issues in managed mental health. In S. Feldman (Ed.), *Managed mental health services* (pp. 245–265). Springfield, IL: Charles C. Thomas.

Bogust v. Iverson, 102 N.W.2d 288 (Wis. 1960).

Brace, K. (1997). Ethical considerations in the development of counseling goals. In *The Hatherleigh guide to ethics in therapy* (pp. 17–35). New York: Hatherleigh Press. Boston: Allyn and Bacon.

Bricklin, P.M. (1993, May). When ethics are law. *The Pennsylvania Psychologists Quarterly., 53(5),* May, 8– 9.

Brown, L.S. (1994). *Subversive dialogues: Theory in feminist therapy.* New York: Harper Collins, Basic Books.

Canter, M.B., Bennett, B.E., Jones, S.E., & Nagy, T.F. (1994). *Ethics for psychologists: A commentary on the APA ethics code.* Washington, DC: American Psychological Association.

Canterbury v. Spence, 464F.2d 772 (1972).

Carkhuff, R. R., & Berenson, B.G. (1977) *Beyond counseling and therapy.* New York: Holt, Rinehart and Winston.

Cavaliere, F. (1995, July). Grassroots efforts stall unfavorable legislation. *APA Monitor,* p. 44.

Chalk, R., Frankel, M.D., & Chafer, S.B. (1980). *AAAS professional ethics project.* Washington, DC: American Association for the Advancement of Science.

Chambless, D.L., Sanderson, W.C., Shoham, V., Johnson, S.B., Pope, K.S., Crits-Christoph, P., Baker, M., Johnson, B., Woody, S.R., Sue, S., Beutler, L., Williams, D.A., & McCurry, S. (1996). An update on empirically validated therapies. *Clinical Psychologist, 49(2),* 5–18.

Coale, H.W. (1998). *The vulnerable therapist.* New York: The Haworth Press.

Cohen, E.D. (1997). Ethical standards in counseling sexually active clients with HIV. In *The Hatherleigh guide to ethics in therapy* (pp. 211–233). New York: Hatherleigh Press.

Corey, G., Corey, M.S., & Callanan, P. (1988). *Issues and ethics in the helping professions* (3rd ed.). Pacific Grove, CA: Brooks/Cole.

Corey, G., Corey, M.S., & Callanan, P. (1993). *Issues and ethics in the helping professions* (4th ed.). Pacific Grove, CA: Brooks/Cole.

Cottone, R.R. (1992). *Theories and paradigms of counseling and psychotherapy.* Boston: Allyn and Bacon.

Crawford, R.L. (1994). *Avoiding counselor malpractice.* Alexandria, VA: American Counseling Association.

Cummings, N.A. (1990). The credentialing of professional psychologists and its implication for the other mental health disciplines. *Journal of Counseling and Development, 68(5),* 485–490.

DeLozier, P.P. (1994). Therapist sexual misconduct. *Women & Therapy, 15,* 55–67.

Denkers, G., & Clifford, R. (1994). *A survey of psychologists' experiences with managed care: Consumer issues.* San Mateo, CA: San Francisco Bay Area Psychologists Task Force on Managed Care.

Deutsch, C.J. (1984). Self-reported sources of stress among psychotherapists. *Professional Psychology: Research and Practice, 15*(6), 833–845.

Dickson, D. (1998). Confidentiality and privacy in social work: *A guide to the law for practitioners and students.* New York: The Free Press.

Doherty, W.J.(1995). *Soul searching: Why psychotherapy must promote moral responsibility.* New York: Basic Books.

Edwards, H.B. (1995, November/December). Managed care and confidentiality. *Behavioral Health Management, 15,* 3.

Eisel v. Board of Education of Montgomery County, 324 Md. 376, 597 a, 2d 447 (Md. Ct. App. 1991).

Elkin, I., Shea, M.T. Watkins, J.T. Imbers, S.D., Sotsky, S.M. Collins, J.F. Glass, D.R. Pilkonis, PA., Leber, W.R., Docherty, J.P., Feister, S.F., & Paroloff, M.D. (1989). National Institute of Mental Health treatment of depression collaborative research program: General effectiveness of treatment. *Archives of General Psychiatry, 46,* 971-983.

Emerich v. Philadelphia Center for Human Development, Slip Opinion #J-253-96 (Pa.Sup.Ct.,Dec 11, 1996).

Emerson, S., & Markos, P.A. (1996). Signs and symptoms of the impaired counselor. *Journal of Humanistic Education and Development, 34,* 108–117.

Engels, D., Willborn, B.L., & Schneider, L.J. (190). Ethics curricula for counselor preparation programs. In B. Herlihy & L.B. Golden (Eds.), *Ethical standards casebook* (pp. 111–126). Alexandria, VA: American Association for Counseling and Development.

Erickson, S.H.. Ethics and confidentiality in AIDS counseling. A professional dilemma. *Journal of Mental Health Counseling, 15(2),* 118–31.

Evans, D.R., & Hearn, M.T. (1997). Sexual and non-sexual dual relationships: Managing the boundaries. In D. R. Evans (Ed.), *The law, standards of practice, and ethics in the practice of psychology* (pp. 53–84). Toronto, Canada: Emond Montgomery Publications, Ltd.

Everstein, L., Everstine, D.S., Heymann, G.M., True, R.H., Frey, D.H., Johnson, H.G., & Seiden, R.H. (1995). Privacy and confidentiality in psychotherapy. In D.N. Bersoff (Ed.), *Ethical conflicts in psychology* (pp. 151–155). Washington, DC: American Psychological Association.

Falicov, C.J. (1982). Mexican families. In M. McGoldrick, J.K.Pearce, & J. Giordano (Eds.), *Ethnicity and family therapy* (pp. 134–163). New York: Guilford Press.

Family Educational Rights and Privacy Act of 1974, 20 U.S.C., sec. 1232(g), (Buckley Amendment).

Farber, B.A. (1983). *Stress and burnout in the human service professions.* New York: Pergamon Press.

Finney, M., & Mitroff, I. (1986). Strategic planning failures: The organization as its own worse energy. In H.S. Sims (Ed.), *The thinking organization* (pp. 317–335). San Francisco: Jossey- Bass.

Fischer, J. (1993). Empirically based practice: The end of ideology? *Journal of Social Service Research, 18*(1/2), 19–64.

Forester-Miller, H., & Davis, T.E. (1995). *A practitioner's guide to ethical decision making.* Alexandria, VA: American Counseling Association.

Freudenberger, H., & Richelson, G. (1980). *Burn-out: How to beat the high cost of success.* New York: Doubleday.

Godkin v. Miller, 379 F. Supp. 859 (ED N.Y. 1974), aff'd, 514 F 2d 123 (2d Cir.1975).

Gorey, K. (1996). Effectiveness of social work intervention research: Internal versus external evaluations. *Social Work Research, 20,* 119–128.

Goss v. Lopez, 419 U.S. 565 (1975).

Gottlieb, A. (1993). Avoiding exploitive dual relations: A decision-making model. *Psychotherapy,* 40, 41–47.

Greenspan, M. (1995, July-August). Out of bounds. *Common Boundary,* 51–56.

Grimm, D.W., (1994). Therapist, spiritual and religious values in psychotherapy. *Counseling and Values, 38(3),* 154–164.

Gutheil, T. G. (1989, Nov./Dec.). Patient-therapist sexual relations. *The California Therapist*, 29–31.

Gutheil, T.G., & Gabbard, G.O. (1993). The concept of boundaries in clinical practice: Theoretical and risk-management dimensions. *American Journal of Psychiatry, 150*(2), 188–196.

Guy, J.D. (1987). *The personal life of the psychotherapists*. New York: Wiley.

Haas, L.J., & Cummings, N.A. (1991). Managed outpatient mental health plans: Clinical, ethical and practical guidelines for participation. *Professional Psychology: Research and Practice, 22*(1), 45–51.

Haas, L.J., & Cummings, N.A. (1995). Managed outpatient mental health plans: Clinical, ethical and practical guidelines for participation. In D.N. Bersoff (Ed.), *Ethical conflicts in psychology*. Washington, DC: American Psychological Association.

Haas, L.J., & Malouf, J.L. (1989). *Keeping up the good work: A practitioner's guide to mental health ethics*. Sarasota, FL: Professional Resource Exchange.

Hackney, H. & Cormier, L.S. (1991). *Counseling strategies and interventions* (3rd ed.). Boston: Allyn and Bacon.

Hammer v. Rosen, 165 N.E. 2d 756 (1960).

Handelsman, M.M., & Galvin, M.D. (1995) Facilitating informed consent for outpatient psychotherapy: A suggest written format. In D.N. Bersoff (Ed.), *Ethical conflicts in psychology*. Washington, DC: American Psychological Association.

Handelsman, M.M., Kemper, M.B., Kesson-Craig, P., McLain, J., & Johnsrud, C. (1986). Use, content and readability of written informed consent forms of treatment. *Professional Psychology: Research and Practice, 17*, 514–518.

Hare-Mustin, R.T., Marecek, J., Kaplan, A.G. & Liss-Levinson, N. (1995). Rights of clients, responsibilities of therapists. In D.N. Bersoff (Ed.), *Ethical conflicts in psychology* (pp. 305-310). Washington, DC: American Psychological Association.

Hedges, L.E. (1993 May-June). In praise of dual relationship, part I. *The California Therapist,* 46–50.

Hedlund v. Superior Court of Orange County, 669, P.2d41, 191 Cal.Rptr. 805 (1983)

Hendrix, D. H. (1991). Ethics and intrafamily confidentiality in counseling with children. *Journal of Mental Health Counseling*, 13, 323–333.

Herlihy, B., & Corey, G. (1996). *ACA ethical standards casebook* (5th ed.). Alexandria, VA: American Counseling Association.

Herlihy, B., & Corey, G. (1997). *Boundary issues in counseling: Multiple roles and responsibilities*. Alexandria, VA: American Counseling Association.

Herlihy, B. & Sheeley, V.L. (1988). Counselor liability and the duty to warn: Selected cases, statutes, trends and implication for practice. *Counselor Education and Supervision, 27*, 203-215.

Hill, M., Glaser, K., & Harden, J. (1995) *A feminist model for ethical decision making*. New York: Guilford Press.

Hipp, M.L., Atkinson, C., & Pelc, R. (1994). *Colorado Psychological Association Legislative Survey*. Denver, CO: Colorado Psychological Association.

Hodgkinson v. Simms (1994). 117 DLR (4th) 161.

Holub, E.A. & Lee, S.S. (1990). *The counselor and the law* (3rd ed.). Alexandria, VA: American Counseling Association Press.

Hopkins, B.H., & Anderson, B.S. (1990). *The counselor and the law* (3rd ed.). Alexandria, VA: American Counseling Association Press.

Horack v. Bris, 474 N.E. 2d13 (1985).

International Association for the Right to Effective Treatment. (1996). The IARET statement of philosophy. *IARET Newsletter, 7*(1), 3.

Ivey, A.E., Bradford-Ivey, M., & Simek-Morgan, L. (1993). *Counseling and psychotherapy: A multicultural perspective* (3rd ed.). Boston: Allyn and Bacon.

Jablonski v. United States, 712 F.2d 391 (9th Cir., 1983).

Jacob-Timm, S & Hartshorne, T.S. (1998). *Ethics and law for school psychologists* (3rd ed.). New York: John Wiley and Sons.

Jaffe v. Redmond et al., WL 315841 (U.S. June 13, 1996).

Jeffrey, T.B., Rankin, R.J., & Jeffrey, L.K. (1992). In service of two masters: The ethical-legal dilemma faced by military psychologists. *Professional Psychology: Research and Practice, 23*, 91–95.

Kalischman, S.C., & Brosig, C.L. (1993). The effects of statutory requirements on child maltreatment reporting: A comparison of two states. *American Journal of Orthopsychiatry, 62*(2), 284-297.

Kalischman, S.C., & Craig, M.E. (1991). Professional psychologists' decision to report suspected child abuse: Clinician and situation influences. *Professional Psychology: Research and Practice, 22*(1), 84-89.

Keith-Spiegel, P., & Koocher, G. (1985). *Ethics in psychology: Professional standards and cases.* New York: Random House

Kitchener, K.S. (1984). Intuition, critical evaluation and ethical principles: The foundation for ethical decisions in counseling psychology. *Counseling Psychologist, 12*, 43–55.

Kitchener, K.S. (1986). Teaching applied ethics in counselor education: An integration of psychological processes and philosophical analysis. *Journal of Counseling and Development, 64*, 306–310.

Klerman, G.L. (1990). The psychiatric patient's right to effective treatment: Implications of *Osheroff v. Chestnut Lodge. American Journal of Psychiatry, 147*, 409–418.

Knapp, S. (1998). Cultural awareness and competence. *The Pennsylvania Psychologist Update.* April 7.

Knapp, S., & VandeCreek, L. (1983). Privileged communications and the counselor. *Personnel and Guidance Journal, 62*, 83–85.

Kuh, G.D., & Whitt, E.J. (1988). The invisible tapestry: Culture in American colleges and universities. *AAHE-ERIC/ Higher Education Report, No. I.* Washington, DC: American Association for Higher Education.

Kurpius, D.J. (1985). Consultation interventions: Successes, failures and proposals. *The Counseling Psychologists, 13*, 368–389.

Kurpius, D.J. (1997). *Current ethical issues in the practice of psychology.* The Hatherleigh guide series, Vol. 10. (pp. 1-16). New York: Hatherleigh Press.

Kutchins, H. (1991). The fiduciary relationship: The legal basis for social workers' responsibilities to clients. *Social Work, 36*, 106–113.

Lazarus, A. (1989). *The practice of multimodal therapy* (2). Baltimore: John Hopkins University Press.

Langwell, K.M. (1992). The effects of managed care on use and costs of health services. (Staff memorandum). Washington, DC: Congressional Budget Office.

Lerman, H. & Rigby, B. (1994). Boundary violations: Misuse of the power of the therapist. In H. Lerman & N. Porter (Eds.), *Feminist ethics in psychotherapy* (pp. 51–59). New York: Springer.

Lowenberg, F., & Dolgoff R. (1988). *Ethical decisions for social work practice* (3rd ed.). Itasca, IL: F.E. Peacock Publishers.

Lewis, G.J., Greenburg, S.L., & Hatch, D.B. (1988). Peer consultation groups for psychologists in private practice: A national survey. *Professional Psychology: Research and Practice, 19*(1), 81–86.

Lipari v. Sears, Roebuck & Co., 497 F.Supp. 185 (D.Neb. 1980).

MacDonald, G., Sheldon, B., & Gillespie, J. (1992). Contemporary studies of the effectiveness of social work. British Journal of Social Work, 2, 615–643.

M.(K.) v. M.(H.), (1992), 96 DLR (4th) 289.

Mazza v. Huffaker, 300 S.E. 2d 833, (1983).

McGuire, J., Nieri, D., Abbott, D., Sheridan, K., & Fisher, R. (1995). Do *Tarasoff* principles apply in AIDS-related psychotherapy? Ethical decision making and the role of therapist in homophobia and perceived client dangerousness. *Professional Psychology: Research and Practice, 26*(6), 608–611.

McInerney v. MacDonald (1992), 93 DLR (4th) 415.

Merluzzi, T., & Brischetto, C. (1983). Breach of confidentiality and perceived trustworthiness of counselors. *Journal of Counseling Psychology, 30,* 245–251.

Miller, D., & Thelen, M. (1986). Knowledge and beliefs about confidentiality in psychotherapy. *Professional Psychology: Research and Practice, 17,* 15–19.

Miller, I. (1996). Ethical and liability issues concerning invisible rationing. *Professional Psychology: Research and Practice, 27* (6), 583–587.

Nally v. Grace Community Church, 47 Cal.3d 378 (1988).

National Association of Social Workers. (1996). *Code of ethics*. Washington, DC: Author.

Newman, J.L. (1993). Ethical issues in consultation. *Journal of Counseling and Development 72,* 148–156.

Newman, R., & Bricklin, P.M. (1991). Parameters of managed mental health care: Legal, ethical, and professional guidelines. *Professional Psychology: Research and Practice, 22*(1), 26– 35.

Norberg v. Wynrib (1992), 92 DLR (4th) 449.

Olarte, S.W. (1997). Sexual boundary violations. In *The Hatherleigh guide to ethics in therapy* (pp. 195–209). New York: Hatherleigh Press.

Owebm G. (1982). Ethics of intervention for change. *Australian Psychologist, 21*(2), 211-218.

Parsons, R.D. (1996). *The skilled consultant*. Boston: Allyn and Bacon.

Parsons, R.D. (1995). *The skills of helping*. Boston: Allyn and Bacon

Parsons, R. (1985). The counseling relationship. In R. Wicks, R. Parsons, D. Capps (Eds.), *Clinical handbook of pastoral counseling*. Mahwah, NJ: Paulist.

Peck v. Counseling Services of Addison County, 499 A.2d422(VT 1985).

Pepper-Smith, R. Harvey, W.R., Silberfeld, M., Stein, E. & Rutman, D. (1992). Consent to competency assessment. *International Journal of Law and Psychiatry, 15,* 13-23.

Peters, M., & Robinson, V. (1984). The origins and status of Action Research. *The Journal of Applied Behavioral Science, 20*(2), 113-124.

Peterson, M.R. (1992). *At personal risk: Boundary violations in professional-client relationships*. New York: W.W. Norton

Pryzwansky, W.B. (1993). Ethical consultation practice. In J.E. Zins, T.R. Kratochwill, & S.N. Elliot (Eds.), *Handbook of consultation services for children* (pp. 329–350). San Francisco: Jossey-Bass.

Pope, K.S., Tabachnick, B.G., & Keith-Spiegel, P. (1987). Ethics of practice: The beliefs and behaviors of psychologists as therapists. *American Psychologist, 42*(11), 993–1006.

Pope, K., & Vasquez, M.J.T. (1991). *Ethics in psychotherapy and counseling*. San Francisco: Jossey Bass.

Reamer, F.G. (1997). Managing ethics under managed care. *Families in Society, 78*(1),96–101.

Reamer, F.G. (1990). *Ethical dilemmas in social service* (2nd ed). Columbia University Press.

Reaves, R.P., & Ogloff, J.R.P. (1996). Liability for professional misconduct. In L.J. Bass, S.T. DeMers, J.R.P. Ogloff, C. Peterson, J.L. Pettifor, R.P.Reaves, T.Retfalvi, N.P. Simon, C. Sinclair, & R.M.Tipton (Eds.), *Professional conduct and discipline in psychology*, (117–142). Washington, DC: American Psychological Association.

Remley, T.P., Jr. (1996). The relationship between law and ethics. In B. Herlihy & G. Corey (Eds.), *ACA ethical standards casebook* (5th ed.; pp. 285–292). Alexandria, VA: American Counseling Association.

Richardson, B.I. (1992). Utilizing the resources of the African American Church: Strategies for counseling professionals. In C.C. Lee & B.L. Richardson (Eds.). *Multicultural issues in counseling new approaches to diversity.* Alexandria, VA: American Counseling Association.

Russell Sage Foundation. (1970). *Guidelines for the collection maintenance and dissemination of pupil records.* Hartford, CN: Russell Sage Foundation.

Salgo v. Leland Stanford Jr. Board of Trustees, 317P.2nd 170 (1957).

Salo, M. & Schumate, S. (1993). *Counseling minor clients.* Alexandria, VA: American School Counselor Association.

Sanderson, W.C., & Woody, S. (1995). Manuals for empirically validated treatment. A project of the Task Force on Psychological Interventions, Division of Clinical Psychology. American Psychological Association. *Clinical Psychologist, 48(4),* 7–11.

Schaffer, S.J. (1997). Don't be aloof about record-keeping; it may be your best liability coverage. *The National Psychologist,* 6(1), 21.

Schein, E. H. (1990). Organizational culture. *American Psychologist, 45,* 109–119.

Schein, E. H. (1991). Process consultation. *Consulting Psychology Bulletin, 45,* 109–119.

Schlesinger, M. (1995). Ethical issues in policy advocacy. *Health Affairs, 14,* 23–29.

Schmidt, J.J. (1991). *A survival guide for the elementary/middle school counselor.* West Nyack, NY: The Center for Applied Research in Education.

Schutz, B.M. (1982). *Legal liability in psychotherapy: A practitioner's guide to risk management.* San Francisco, CA: Jossey-Bass.

Schwitzebel, R.L., & Schwitzgebel, R.K. (1980). *Law and psychological practice.* New York: John Wiley and Sons.

Seppa, N. (1996, August). Supreme court protects patient-therapist privilege. *APA Monitor, 27*(8), 39.

Sexton, T.L., Whisten, S.C., Bleuer, J.C., & Walz, G.R. (1997). *Integrating outcome research into counseling practice and training.* Alexandria, VA: American Counseling Association.

Shani, A.B. (1990). Solving problems bureaucracies cannot handle. In G. Bushe and A.B. Shani (Eds.), *Parallel learning structures.* Reading, MA: Addison-Wesley.

Shore, M. (1996, January). Impact of managed care. *New England Journal of Medicine,* 116–118.

Simon, R.I. (1992a). *Clinical psychiatry and the law* (2nd ed.). Washington, DC: American Psychiatric Press.

Simon, R.I. (1992b). *Concise guide to psychiatry and the law for clinicians.* Washington, DC: American Psychiatry Press.

Skorupa, J., & Agresti, A.A. (1993). Ethical beliefs about burnout and continued professional practice. *Professional Psychology: Research and Practice, 24*(3), 281–285.

Smith, D., & Fitzpatrick, M. (1995). Patient-therapist boundary issues: An integrative review of theory and research. *Professional Psychology: Research and Practice, 26*(5), 499–506.

Smith v. Seilby, 72 Wash.2nd 16 (1967).

Snider, P.D. (1987). Client records: Inexpensive liability protection for mental health counselors. *Journal of Mental Health Counseling,* 9, 134–141.

Speight, S.L., Myers, L.J., Cox, C.I., & Highlen, P.S. (1991). A redefinition of multicultural counseling. *Journal of Counseling & Development, 70,* 29–36.

St. Germaine, J. (1993). Dual relationships: What's wrong with them? *American Counselor, 2,* 24-30.

Stadler, H.A. (1990). Counselor impairment. In B. Herlihy & L.B. Golden (Eds.), *AACD ethical standards casebook* (4th ed.; pp. 102–110). Alexandria, VA: American Association for Counseling and Development.

Stake, J.E. & Oliver, J. (1991). Sexual contact and touching between therapist and client. A survey of psychologists' attitudes and behaviors. *Professional Psychology: Research and Practice,* 22(4), 297-307.

Stanley, B. (1987). Informed consent in treatment and research. In I.B. Weiner & A.K. Hess (eds.), *Handbook of forensic psychology* (pp. 63–85). New York: Wiley.

Strasburger, L.H., Jorgenson, L., & Sutherland, P. (1992). The prevention of psychotherapist sexual misconduct: Avoiding the slippery slope. *American Journal of Psychotherapy, 46*, 544–555.

Stromberg, D., Stone, G., & Claiborn, C. (1993). Informed consent: Therapists' beliefs and practices. Professional Psychology: Research and Practice, 24, 153–159.

Stromberg, C., and his colleagues in the Law Firm of Hogan & Hartson of Washington, DC. (1993, April). Privacy, confidentiality and privilege. *The psychologist's legal update*. Washington, DC: National Register of Health Service Providers in Psychology.

Sue, D.W., Arrendondo, P., & McDavis, R. (1992). Multicultural counseling competencies and standards: A call to the profession. *Journal of Counseling & Development, 70*, 477–486.

Sue, D.W., Ivey, A.E., & Pedersen, P.B. (1996). *A theory of multicultural counseling and therapy.* Pacific Grove, CA: Brooks/Cole

Sue, S., & Morishma, J.K.(1982). *The mental health of Asian-Americans.* San Francisco: Jossey-Bass.

Sue, D.W. & Sue, D. (1990). *Counseling the culturally different* (2nd ed.). New York: John Wiley and Sons.

Sullivan, T., Martin, W., & Handelsman, M. (1993). Practical benefits of an informed-consent procedure: An empirical investigation. *Professional Psychology: Research and Practice, 24,* 160–163.

Tarasof v. The Regents of the University of California, 551 P.2d 334 (Cal.Sup.Ct., 1976).

Task Force on Promotion and Dissemination of Psychological Procedures. (1995). Training in and dissemination of empirically-validated psychological treatments: Report and recommendations. *Clinical Psychologist, 48*(1), 3–23.

Tepper, A.M. & Knapp, S.(1999, February). Pennsylvania recognizes an affirmative duty to warn third party victims. *The Pennsylvania Psychologists Quarterly.*

Thomason, T.C. (1993). Counseling Native Americans: An introduction for non-Native Americans. In D.R. Atkinson, G. Morten, & D.W. Sue (Eds.). *Counseling American minorities: A cross-cultural perspective* (pp. 171–187). Dubuque, IA: Wm. C. Brown.

Thomson, A. (1990). *Guide to ethical practice in psychotherapy.* New York: John Wiley and Sons.

Thoreson, R.W., Shaughnessy, P., Heppner, P.P., & Cook, S.W. (1993). Sexual contact during and after professional relationship: Attitudes and practices of male counselors. *Journal of Counseling and Development, 71*, 429–434.

Thyer, B.A. (1996). Forty years of progress toward empirical clinical practice? *Social Work Research, 20,* 77–81.

Tomm, K. (1991, winter). The ethics of dual relationships. *The Calgary Participator*, pp. 11–15.

Totten, G., Lamb, D.H., & Reeder, G.D. (1990). *Tarasoff* and confidentiality in AIDS-related psychotherapy. *Professional Psychology: Research and Practice, 21*(3), 155–160.

Treppa, J.A. (1998). A practitioner's guide to ethical decision-making. In R.M. Anderson, T.L. Needels, & H.V. Hall (Eds.), *Avoiding ethical misconduct in psychology specialty areas* (pp. 26–41.), Springfield, IL: Charles C. Thomas.

Truax, C.B., & Carkhuff, R.R. (1965). The experimental manipulation of therapeutic conditions. *Journal of Consulting Psychology, 29,* 119–224.

Tutty, L. (1990). The response of community mental health professionals to client's rights: A review and suggestions. *Canadian Journal of Community Mental Health, 9*(1), 1–24.

Valentich, M., & Gripton, J. (1992). Dual relationships: Dilemmas and doubts. *Canadian Journal of Human Sexuality, 1,* 155–166.

Van Maanen, J., & Barley, S.R. (1985). Cultural organization: Fragments of a theory. In P. Frost, L. Moore, M. Louis, C. Lundberg, & J. Martin (Eds.), *Organizational culture* (pp. 31–54). Beverly Hills, CA: Sage.

Vesper, J.H., & Brock, G. (1991). *Ethics, legalities and professional practice issue in marriage and family therapy.* Boston: Allyn and Bacon.

Viederman, M. (1991). The real person of the analyst and his role in the process of psychoanalytic cure. *Journal of the American Psychoanalysis Association, 39,* 451–489.

Wigmore, J.H. (1961) Evidence in trials at common law. In J.T. McNaughton (Ed.), *Rules of evidence* (Vol 8, rev.ed.). Boston: Little, Brown.

Wilson v. Corbin, 41 N.W., d.702 (1985).

Winick, B.J. (1991). Competence to consent to treatment: The distinction between assent and objection. In D. B. Wexler & B.J. Winick (Eds.), *Essays in therapeutic jurisprudence* (pp. 41–81). Durham, NC: Carolina Academic Press.

Woody, R.H. (1997). *Legally safe mental health practice: Psycholegal questions and answers.* Madison, CT: Psychosocial Press.

Younggren, J.N. (1993). Ethical issues in religious psychotherapy. *Register Report,* 19(4), 1–8.

APPENDIX A

Professional Organizations

American Counseling Association (ACA), 5999 Stevenson Avenue, Alexandria, VA 22304-3300.

National Board of Certified Counselors (NBCC), 3-D Terrace Way, Greensboro, NC 27403.

American Psychological Association (APA), 750 First Street, N.E., Washington, DC 20002-4242

American Board of Professional Psychology (ABPP), 2100 East Broadway (Suite 313), Columbia, MD 65201

American Association for Marriage and Family Therapy (AAMFT), 1100 17th Street, Washington, DC 20036-4601.

National Association for Social Work (NASW), 750 First Street N.E., Suite 700, Washington, DC 20002-4241.

APPENDIX B

Codes of Ethics and Standards of Professional Practice

Within the body of this text, specific sections of the most recent versions of the Codes of Ethics for (1) the American Counseling Association, (2) the American Psychological Association, (3) the American Association of Marriage and Family Therapists, and (4) the National Association of Social Workers have been identified. However, as noted throughout the text, professional codes of ethics evolve in response to contemporary issues facing that profession. Thus, Appendix B includes the Introduction/Preambles for each of the four professional associations discussed throughout the text along with web site references for the full codes and standards. The reader is directed to the listed web sites for each of these professional groups to receive the current Standards of Practice and Codes of Ethics.

American Counseling Association Code of Ethics and Standards of Practice

Preamble

The American Counseling Association is an educational, scientific, and professional organization whose members are dedicated to the enhancement of human development throughout the life-span. Association members recognize diversity in our society and embrace a crosscultural approach in support of the worth, dignity, potential, and uniqueness of each individual.

The specification of a code of ethics enables the association to clarify to current and future members, and to those served by members, the nature of the ethical responsibilities held in common by its members. As the code of ethics of the association, this document establishes principles that define the ethical behavior of association members. All members of the American Counseling Association are required to adhere to the Code of Ethics and Standards of Practice. The Code of Ethics will serve as the basis for processing ethical complaints initiated against members of the association.

Online: http://www.counseling.org/resources/codeofethics.htm

American Psychological Association Ethical Principles of Psychologists and Code of Conduct

Preamble

Psychologists work to develop a valid and reliable body of scientific knowledge based on research. They may apply that knowledge to human behavior in a variety of contexts. In doing so, they perform many roles, such as researcher, educator, diagnostician, therapist, supervisor, consultant, administrator, social interventionist, and expert witness. Their goal is to broaden knowledge of behavior and, where appropriate, to apply it pragmatically to improve the condition of both the individual and society. Psychologists respect the central importance of freedom of inquiry and expression in research, teaching, and publication. They also strive to help the public in developing informed judgments and choices concerning human behavior. This Ethics Code provides a common set of values upon which psychologists build their professional and scientific work.

This Code is intended to provide both the general principles and the decision rules to cover most situations encountered by psychologists. It has as its primary goal the welfare and protection of the individuals and groups with whom psychologists work. It is the individual responsibility of each psychologist to aspire to the highest possible standards of conduct. Psychologists respect and protect human and civil rights, and do not knowingly participate in or condone unfair discriminatory practices.

The development of a dynamic set of ethical standards for a psychologist's work-related conduct requires a personal commitment to a lifelong effort to act ethically; to encourage ethical behavior by students, supervisees, employees, and colleagues, as appropriate; and to consult with others, as needed, concerning ethical problems. Each psychologist supplements, but does not violate, the Ethics Code's values and rules on the basis of guidance drawn from personal values, culture, and experience.

Online: http://www.apa.org/ethics/code.htm

American Association for Marriage and Family Therapy Code of Ethics

The Board of Directors of the American Association for Marriage and Family Therapy (AAMFT) hereby promulgates, pursuant to Article 2, Section 2.013 for the Association's Bylaws, the Revised AAMFT Code of Ethics, effective July 1, 1998. The AAMFT Code of Ethics is binding on Members of AAMFT in all membership categories, AAMFT Approved Supervisors, and applicants for membership and the Approved Supervisor designation (hereafter AAMFT Member). If an AAMFT Member resigns in anticipation of, or during the course of an ethics investigation, the Ethics Committee will complete its investigation. Any publication of action taken by the Association will include the fact that the Member attempted to resign during the investigation. Marriage and family therapists are strongly encouraged to report alleged unethical behavior of colleagues to appropriate professional associations and state regulatory bodies.

Online: http://www.aamft.org/about/ethics.htm

National Association of Social Workers Code of Ethics

Preamble

The primary mission of social work profession is the enhance human well-being and help meet the basic human needs of all people, with particular attention to the needs and empowerment of people who are vulnerable, oppressed, and living in poverty. A historic and defining feature of social work is the profession's focus on individual well-being in a social context and the well-being of society. Fundamental to social work is attention to the environmental force that create, contribute to, and address problems in living.

Social workers promote social justice and social change with and on behalf of clients. "Clients" is used inclusively to refer to individuals, families, groups, organizations, and communities. Social workers are sensitive to cultural and ethnic diversity and strive to end discrimination, oppression, poverty, and other forms of social injustice. These activities may be in the form of direct practice, community organizing, supervision, consultation, administration, advocacy, social and political action, policy development and implementation, education, and research and evaluation. Social workers seek to enhance the capacity of people to address their own needs. Social workers also seek to promote the responsiveness of organizations, communities, and other social institutions to individuals' needs and social problems.

The mission of the social work profession is rooted in a set of core values. These core values, embraced by social workers throughout the profession's history, are the foundation of social work's unique purpose and perspective:

service

social justice

dignity and worth of the person

importance of human relationships

integrity

competence

This constellation of core values reflects what is unique to the social work profession. Core values, and the principles that flow from them, must be balanced within the context and complexity of the human experience.

National Association of Social Workers
Purpose of the Code of Ethics

Professional ethics are at the core of social work. The profession has an obligation to artic-ulate its basic values, ethical principles, and ethical standards. The *NASW Code of Ethics* sets forth these values, principles, and standards to guide the social worker's conduct.

The *Code* is relevant to all social workers and social worker students, regardless of their functions, the settings in which they work, or the populations they serve.

The *NASW Code of Ethics* serve six purposes:

The *Code* identifies core values on which social work's mission is based.

The *Code* summarizes broad ethical principles that reflect the profession's core val-ues and establish a set of specific ethical standards that should be used to guide social work practice.

The *Code* is designed to help social workers identify relevant considerations when professional obligations conflict or ethical uncertainties arise.

The *Code* provides ethical standards to which the general public can hold the social work profession accountable.

The *Code* socializes practitioners new to the field to social work's mission, values, ethical principles, and ethical standards.

The *Code* articulates standards that the social work profession itself can use to assess whether social workers have engaged in unethical conduct. NASW has formed pro-cedures to adjudicate ethics complaints filed against its members.[1] In subscribing to this *Code*, social workers are required to cooperate in its implementation, participate in NASW adjudication proceedings, and abide by any NASW disciplinary rulings or sanctions based on it.

The *Code* offers a set of values, principles, and standards to guide decision making and conduct when ethical issues arise. It does not provide a set of rules that prescribe how social workers should act in all situations. Specific applications of the *Code* must take into account the context that is being considered and the possibility of conflicts among the *Code's* values, principles, and standards. Ethical responsibilities flow from all human rela-tionships, from the personal and familial to the social and professional.

Further, the *NASW Code of Ethics* does not specify which values, principles, and standards are most important and ought to outweigh others in instances when they conflict. Reasonable differences of opinion can and do exist among social workers with respect to the ways in which values, ethical principles, and ethical standards should rank ordered when they conflict. Ethical decision making is a process. There are many instances in social work where simple answers are not available to resolve complex ethical issues. Social workers should take into consideration all the values, principles, and standards in

---

[1] For information on NASW adjudication procedures, see *NASW Procedures for the Adjudication of Grievances.*

this *Code* that are relevant to any situation in which ethical judgment is warranted. Social workers' decisions and actions should be consistent with the spirit as well as the letter of this *Code*.

In addition to this *Code*, there are many other sources of information about ethical thinking that may be useful. Social workers should consider ethical theory and principles generally, social work theory and research, laws, regulations, agency policies, and other relevant codes of ethics, recognizing that among codes of ethics social workers should consider the *NASW Code Ethics* as their primary source. Social workers also should be aware of the impact on ethical decision making of their clients' and their own personal values and cultural and religious beliefs and practices. They should be aware of any conflicts between personal and professional values and deal with them responsibly. For additional guidance social workers should consult the relevant literature on professional ethics and ethical decision making and seek appropriate consultation when faced with ethical dilemmas. This may involve consultation with an agency-based or social work organization's ethics committee, a regulatory body, knowledgeable colleagues, supervisors, or legal counsel.

Instances may arise when social workers' ethical obligations conflict with agency policies or relevant laws or regulations. When such conflicts occur, social workers must make a responsible effort to resolve the conflict in a manner that is consistent with the values, principles, and standards expressed in this *Code*. If a reasonable resolution of the conflict does not appear possible, social workers should seek proper consultation before making a decision.

The *NASW Code of Ethics* is to be used by NASW and by individuals, agencies, organizations, and bodies (such as licensing and regulatory boards, professional liability insurance providers, courts of law, agency boards or directors, government agencies, and other professional groups) that choose to adopt it or use it as a frame of reference. Violation of standards in this Code does not automatically imply legal liability or violation of the law. Such determination can only be made in the context of legal and judicial proceedings. Alleged violations of the *Code* would be subject to a peer review process. Such processes are generally separate from legal or administrative procedures and insulated from legal review or administrative procedures and insulated from legal review or proceedings to allow the profession to counsel and discipline its own members.

A code of ethics cannot guarantee ethical behavior. Moreover, a code of ethics cannot resolve all ethical issues or disputes or capture the richness and complexity involved in striving to make responsible choices within a moral community. Rather, a code of ethics sets forth values, ethical principles, and ethical standards to which professionals aspire and by which their actions can be judged. Social workers' ethical behavior should result from their personal commitment to engage in ethical practice. The *NASW Code of Ethics* reflects the commitment of all social workers to uphold the profession's values and to act ethically. Principles and standards must be applied by individuals of good character who discern moral questions and, in good faith, seek to make reliable ethical judgments.

Online: http//www.naswdc.org/code.htm

INDEX